UNLCKING
CONSCIOUSNESS

Lessons from the Convergence of Computing and Cognitive Psychology

UNL🔒CKING CONSCIOUSNESS

Lessons from the Convergence of Computing and Cognitive Psychology

Charles T. Ross
British Computer Society, UK

World Scientific

NEW JERSEY · LONDON · SINGAPORE · BEIJING · SHANGHAI · HONG KONG · TAIPEI · CHENNAI · TOKYO

Published by

World Scientific Publishing Europe Ltd.

57 Shelton Street, Covent Garden, London WC2H 9HE

Head office: 5 Toh Tuck Link, Singapore 596224

USA office: 27 Warren Street, Suite 401-402, Hackensack, NJ 07601

Library of Congress Cataloging-in-Publication Data

Names: Ross, Charles (Charles Trevor), author.

Title: Unlocking consciousness : lessons from the convergence of computing
    and cognitive psychology / Charles T. Ross (British Computer Society, UK).

Description: New Jersey : World Scientific, [2018] | Includes bibliographical references and index.

Identifiers: LCCN 2017044675 | ISBN 9781786344687 (hc : alk. paper)

Subjects: LCSH: Artificial intelligence. | Cognitive science. | Cognitive neuroscience. |
    Conscious automata. | Consciousness.

Classification: LCC Q335 .R677 2018 | DDC 006.3--dc23

LC record available at https://lccn.loc.gov/2017044675

British Library Cataloguing-in-Publication Data

A catalogue record for this book is available from the British Library.

For any available supplementary material, please visit
http://www.worldscientific.com/worldscibooks/10.1142/Q0136#t=suppl

Desk Editors: Anthony Alexander/Jennifer Brough/Shi Ying Koe

Typeset by Stallion Press
Email: enquiries@stallionpress.com

Printed in Singapore

Dedicated to my wife, Louise
for her unlimited support

The Universe is a mass of patterns waiting for us to discover them.

Einstein

PREFACE

The difficulty is not in new ideas, but in escaping from old ones, which ramify for those brought up as most of us have been, into every corner of our minds.

John Maynard Keynes, Dec 1935

Computers are more than just the most sophisticated tools we have ever invented. As well as starting to emulate intelligence, we have begun to learn how we can enhance our own individual personal abilities, then design prosthetic brains, grow organoids using synthetic biology and edit the next generation's genes to expand the abilities of the whole community.

These exciting developments depend on unlocking the secrets of intelligence, the structure of the information upon which all processing depends, meaning and even consciousness.

In the last few years, we have seen a genuine convergence of biogenetics, cognitive neuroscience and computing. The systems that are involved in the formation of the genome and the development of the foetus, and its continuous development through to puberty and adult behaviour all involve information processing, memory formation, access and recall.

In parallel, there is a rising tide of public interest in the possibilities, potential and problems of *artificial intelligence* (AI). Well-renowned scientists are speculating on whether we can build computers that are so much cleverer than us that they will make us redundant; lawyers are wondering if we should start to draw up laws to limit the power of robots, while the Astronomer Royal reports on debates with groups of Nobel Prize winners that "we may be bumping up against the limits of what our biological brains are capable of understanding".

Whether computing turns out to be a great force for good or bad is entirely in our hands. The convergence of knowledge of both human and AI helps both sciences forward.

Computers are the first invention of our civilisation that can actually expand, extend, augment and improve our natural inherited capabilities, even affect our evolution. This raises significant economic, employment, educational and ethical problems that our civilisation has never had to address before.

If we are to successfully meet these challenges, gain the extraordinary benefits and prepare to mitigate or negate the risks and problems, the first key task must be to widen, extend, strengthen and enhance our knowledge of how our brain mind operates.

Fundamental to all our intellectual abilities is that remarkably illusive capability — intelligence.

If we are to understand how we learn and think, we must understand intelligence: what it is and how to categorise it, describe it, measure it and define it? If we are going to build artificially intelligent systems, let alone sentient robots, we must develop comprehensive definitions of intelligence to illuminate our endeavours and measure our success.

This is no easy task. Over the millennia, the greatest brains have been frustrated in their struggles to define intelligence — there are many very different definitions. More than 20 of the most disparate are listed in Appendix 2 (hosted on the website www.BrainMindForum.org/appendices). Why are they so different? Why is there no consensus? Why are so many people in the scientific community so apprehensive about this subject? Maybe the unique perspective of the humanities can help?

Based on some 50 years' experience of computer systems analysis, in the context of the perennial questions asked by the philosophers and insights from the arts and psychologists, we will present the argument that many of these historic descriptions and definitions of intelligence are *true,* but that for assorted reasons they are incomplete. The word "intelligence" is used by different people to mean different things, in different situations, at different times.

When we can synthesise these definitions, we will have a basis to explore the biggest question of them all. "How are we sentient and aware of our surroundings and of ourselves? How are we conscious?"

List of Appendices

All appendices referred to within this text are hosted on the Brain Mind Forum website and can be accessed at this address: www. BrainMindForum.org/appendices.

ABOUT THE AUTHOR

I have been fortunate to live through the battles at the dawning of the age of computing, and be directly involved in many of its major developments.

I was born in North London in 1936, the year Alan Turing presented "On Computable Numbers, with an Application to the *Entscheidungs-problem*" to the Royal Society, and John Maynard Keynes published *The General Theory of Employment, Interest and Money*. I was educated at Highgate School, the Royal Artillery and the Regent Street Polytechnic (now part of Westminster University) with the intention of following a banking career in Coutts & Co. After reading law, accounting and economics, I thought computing sounded more interesting so, in 1958, I left the bank to become a trainee computer programmer. In 1960, my first major task was to help write the machine code program to calculate the daily stock market indices for the *Financial Times*. I was not a very accurate programmer so I wrote a trace program to find my errors.

In 1963, a colleague and I started our first company, and in 1966, we launched one of the world's first systems linking terminals on customer's desks to a central computer — Stockmarket Computer Answering Network (*SCAN*). A second company automatically typeset the monthly *World Airways Guide* — arguably the beginning of computer typesetting.

With the arrival of desktop personal computers in the 1980s, I helped design one of the first programming languages to enable these machines to be used as word processors. We designed some proportional, Cyrillic and Arabic typefaces for the first laser printers. Commands and Layouts for the User made Easy (*CLUE*) won a British Computer Society Silver Medal. In 1994, I helped publish the December edition of *The Computer Bulletin*, the first magazine to be typeset from the voice of the editor, for the British Computer Society and the Oxford University Press.

I have been interested in how my brain did (or did not) do things since experimenting with better ways of learning poetry homework at school. In 1990, I started to study cognitive neuroscience as, together with colleagues in the Real Time Club, we began to realise that what we were learning as we designed our computer systems was helping us to better understand how our brain did similar tasks.

In 2002, we studied the credentials of some 2,000 software specialists for the (then) Department of Trade & Industry. Skills, Capabilities, Aptitude and the Learning Environment in the 21st Century (SCALE 21) which showed that the skills needed for computing were significantly different to many traditional careers. Not better, not worse, but definitely different. The general state education did not appear to be a particularly helpful preparation.

In 2005, together with colleagues at Oxford and the *New Scientist*, we published a set of *21 Questions for Cognitive Neuroscientists in the 21st Century* borrowing from Hilbert's *Questions for Mathematicians* from a century earlier. In 2008, Shirley Redpath and I published *Biological Systems of the Brain* suggesting how memory is formed and the neural mechanism of sleep.

Also in the 1990s, I started studying quantum physics and helped propose, set up and manage the Quantum Computing in Europe Pathfinder Project for the European Commission. As a result, Framework V included some 34 million European Currency Units (ECU) for quantum computing research.

At a dinner in 2015 with professor Daniel Dennett, our newly formed Brain Mind Forum started to discuss a collaboration with professor A.C. Grayling's New College of the Humanities. Out of these dinners, debates and discussions have come some of the concepts in this book.

I hope this book stimulates numbers of ideas to build better computer systems, helps as many people as possible expand their individual personal abilities and stimulates discussions about some of the ethical complications arising at the dawn of the age of computing.

Charles Trevor Ross
Honorary Fellow, British Computer Society
Chartered Information Technology Professional Fellow
Royal Society Arts

CONTENTS

INTRODUCTION

We look with awe and wonder at the staggering beauty of this world in which we find ourselves. Each one of us is born a unique combination not just of our two parents but of generations of our forebears, always in search of better, brighter, cleverer, stronger individuals aiming for perfection, but with a sense, we still have far to travel and much to learn.

We come into this world able to do almost nothing, but we have the power and capacity to learn to do almost anything. Our forebears set off over every horizon to discover the geography of our planet. Increasingly, we can look inward to discover the intricacies of our own bodies, how we learn, think, are creative, make decisions and cope with the world about us.

We can look out into the sky at the breath-taking immensity of our universe, and study the clues about how life forms began and evolved into our human form. We speculate how we developed the ability to communicate one with another, by languages that allow us to reminisce about the past, make the best we can of the present and imagine, argue and debate how the future might develop — make provision for possible eventualities, even how to make things better.

We can study our history of recorded time and all the tools we have invented to smooth our path and make the best use of our energy, from the plough and wheel to help us produce a good reliable and regular diet; to the machines that help us make and manipulate more things to ameliorate the tasks of daily life and travel widely. All these tools supplement our muscles, enabling puny mankind to move mountains, redirect rivers and build massive buildings. We wonder at the equipment we have invented to extend the capacity of our senses — microscopes, telescopes and television to enhance our eyesight, telephones and radio to enhance our hearing, cars to travel ever faster, ships to sail the seas, aeroplanes to fly and rockets to explore space — to begin to control our environment. However, since the first civilisations, particularly in ancient Greece — one thing — perhaps the most beguiling, always the most inscrutable has proved the most difficult to explore — ourselves.

We can see the framework of our skeletons that give us stability and form, within the envelope of our skin that protects us from the outside. We can study all the organs and their individual and cooperative roles — the sensory organs continuously monitoring the soundwaves and airwaves, and the patterns of light and chemicals in the atmosphere that enable us to be aware of our environment and each other. We can see the networks of neurons of our internal communication system that coordinates everything to operate as one cooperative synchronised whole, and the transport system that pumps blood around the arteries and veins distributing nutrients and hormones; but then we come to that extraordinary group of abilities that enable us to learn, to think, to be creative and conscious of who we are, our place in the firmament and to be alive and responsible for controlling ourselves and our behaviour.

The Invention of Computers

Our generation has been particularly fortunate to have lived to invent the most exciting and sophisticated tool the human race has ever invented. We have for the first time a machine that supplements and enhances our brain — our computers.

We have barely scratched the surface of their potential. In not quite one generation we have come a very long way, but learned enough to begin to realise the vast potential and how much we still must learn. Thanks to these extraordinary devices, every field of research in all the sciences, medicine and agriculture, and in government, politics, manufacture, trade, education, employment, economics, everything is on the cusp of major breakthroughs, substantial changes and a cumulative transformation.

At the centre is our brain and mind that has so fascinated our forebears. Now, we have a partner on our journey of discovery and understanding.

This book is arranged to set out to explore:

(1) How we gradually invented computers — the first 2,000 years and the contribution today's computers can make to our knowledge.

(2) The state of the art of our burgeoning knowledge of cognitive neuroscience.

(3) Then we reconnoitre the science of information, and how we have learned to represent and process text, numbers, images, art, drama and music.

(4) How do we give information meaning? How do we build and grow memories of our expanding knowledge?

(5) This gives us a foundation on which to build and to bring together all our knowledge and experience to puzzle out how we ourselves operate, and a framework and structure to explore what we call "intelligence".

(6) Then we can start to study what it means to be aware of our surroundings and ourselves, what it means to be alive and what we experience as "consciousness".

Hopefully, this will give us the means to help us better control our own behaviour and work towards living together in peace with everyone else.

The better we understand ourselves and how we operate, the better computers we can design, build and program.

Maybe we can only ask more questions, but maybe they will help others formulate better answers.

Now we have a partner with which to share our planet

Over the millennia, we have learned to nurture our young, our successors. Now we have to learn how to train our new-found partners to do our bidding — to help us, support us, to do the work we cannot do, then the work we do not want to do, and steadily raise the quality of our lives and the environment we live in.

We can already see that our new partners will come in many forms: massive systems, large as office blocks, pocket computers with wristwatch interfaces and everything in between. Early robots are being designed to look familiar and never threatening. Editing our genes will gradually rid us of inherited diseases and align our intelligences to enhance our natural talents, widening the scope of the whole community. Ever more sophisticated prosthetics will enable us to make man–machine connections that enable us to access the entire body of human knowledge, art, culture, commerce, skills, crafts, teaching, training and emotions directly online. Groups will be able to cooperate together and gain the benefits of specialisation and the division of labour. Already we can construct synthetic biological cells and the growing of the first "organoids" is being reported, and the first step on the path to building reliable, durable, replaceable organs.

We have a partner we can entirely bend to our will for good or bad. We can create a whole new species that can take all the strain, stress and tedium out of our lives, or possibly create a monster that can harm us. As always, the future is in our hands.

Our engineers are beginning to build devices we can send to places where our flesh and blood cannot now travel. We can send our robot partners on journeys of unlimited length. We can send them to explore the universe, travel to distant planets and build facilities to welcome us as we arrive to join them.

For the first time in the history of our species, we have a partner that can join us on our journey as we spin through space on our small planet.

Predator or partner the choice is ours.

PHILOSOPHY

For the first time in our civilisation, we have a partner in our quest for knowledge. The collateral benefit of our computers is that they are completely and precisely logical. We instruct our computers exactly what we want them to do, which, often irritatingly, is not always what we intended them to do, thus exposing the first errors in our thinking.

We are the only two entities that can process information. In our brain, mind and bodies, information has evolved to enable all the organs to operate as one cooperative coordinated whole. We have designed our computers exclusively to process information and nothing else.

One subtext of this book is how to use our computers to improve our own individual personal ability, and, in particular, to think. Then use our new-found knowledge to build cleverer computers.

From the beginning of recorded history, mankind has thought in broadly four perspectives. Those of a religious persuasion believe gods or superior intelligences created everything in this world, and we should be happy to leave them with the responsibility of disclosing their wisdom to us. There are the scientists who work to understand how things operate. They observe, record and seek for patterns with meticulous care. They experiment, construct replicas and build up a body of knowledge of how things operate that stand the test of time. There are those that frame the problems of the world as questions and seek to imagine, predict and invent possible answers. Then there are the philosophers who ask "why?" There are plenty of people who can straddle two or all four ways of thinking — and be scientists 5 days a week, inventers on Saturday, attend religious ceremonies regularly on Sunday and be philosophers on holiday.

Sometimes Logic is Insufficient

Our engineers can build us integrated circuits and our neuroscientists can describe ever more accurately how individual neurons operate, but we know that no transistor can do more than be in one of two states, and neurons can only transmit an electrochemical signal or not. The cog wheels in a clock cannot tell the time. Only in complex combinations and patterns, can neurons and transistors process information and execute algorithms — and cog wheels display the time. Both neurons and transistors can be organised to carry out a simple task. Hierarchies of these modules of tiny tasks build into ever more complex structures, which in due course can plot a route to the moon or develop democracy. To do this, we have evolved the abstract concept of *the system* which is neither religious nor really science, nor something imaginary, because although it might not be testable in a test tube and it might be abstract, a system is very real. It is pure philosophy. Systems are the knowledge of structures, processes, patterns, relationships and sequences.

Systems are the foundation and architecture of all software. The complex software systems we have built for our computers have helped us understand the complex systems that have evolved in our brain, minds and bodies.

Another abstract concept without which, certainly meaning, and perhaps even intelligence might not be possible in the brain mind, is the phenomenon of *emergence*: the remarkable notion that the whole is greater than the sum of its parts. Logically impossible? But, an essential ingredient of thought and information processing. Emergence is referred to often below. Appendix 25 (www.BrainMindForum.org/appendices) sets out its power and gives an example that enables everyone to experience this insight. Could the concept of emergence help us understand how we describe qualia?

Then there is the art of simplicity. For every complex solution, there is always a simpler one. Equally, whenever we make a great breakthrough in our knowledge, we discover a new world of complexity that lies below that supports the old theories, but opens a whole new dimension to explore. We thought we had made a very elegant breakthrough, when we discovered that atoms contained a nucleus surrounded by orbiting electrons. Thus, the very large was like the very small. Now, every school student is familiar with quarks, and the next generation may well be learning about axions in the scale of the Plank constant!

Most people are more familiar with the hardware of computers than with the software. Software started life as a simple set of instructions to operate the functions of the hardware in the correct sequence to achieve a desired result. The big breakthrough was being able to store those programs of instructions in the hardware in an identical format to information. These "stored programs" enable programmers to design programs that can program programs, and therefore learn from experience.

Software is a highly stylised form of thinking. However, we can store this thinking, edit it, correct it and perfect it. Once in place, it is available for anyone to use. Thus, with huge effort we have designed programs that enable computers to beat chess masters. Those programs are now available to everyone, with a similar computer.

Thinking has a long and proud tradition. As usual, the ancient Greeks did a lot of the spadework (see Appendix 20 www.BrainMindForum.org/appendices). Solving the most complex problems starts with the simplest step. Every software designer recognises the syllogism in Aristotle's *Organon*: "All men are mortal, Socrates is a man, Therefore, Socrates is mortal". The bottom-up inductive approach: build from the detail to the general. Leibnitz began to dream of a concept language. In the nineteenth century, George Boole in his *Laws of Thought* set out to build the fundamental laws of the operation of the mind by which reasoning is performed and express them in a symbolic language upon which to build a science of logic — mathematical logic, or "Boolean logic" which is one of the foundations of today's computers. Meanwhile Bayesian modelling extended Plato's "top-down" deductive approach starting with a possible theory and continuously updating it.

Many famous philosophers and mathematicians have made significant contributions, but the great breakthrough came in the 1930s when Claude Shannon, the father of information theory, mapped Boolean logic onto electrical circuits, that could be used to power the mathematical model for an all-purpose computer that Alan Turing described in "On Computable Numbers, with an Application to the *Entscheidungsproblem*".

It then took John Von Neumann (and others) to use Boole's logic, Shannon's circuits and Turing's algorithm, and, incidentally, Morse's coding system, to design the "stored program computers" of today.

From Leibnitz onwards, all the great philosophers have tried to devise specialist languages to help structure and express our thoughts. Most adopted Gottleeb Frege's concept script. The first act of the computer programmers was to devise a programming language. There is now a tower of babel of programming languages. The last chapter outlines the possible next generation of programming languages: an amalgam of verbal language and computer programming language to "command" our robots and AI systems.

Immanuel Kant was the first to argue that intelligence and thinking are different. Intelligence is about carrying out tasks we have learned, as efficiently as possible. Thinking is about creating innovative ideas and solutions. In the computing world, intelligence is the equivalent of efficiently executing, or running existing programs. Thinking is the equivalent of designing and writing new programs.

While initially, the clear majority of attention was directed at designing the hardware of computers and telecommunications, the attention now is moving towards the software. We are close to the hardware being merely a vehicle to process software.

It is tempting to speculate if the brain may one day become just a vehicle for the mind, but this conjecture draws attention to a crucial difference. In computing, hardware and software are quite separate and independent, whereas our brains and our minds are both integral parts of our whole bodies. Separate our minds from our bodies and we cease to exist.

Software is evolving. Initially, programming followed Aristotle's inductive logic, building from the bottom up. More recently, Plato's deductive logic has been yielding big dividends by analysing, top down, ever larger volumes of records or data to identify patterns or rules. This helps us understand how the brain, mind and body identify information and is explored in Chapters 4–6.

Many people are trying to give titles to this century as it begins to unfold, "the age of the computer" or the "computer revolution". The World Economic Forum at Davos seems to think we are still in the industrial revolution, just its fourth phase.

There is a compelling argument that, like never before, the role of the philosopher will be paramount. Not just in exploring and developing better ways of thinking but in recognising and preparing the community for huge changes in the way we live, work, educate ourselves, manage our economies and governments, and all the ethical and moral problems that swift change will inexorably cause, provoke and aggravate. This is more than the age of computing.

In parallel, this is the dawning of the age of the philosophers.

PART I
CONVERGENCE

CHAPTER ONE

CONTRIBUTION OF COMPUTERS: PREDATOR OR PARTNER?

Give me a fulcrum and I will move the World.

Archimedes

What are these machines we have invented? Why are they so special?

Let us first look briefly at where computers have come from. We can learn a lot from this history.

Most people think that computers slid unobtrusively into the world after the Second World War. Some claim that the first computer was the Colossus machine built to break German codes. In many ways it was, but it could only do the job it was designed to do. After the war, various machines were designed, but the first general purpose, stored program, binary digital computer — variously claimed by a number of universities in the UK and USA around 1948 — was the watershed moment in human history.

The First Known Mechanical Calculator — First Century BC

However, various types of computers, calculators, controllers and early information processors have been in existence since the days of the Greek ascendency. To everyone's surprise, a very much corroded "machine" was retrieved from a wreck on the bottom of the Aegean Sea earlier in the twentieth century. It was undeniably made about the first century before the Christian era. Thanks to recent scanning techniques, it has been possible to study it without risking damage and as a result various reconstructed operating models are now working. The engineering is extraordinary with precision gear wheels not seen again till the Swiss started to make watches. The Antikythera can compute many astronomical events, in particular, the dates, even times of eclipses, and the dates for human events like the Olympic Games.

Sundials did not have moving parts, but they accurately displayed the time and proved that either the earth or the sun must move. Eratosthenes argued that the earth moved and is a sphere. He then went on to measure its diameter remarkably accurately, again, about the first century BC.

The Abacus

The abacus established the concept that the position of a number was as significant as its value. Addition (and multiplication) could be done by swapping rows of balls between parallel shafts. As soon as one row is full, it triggers moving a ball to the next row. Essentially, this is the same basic process of arithmetic used in the most modern mainframe computers today.

Mills

Windmills and watermills enabled a large wheel powered by wind or water to turn a shaft, and the invention of gears enabled that shaft to move other shafts faster or slower and even change direction — a horizontal water wheel turning a vertical mill wheel, for instance.

Clocks

The next big advance was clocks. Displaying the passage of time was useful and enabled people to say their prayers regularly. Various solutions preceded the pendulum as a form of regular release, as a heavy weight provided the power to move the gear wheels to move the hands on a dial. Sounding a bell on the hour soon followed. Arguably, the first example of a general purpose machine was when one mechanism was invented that could ring a different number on each hour.

Very little happened in the 1,000 years of the Roman Christian era as no one could, or can to this day, process roman numerals — even modern computers find them inscrutable!

Beginning of Automation

In the eighteenth century, a weaver in Lyon in France came up with a groundbreaking invention.

On Jacquard's looms, his weavers followed a continuous series of monotonous movements as they threw bobbins of different coloured thread across the fixed threads which made the patterns in the cloth his customers wanted to buy. He realised that the positions of a series of holes in a long strip of cardboard could be used to select the next bobbin. Link up the cardboard into a ring, and the machine would reproduce the required pattern continuously — automation, punched-card technology, even the beginning of digital imagery, dots of assorted colours between the warp and weft. The basis of television images today.

Automatic Organ Music

Fairground organs provided a similar opportunity. Holes in a continuous concertina of cards allowed air to flow into the organ pipes in different patterns and sequences — playing the tunes of pieces of music. The length of the holes determined the length the note played. Take out one card pack, insert another and the organ played a different tune, without further human interference — a general-purpose system.

Steam Power

In the tin mines of Cornwall steam power was harnessed to push pistons, to turn wheels, to replace unreliable wind to power pumps, to lift water and to stop mines flooding. Steam power was working increasingly efficiently long before the science was understood. For a century, a substance called *phlogiston* was thought to be responsible for fire. Although this was soon disproved, it led to the formulation of the laws of thermodynamics. There is a persuasive argument to start to consider whether our growing knowledge of information could lead to the formulation of some Laws of Infodynamics.

The Babbage Difference Engine

In the nineteenth century, Babbage famously tried to pull the two technologies of machines capable of computation and machines capable of generating energy together to design and power his difference engine. (The reconstruction in the Science Museum is now driven by electricity — not known in Babbage's time.) The difference engine used the information-processing concepts of the abacus and the engineering of clocks to compute numbers.

His greater breakthrough was to incorporate interchangeable gear wheels, so that his machine could compute different algorithms, different maths tunes! He never made his system work, but his colleague, Ada Countess of Lovelace, arguably the first programmer, appreciated the significance of this invention.

It is interesting that for a number of years in the 1950s and 1960s, many girls were programmers. Sadly, our education system has discouraged girls, even more than boys to take up programming.

Tabulators

Later in the nineteenth century, Hollerith and others designed mechanical systems reminiscent of the abacus but now driven by electric motors. Using individual cards in packs, usually with 80 columns of 12 rectangular holes, these machines used pins to recognise holes which then turned cog wheels or opened gates to let cards fall though. In combination, these machines could sort and add the values of packs of cards, punch the totals into "output" or "memory" cards and drive simple printing machines. By the end of the 1930s, interchangeable wiring panels were introduced which enabled a standard tabulator to be programmed to do different jobs. Ingenious wiring panel programs were carrying out very sophisticated applications.

In many ways, but in a higher league, this is where the artificial intelligence (AI) leaders have reached today. They are writing brilliant applications programs, but like their wiring panel forebears their programs and panels can only do one application. We can learn a lot from this about what we mean by "general intelligence" both in our computers and our brains.

Electronics

The big breakthrough was when semiconductors replaced gears. Ten teeth on a gear wheel could be represented by 10 thermionic valves (and later transistors). Gear wheels had to be inserted and replaced. Valves or transistors could be programmed to switch on or off automatically in ever-more complex patterns and sequences — the dawn of software. A sequence of information looks the same as a sequence of instructions, so it is possible to store programs in the memories of computers. Hence, the crucial importance of the general purpose *stored program* computer.

One thermionic valve was about the size of an iPhone. There are more than a billion transistors in an iPhone!

Overture

Everything about the work at Bletchley Park, Colossus and the Bombs were covered by the Official Secrets Act for decades after the war ended. In the late 1940s, however, teams in Manchester, Cambridge, the National Physical Laboratory and America started work on a variety of systems. Funding in near bankrupt Britain was scarce and most was directed towards building atomic power stations. Everyone aimed at providing fast, flexible calculating capability. Cambridge planned their system to be a service to the whole university, and to help people use it, they devised a basic machine code set of about 10 instructions — the first proto programming language. In the early 1950s, the Lyons catering company, working with Manchester University and the Ferranti Company, started to design machines for commercial applications. International Computers and Tabulators started to attach more complex processors to their tabulators.

In the USA, International Business Machines Corporation did the same. The US government placed a series of orders with both IBM and Univac, an offshoot of Remington Rand, and Hewlett Packard who started to build a solid commercial base. The National Cash Register Company tied up with Elliott Automation in the UK for the latter to design and build and the former to sell the EA 400 series computers.

These early machines were the size of whole offices and housed in air-conditioned rooms. They had specialised operators, who wore overalls to minimise any problems with dust, to load information and programs into the systems and bring out the results.

The arrival of semiconductors or transistors — solid-state electronics reduced the size of systems by about 80% and widened their applications. The basic design architecture of these systems has not changed much, with just two exceptions. The ability to control and process terminals, process a number in parallel and of great significance, random access memory (RAM) systems. In 1966, the first systems for the financial community with teleprinter terminals in banker's and broker's offices linked to a central computer providing minute-by-minute stock market prices and valuing and analysing portfolios were operating, first in London and then in New York.

In the 1960s, IBM marketed a range of systems — the 360 family — a small system then a "ladder" of larger machines that buyers could acquire as they expanded their knowledge and usage. They decided to provide a basic operating program that would be standard up this range. This turned out to be vastly more difficult than expected and cost IBM a great deal of money and resources.

The development of computer operating systems plays a major role in how we think about and widen our understanding of our background general intelligence.

By the middle of the 1970s, commercial computing was a substantial business in the UK with over 100,000 staff in the hardware and software sides of the technology. Universities were beginning to offer courses in the design and programming of software. This alarmed the teaching profession, and some Local Education Authorities tried to ban their use in schools.

Why Does This Help Us Understand How Our Brain and Mind Work?

We learn a lot by analogy. If an abacus does arithmetic that way, does this throw any light on how our mind does arithmetic? Nine tenths of invention is getting the community to accept something new. Democracy is much more than a voting system. Equally important is the toleration of new ideas.

The First Act of the Computer Revolution

Bright teenagers and undergraduates bought components and wired up small processors. Others attached commercial television screens. The technology of record players was converted to recording and playing data. Add a keyboard — wire up a standard electric typewriter. It all went on a bedroom desk. Adverts in technical magazines generated a profusion of orders. An aptly called BASIC programming language enabled anyone to communicate with their own micro-computer. The mainframe manufacturers initially ignored these trivial upstarts. Scare stories circulated about the damage to teenagers spending too much time playing games with their computers. The British Government instructed the research councils not to fund any proposals that included using these "toys" to keep them out of the universities. If schools wanted them, the parents would have to buy them with loyalty points from the local Tesco. The BBC marketed a system — the famous BBC Micro — and was overwhelmed with orders. This upset everyone. The BBC was not supposed to compete with business and did not proceed.

Nobody in "the establishment", however one defines that group, could believe that the whole community would soon have them in their homes, let alone in their pockets. Is it psychologically interesting that the establishment could not comprehend that "ordinary" members of the public, especially their children could not only understand, but also push out the frontiers of something like computing.

In the event, it is the establishment that has signally failed to grasp the opportunities that this new science, technology, business and commercial opportunity have offered. It is embarrassing to the nation of Newton, Darwin, Brunel, Turing and Berners-Lee that not one single major national computer system has been installed to specification, on time and within budget. After long continuous lobbying, some aspects of computer programming were included in the National school's curriculum in 2015. It is more surprising still, that no one across government seems to be much concerned about this record. The behaviour of some groups, industries, whole professions even, seem as though they are in denial.

The great breakthrough in human development was language — an efficient means of communication. The great breakthrough in computing was the combination of a keyboard, screen and processor. We could communicate with our machines.

Computers Come of Age

Computers now dominate the scene, and it is useful to study some of the component industries and sciences, and the advantages and disadvantages of the internet and the World Wide Web. Plato was not too keen on the early democracy, where a good orator could sway the Agora to make terrible decisions. No doubt there are many "remainers" in the UK, and voters in the USA, that might be tempted to think that "social media" has similar drawbacks and agree with him.

It is well known that the two most powerful drivers of technology are war and sex. The Second World War gave us *Colossus*. The World Wide Web has made the development of search engines and *Wikipedia* possible, but initially the widespread development of the internet was made economically possible by the proceeds of widely popular online pornography.

The Second Act of the Computer Revolution

In the last 50 years, computing has generated more wealth than any other invention in history, but almost every usage has been as a tool. A very sophisticated tool, but a tool, nonetheless.

Now, in the same way that the components of micros slipped into the market, computing is changing again, and this time these developments are orders of magnitude greater. One of the main themes of this book is that for the first time in the history of civilisation, we have a tool that can enhance our own personal individual abilities. Robots are turning conventional ideas of economics, employment, education and ethics upside down. Prosthetic links to the brain are working, synthetic biologists are linking animate to inanimate cells, and biogeneticists are beginning to edit deoxyribonucleic acid (DNA).

But that is largely the background to the rest of this book. Back to the components that brought us this far.

Telecommunications and the Beginning of Coding Systems

The invention of the telegraph and telecommunications played an indirect major role.

The first telegraph systems were very limited in the signals they could transmit. Samuel F. B. Morse devised a signalling system to transmit letters and numbers over the network. Morse used groups of five on–off signals which provided 32 combinations. Using one code to change shift enabled 62 combinations so that numbers and punctuation could be included. Extended to groups of eight codes, all computers to this day use Extended Morse as the International Standard (ISO). Teleprinters were simplified electric typewriters capable of both sending and receiving the telegraph signals. One early addition was a paper tape punch and reader to store streams of signals — a descendant of packs of punched cards that were reels of five channel paper tapes. Originally a paper tape was read by five pins falling through holes if they were present. Soon they were read by light, which was much faster — always the pressure for speed.

There are no numbers or letters in our computers, only patterns of bits. We will explore how this helps us understand how we process letters and numbers in our brains and minds.

Computer Terminals

Teleprinters were attached to many early computers to enable operators to input program and sort out problems. The printer function provided an "audit trail". In the early 1960s, it occurred to programmers that it would be possible to attach teleprinters to mainframe computers at any distance by using a standard teleprinter telephone line. Teleprinters were very slow, so 10, 20, even a 100 teleprinters at any distance could be connected to one computer. This needed some fairly complicated queuing software: the era of terminals had dawned. Now every computer is connected to networks by antique British Telecoms (BT) copper pairs, fibre, terrestrial wireless links or satellites. In the long run, all telecommunications may be by satellite.

Parallel Programming

Computer processors are all sequential, even the largest modern computers — they carry out instructions one at a time. Because they can carry out millions of instructions per second (MIPS), they often give an observer the impression they are doing lots of things at the same time. For instance, 100 terminals might all appear to be working in unison. The software breakthrough was to design a queuing system, known as *the stack*. In the terminal processing example, each time a terminal is activated (an operator starts keying a question) an interrupt instruction is placed in the stack. Every time the processor completes a piece of program, it accesses the stack for the next interrupt in the queue. When our interrupt reaches the head of the queue, the processor picks up the query from our terminal, processes the query and transmits the answer. Often this process may involve retrieving information from the data systems, thus our query may pass through the queue in the stack a number of times, but it is so fast we do not notice.

The brain appears to be a *parallel* system. Lots of neural activity happens concurrently. Magnetic resonance imaging (MRI) scans suggest the whole brain is continuously in a low-level state of activity, while various sub-sections of the brain are on gradients of increasing activity according to the tasks being carried out, up to focussed concentration. For instance, the brain is continuously processing signals from the sensory and other organs as they monitor the outside world and our body's operation. An important question is how does the brain determine the sequence of neural activity? What is the process that determines priorities? It is observable that the brain and computers operate in completely different ways, but the question is still valid. We know how the machine does this job. How does the neural biological system solve this problem?

Convergence of Technologies

In the middle of the century, most mathematical calculations were made by mechanical devices with hand-rotated gear wheels.

A number of technologies converged. The key was the cathode ray tube developed for television, which provided a "window" into what the computer processor was doing. Add one of these screens, a keyboard, an electric typewriter and a memory unit to a simple processor, include some software and the word processor was born. Overnight the entire secretarial community was obsolescent. Laser, then inkjet printers, first black and white, then quickly in colour, and the whole printing industry was turned up-side down. Hand calculators, accounting machines, mechanical tills and typewriters quietly vanished. What happened to those communities should help us prepare for the obsolescence of our lawyers, accountants, administrators, regulators, and the notable change of role of teachers and lecturers.

Both computer processors and cathode ray tubes operate exclusively in streams of dots. All pictures were digitised. Sound engineers were developing digitised sound.

Now we live in a digital world. All Information, speech, program, text, mathematical formulae, algorithms, pictures and sound are just one identical stream of dots and dashes, electrical signal patterns, either actively operating or passively stored in memory.

This technology greatly helps us understand how the eyes and ears process light and sound.

Software

Software, or the art of programming, is central to all computing. For those interested in more details, Appendix 32 (all appendices are hosted on the website, www.BrainMindForum.org/appendices) describes how a Turing machine which is only able to add, subtract and question can be programmed to beat chess masters. Appendix 32-H (all appendices are hosted on www.BrainMindForum.org/appendices), describes how a computer's central processor executes program instructions, and thus how programs can be designed to build programs — the essential ability of every type of artificial (or machine) intelligence.

The brain and mind only has neurons. Can they add and subtract? Programs writing programs sounds like how we think. Does this help us understand how we think? We can learn to program; does this mean we can learn to think?

The earliest programs were written quite literally in the sequence of *codes that the processor used. At Cambridge*, the designers of the *Electronic Delay Storage Automatic Calculator* (EDSAC) computer was planned as a service bureau, so they provided one of the first "machine code" proto programming languages. This expanded the simple plus and minus commands to provide a more user friendly 10 or so instructions moving data to and from an accumulator. Later versions moved data to and from various "registers". More sophisticated machines had multiplication and division functions designed into the hardware, while others provided software subroutines — slower but cheaper. Two levels of memory storage were provided. Long-term memory, often reels of magnetic tape, and short-term memory, which was much quicker to access, but very much smaller, fixed length and designed as a store to hold sections of program. Does the brain have levels of memory? It is the subject of much debate.

Solving the Difficulties of Programming

Machine code is difficult because any mistakes are usually hard to correct. Often corrections create more errors. Programmers began to design programs to help programmers write programs and find the errors in their programs. Computer processors consist of a series of registers that contain a string of on–off bits. These can be either data or instructions. Programs access these registers by using a sequence controller. A simple program executes each instruction then automatically uses this controller to access the next instruction in turn. A conditional jump instruction, therefore, either selects the next instruction in sequence if the condition is true, or if the condition is false, instructs the controller to jump to a specified instruction. This ability to choose from two alternatives gives computers their unique power to make decisions.

If the programmer makes an error and the jump instruction leads to a register containing data, the processor will attempt to decipher the data as an instruction with potentially devastating results.

However, this remarkably powerful feature means that a programmer can write multiple programs, intentionally executing instructions from different programs. Thus, a master program might intentionally change the contents of a register containing a slave program as though it were data, then intentionally use the controller to execute that amended program. As mentioned above, this procedure is set out in detail in Appendix 32-H (all appendices are hosted on www.BrainMindForum.org/appendices).

This was a very significant development because it demonstrates the power of both program and information being stored in the same format, and in the same memory structures. The key point of this is that any program can be processed by other programs as though it was information. This means that programs can be written specifically to vary programs in the light of events.

Because computers store their own programs, they can be programmed to learn. Is this how the brain, mind and body learn?

Programming Languages

Programs to write programs soon developed into programming languages specifically designed to help process different classes of problem. One of the first programming languages, probably the most famous and still used today is FORTRAN, or FORmula TRANslation. Mathematical programs tend to be easier to write as the problems are usually more clearly defined.

Commercial applications are often less rigorous with multiple alternatives that humans using the system may try and take. Also, people using computers make mistakes, inadvertently pressing the wrong keys, even accidently switching off the power. "Did you back up your data?" was a frequently heard cry. Thus, quite often 90% of commercial programs that the public might use, are defensive program, designed to cope with every error and mistake a tired operator might inadvertently make.

Programs that help programmers write programs proliferated and a veritable tower of babel of programming languages exists and is continuously expanding.

Compiled Programs

There are two distinct types of programming language, and this is of considerable significance to studying how the brain operates. There is a persuasive argument that this is how we learn.

We can outline the principles here, but we can learn a lot about how the brain does something remarkably similar in greater detail later.

Programs that carry out tasks that are precisely defined and involve little or no human input other than by trained skilled operators are written in the program language. When this is complete, a "complier" program converts the language steps into a machine code program. This is fixed and cannot be edited. Corrections or later amendments can only be made to the language version and recompiled from scratch. This system is inflexible but the programs run very fast.

Interpreted Programs

Many applications require more flexibility. These programming languages allow the operator to insert alternative parameters, different every time the application is used. For example, the word processor programs being used to write these words has both "compiled" and "interpreted" sections. The compiled part carries out all the functions to turn the keystrokes into text, stores this text, accesses it, prints it out and generally does all the heavy lifting. However, nowadays, every text can be in a multitude of typefaces, point sizes and layouts. The author and editor can change a great deal at will. To change the next two lines to Arial Italic 12 point requires me to point to those changes:

In the stream of text this will embed three program instructions, "Change to Arial", "Change to Italic Typeface" and "Change to 12 point".

As the program processes this stream of text it "sees" these program instructions and "interprets" them and carries out the instructions.

Now I have changed them back and the new (original) instructions have been interpreted as program. Early word processors allowed the operator to insert these program instructions. They might have looked to the operator on the screen something like this: #TF Arial~, #italic~, #12pt~. # to indicate the next characters are program. TF = type Font and so forth. Program instructions like these are out of sight on all modern systems, but they are still there embedded in the text and are still interpreted in the same way, only many hundreds of times faster. On older systems, it was possible to display them. There were often many more program instructions that text characters.

The brain operates the same way. When we learn to drive a car, all the finicky movements of the clutch and gear lever slip into compiled mode, usually called *background mode*, and we do them without thought. Moving the indicator to turn at a corner is still entirely in our hands. This *foreground mode* is always manual or interpreted.

Multitasking

This is the basis of how our brain mind enables us to do more than one task at a time. We can drive a car in background mode and talk to our passenger in foreground mode. When we come to a junction, we slot turning the indicator into the foreground conversation.

Early Programming

In early computers, the applications programmers wrote all the programs, including the allocation and the storage areas needed. They had to write all the program steps to input information, perhaps from a paper tape on a teleprinter, instruct the processor and control the printer. Memory systems were very simple. If the application involved updating customer accounts for instance, the whole file of all customer accounts was run through the memory reader *input* unit. The relevant customer account was updated and a complete new file of all customer accounts was created through the memory writing *output* unit. To make this process acceptably efficient, all work to be done that involved updating memory files was batched together and processed in one session. This had the advantage that a series of "grandfather", "father", and "son" files could be stored and accessed if a subsequent error occurred.

For instance, in a bank application, all the transactions during the day, could be batched together and processed during the night. Provision was made to ensure that wily customers did not draw out a number of amounts during the day that individually were less than the previous overnight balance, but cumulatively was greater than their balance, as this would not come to light till the following morning.

Memory Systems

One of the great breakthroughs of the micro revolution was the invention of 'Random Access Memory' or RAM systems. It is easy to see that a tape recorder could be used to key an article or book, but the whole process would be impossibly unwieldy if the whole tape recording had to be updated to insert one new word, or even just one lowly comma!

The technology of the gramophone was merged with the tape recorder. A magnetic disc had a series of read–write heads instead of one stylus. Each head read or wrote a magnetic pattern on to a magnetic ring on the disc. The software had to be quite sophisticated. If some words needed to be inserted to a paragraph, the new file could be longer than the original. How could it be slotted back into the space from whence it came?

The solution was to break up every file into fixed length blocks of say 128 characters each. These were then "written" onto the disc and an *index* kept of where each block was located. When the file was needed, the program consulted the index and collected each block in turn to reassemble the file. Adding or deleting words and paragraphs meant that when the file had blocks that were a new size they were located elsewhere. The old blocks were released to the index controller and so were available for reuse for another block of that file, or any other.

Disks take time to rotate, so database management programs are optimised to place blocks in the correct position on different rings to maximise the speed of reading and writing. Thus, the text of even a simple letter is likely to be spread all over a random access disk. The quality of the indexing systems becomes paramount. Old information is not removed. The file delete instruction only removes the entries in the index. New data is simply written over the old. The technology of magnetic patterns is such that the latest message written is the easiest to read. However, sophisticated equipment can read levels of magnetic messages, thus files thought to have been deleted can be read at any time in the future. Beware!

Our brains are random access systems. A whole body of psychology has been built on the theory that memories can be buried deep in the brain.

Packet Switching

This is the same technology used to transmit messages over the internet network. A message is divided up into packets. Each packet is sent by a different route through the network and the whole message is reassembled at the destination. This technology maximises the efficiency of the overall system, and no long message can cause congestion.

One of the principal functions of the brain is to manage the memory system. The brain is continuously accessing, processing, updating and restoring memories. How does the brain cope with variable length records that are continuously changing?

As we commented above, it is observable that the brain and computers operate in completely different ways, but the question is still valid. We know how the machine does this job. How does the neural biological system solve this problem?

Operating Systems

Early computer manufacturers supplied users with a library of "subroutines" to input data, store data, carry out certain standard, frequently used processes, and output programs to help assemble data to be printcd with increasing complexity. Similarly, the number of programming languages proliferated. In the late 1960s IBM undertook an ambitious campaign to manufacture a range of computers; small versions for starters, medium-sized systems geared to commercial or scientific use and large systems for large organisations — the 360 range. To help customers pass up this gradient they set up a team to bring together all the sub-routines to control all the different peripherals. The brilliant idea was to enable good applications programs to be moved up to bigger processors as the demand increased. It proved a mammoth task and eventually some thousands of staff were involved.

Along came the Micros and the entire process started again, with one very big difference. All the 360 family and their competitors were essentially batch processing systems. Once programs were started operators had very little idea of what was happening and few facilities to adjust the process.

Micros had a screen so the operator could see exactly what was happening and a keyboard to control the process, as well as input information and store it on memory disks. Writing the programs to manage the data on these new RAM disks was beyond the reach of early micro users, so all machines were sold with a software '*disk operating system*', or DOS. At the beginning of the 1980s, there were several competing operating systems which was a major problem to suppliers of applications products. Microsoft offered an efficient cheap and cheerful system which included screen and keyboard control programs as well as optimised disk operation programs. It established a world standard and within 5 years was the richest corporation in the world. Even early DOS systems already had some 40,000 instructions.

To those interested in the history of computing, this development completely changed the computing industry. Up to this watershed, the hardware manufacturers were the senior partners. Nowadays, software applications are the centre of attention, and the manufacturers of hardware

are in business to provide just the kit to run programs. Today, transistors; tomorrow, quantum bits; in a decade..., DNA?

To those interested in how computing can shed light on the underlying working of the brain and mind, this development is a paradigm shift in our understanding. The brain has evolved a form of background operating system that does all the standard everyday neural chores, continuously monitoring the environment and coping and responding to events, leaving a substantial part of the brain and mind to think, solve problems, make decisions and generally be creative. A significant part of this book is devoted to exploring this hypothesis and studying the extended *autonomic* functions of the central nervous system. It is certainly a candidate for the *general intelligence* that everyone is seeking.

Implications of Online Real-Time Continuous Processing

Old fashioned batch processing had the advantage that if, and when things went wrong there was always a datum point to return and start again. Real life is not susceptible to processing in discreet timed units. Real life is as it happens. One cannot go back and try again.

Two obvious examples are financial transactions where, when money is transferred, the relevant accounts need to be credited and debited immediately. Another is air traffic control. Controllers cannot ask all pilots in the system to go back 5 miles and fly that routine again! Money transfers are a subtler problem. At any time that, say, Bank A is transferring £x from their customer to Bank B for the credit of their customer. The transaction can have left A and be wholly or partly en route to Bank B. The transaction can have arrived at the Head Quarters (HQ) of Bank B but not have reached the customer at B. Both banks have sophisticated back-up systems so that when the transaction is complete B's customer's account will have been credited and A's customer debited, but during the transaction, which might take less than a microsecond the money may be in one bank or the other, or on neither customer's account, or somewhere in the middle. The back-up process may even complicate the issue, because the transaction may or may not have reached either bank's back-up files. An obvious precaution is to site back-up facilities in a safe remote site. In the event of a crash, partial crash or failure at either bank, in the communication system between them, or the back-up systems of either bank, or the communications between each bank and their back-up facilities, which records are correct?

In the 9/11 disaster, the HQ systems of a number of major banks were destroyed. It took some thousands of skilled staff to recreate the systems over the following weeks.

When links in the internet network fail, a similar problem arises.

There is a similar problem in neural systems. Two people talking can very easily come away quite genuinely with a very different view of what was said. Twenty people witnessing a car crash or other event can easily submit quite different reports of what they are quite sure they witnessed. All those memories are different.

At first sight, brains do not have formal back-up systems like the bank examples, but it is a well-established fact that people who lose memories in an accident or stroke can often gradually retrieve them over time. More frequently observed, is the temporary loss of a word or phrase, which is often of concern or worry to older people. Usually the misbehaving word or phrase surfaces a short while later. People are beginning to call this "senior citizen syndrome". The problem may be a temporary failure of the power supply. If a particular word regularly misbehaves, then we can develop strategies to recall that word by other means.

There is plenty of scope for research to learn from computer safety experience to develop neural back-up strategies to augment the brain's natural abilities.

Search for Artificial Intelligence

If intelligence could be programmed, then computers could replace boring jobs and release people for more interesting occupations. More intelligent processing of information could lead to better decision making and a more efficient community. Could intelligent programs be written to control robots?

The thrust of Alan Turing's 1936 paper to the Royal Society, "On Computable Numbers" was that if we could "define precisely the way a problem could be solved, write out the formula, list the steps in the algorithm, then any 'computer' could solve that problem".

Building on this insight, a group of leaders in computing research met in Dartmouth College in the USA in 1956, funded by the Rockefeller foundation. Marvin Minsky, information theorist, who later coined the term "artificial intelligence" while at the Media Lab at Harvard; Claude Shannon, famous for the design of the adding circuit and his work on the technology of the transmission of information over telephone circuits; Herbert Simon and John Nash, both later Nobel Prize Winners, wrote in their funding application "every aspect of learning or any other feature of intelligence can, in principle, be so precisely described that a machine can be made to simulate it". In other words, "if…intelligence can be precisely defined then a machine can be made to simulate it". They went on to ask for funding for a 10-man group to spend 6 months to specify intelligence, including making machines use language, form abstractions and concepts, solve kinds of problems now reserved for humans and improve themselves.

Sixty years and many millions of dollars later, we have successfully written programs that can beat chess masters, win quiz competitions and learn to play the game *Go*. However, neither the cognitive neuroscientists, nor the biogeneticists, nor the cognitive psychologists, nor the scientific community generally, have been able to specify a definition of "intelligence".

Lord Kelvin argued that the first step to knowledge was description, plus measurement leading to a definition verifiable by experiment. The software community paraphrase Archimedes by saying "give us a definition and we will program the world".

Convergence of Computing

The convergence of computing, cognitive neuroscientists, biogenetics and cognitive psychology can make some very useful contributions to our understanding of the brain mind, both directly and indirectly through analogy, by posing questions and by studying the systems problems that both encounter.

Brain Mind Duality

The first and perhaps the most useful contribution of computing is to finally lay to rest the long debate over the duality of the human brain and the definition of mind.

The ancient Egyptians identified a life force or *ka* that clearly left the body at death. Many civilisations speculated about the body that seemed to do things and the brain that seemed to think about things. Fast forward to Rene Descartes, who coined the famous foundation of cognitive neuroscience, *Cogito ergo sum*, or "I think, therefore I am" (the whole quote is in Appendix 3, all appendices are hosted on www.BrainMindForum.org/appendices). He receives a lot of flak for his division into an inert body and an active brain or mind, and use of religious words like soul, but it should be remembered that he was a contemporary of Galileo who narrowly escaped being burnt at the stake for propounding anything that appeared to contradict Holy Writ. At the time, however, neither Descartes nor Holy Writ was particularly well versed in electricity.

Computing has solved this problem completely and elegantly.

Hardware is the mass of circuits we can see and touch in our computers and the mass of neurons we can see and touch in the whole central nervous system throughout the whole body, with large numbers of networks concentrated in the skull. This is the *brain*.

Software is the patterns of program signals that activates and drives our computer systems and the patterns of electrochemical signals that flow over the neurons, generating electromagnetic fields. This is the *mind*.

In both computing and humans, neither hardware nor software can achieve anything at all without the other. They are both truly symbiotic. Look at a computer with its power off and it is inert. Look at a brain seconds after death, the whole network of the central nervous system and the brain can still be complete and perfect, yet capable of nothing.

This is particularly helpful because we can say with some confidence that, just as we know the brain does not feel pain or hunger, so the brain is not intelligent, does not create memory, is not the seat of meaning and is not conscious. All these life-defining properties are functions of the mind.

The neurons of the central nervous system evolved and still provide the communication system linking up all the sensory and other organs and the muscles and glands. The neural networks of the brain coordinate the whole body. The brain is also the learning engine of the whole human system.

Thus, we can say that computers have already helped cognitive neuroscience halve the target area to search for these attributes.

Information

The brain mind and computers are the only information processors we know about in the universe.

Just as we are only beginning to scratch the surface of our knowledge of cognitive neuroscience, we realise we know equally little about the science of information. As we have commented above, the steam engine led to the discovery of the laws of thermodynamics. Science explained the invention *ex post facto*. By studying the acquisition, storage and processing of information in our computers we can, at least ask useful questions about how the brain and mind learn about information. We can ask the physicists to speculate about the measurement of the smallest measurable unit of information and to start to postulate some Laws of Infodynamics to explain what we see and use every day.

However, of more immediate value is to use our computers to study how information is represented in the brain mind. As we noted discussing the origins of telecommunications, there are no letters, words, numbers, pictures or music in any computer ever made. Again, this narrows the target area to search for and discover how the brain represents information.

We can spend time later studying information in detail, but one key insight is important to draw attention to now.

Let us emphasise the point that information can *mean things* such as facts, measurements, or values: passive data; or it can *do things* such as instructions, activities, recipes or as scientists prefer — algorithms or active directives. Furthermore, both types of information can be stored in identical form and processed interchangeably. Indeed, they are not "different types". They are different manifestations of the same phenomena.

The paradigm shift, the game changer, the unique selling point (in management speak) of computing is the stored program capability of computers. It draws our attention to the central foundation of our understanding of the brain mind. The brain swops jobs, varies priorities and learns new things and activities. Knowing how computer programs cope helps us understand how our brains do this.

Computers have fixed memory capacity, a fixed instruction set, they are digital, sequential and binary. This draws into a sharp focus the differences. The brain has an infinite capacity to *grow memory*. At birth, we have a billion neurons in the brain part of the central nervous system. A mature brain has grown upwards of a trillion new neural links and structures. The brain can store experiences and can create — learn — new responses, new tasks, new functions, new skills and new abilities.

The brain is not digital, it is analogue. A computer uses codes to define exact values. The brain represents values by the quantity and strength of electrochemical signals and the ambient hormone mix. Quite a good analogy is that arithmetic is precise. Twelve inches make a foot, always and exactly. In literature, different combinations of similar words in different circumstances generate quite different emotions and meanings.

Similarly, the brain is not binary. We explore the coding systems of computers and the absence of any coding system in the brain in Chapter 6. The representation and processing of letters and words seems to be relatively similar in both computers and brains, whereas the representation and processing of numbers seems to be completely different.

The brain is not sequential. It is massively parallel, with many activities going on concurrently, mostly in "background mode". Exploring how we have invented ways to integrate and prioritise multiple programs, enables us to appreciate the scale of the problem our brain mind faces minute by minute and day by day, and at least delineates the problem that we are trying to solve.

There is One Last, Rather More Subtle Comparison

The history of civilisation is one long progression from the strongest ruling the community to the cleverest, or most intelligent assuming the leading roles.

Had we been researching and discussing comparative skills and started to look for "intelligence" as a way to select the brightest, best and most useful to society before the rise of ancient Greece, throughout the Roman empire, and pretty much up to the Renaissance, we would have begun by listing the strongest, the most coordinated, the most agile, the fastest and the fittest. We would look for the way some people were able to learn new skills faster than others, especially fighting skills. Who would we rather stand next to in battle? We might have invented tests of eye and muscle coordination. The ability to read and write, although undoubtedly useful, was rather of secondary significance — the priests could do that. Eton was started because Henry VI thought it useful if his Barons could read and write.

Would we have looked for the most valuable attributes of "intelligence" among the tiny number of academics, orators and teachers? "Yes, Cicero was a clever chap, but how useful would he be when push came to shove?"

Early histories name the kings, emperors, dictators. Only with the beginnings of thinking do we hear of the Aristotle's, Plato's and Archimedes'. After the renaissance, it is the scientists we begin to know about, as the hereditary leaders begin to fade away. Now it can be inventers, originators, artists, musicians and most recently sportsmen.

The first computers were all about the hardware, with the software the minor partner. Progressively it is the designers of systems and the programmers who push out the frontiers. Now the hardware manufacturers just make the equipment for the software cohorts to run their algorithms.

All our early inventions were machines to supplement our muscles, now the inventions that matter most, supplement our brain minds. When we hunt for intelligence we should not forget that while we give preference to academic and literate abilities, there are other skills that should not be forgotten.

It is not difficult to forecast the trend. Engines changed the role and monopoly of the importance of muscles. Computers, robots and AI are changing the role and monopoly of the importance of brains.

Time to look at the state of the art of our knowledge of cognitive neuroscience.

CHAPTER TWO

STATE OF THE ART: COGNITIVE NEUROSCIENCE

The convergence of computing, biogenetics, cognitive neuroscience, and cognitive psychology has stimulated two major reappraisals of our understanding of the brain, the mind and its relationship to the whole body:

(1) The brain is not an organ on its own but an integral part of the holistic system of the whole body.
(2) Because we have largely thought about the brain in isolation, we have tended to ascribe functions to the brain that, on more careful study, may be functions of other organs and systems.

The body consists of six major systems:

(1) The **central nervous system** that provides the communication infrastructure that connects every organ and every muscle enabling the body to operate in equilibrium as one cooperative, coordinated, synchronised whole.
(2) The **brain mind** that organises responses to internal and external events and modulates behaviour. It is the memory and learning system and the seat of intelligence, thinking and creativity.

(3) The **cardiovascular** system that includes the heart and lungs, and manufactures and circulates the blood through the arteries and veins to supply the body with nutrients, oxygen, water, the hormones and other secretions of the glands of the endocrine system; the "emergency services" to repair damage to the fabric of the body and remove waste. The lymphatic system that circulates liquids throughout the body can be thought of as part of the cardiovascular system or a system in its own right. For our purposes this is not significant.

(4) The **endocrine** system which includes some one hundred known glands and potentially a further hundred that supports the other systems in transmitting information, modifies the activities of those other systems and generates the perceptions, sensations, impressions and emotions that enable us to be aware of events taking place in our bodies, and being part of the environment around us — that we are hungry, angry, aroused, and a myriad other feelings of being alive.

(5) The **immune** system which defends the body from foreign bacteria and viruses maintains facilities to recognise and exclude these invaders should they return and is thought to manage the biome.

(6) The **gastrointestinal, enteric nervous system**, consisting of some 500 million neurons. It is the second largest agglomeration of neurons which controls the conversion of food into nutrients by regulating the selection, supply and temporary storage in the light of events, and expels waste.

The Central Nervous System

Autonomic Functions

In the earliest life forms, a number of cells began to group together for safety and mutual support. Individual cells began to specialise. Neurons evolved to link all the other cells together so that they could communicate and they could begin to work together as one coordinated organism.

Babies born today have about two billion neurons. About half are concentrated in the brain. Some five hundred million form a "secondary brain" in the intestines, and the remaining five hundred million connect every organ and muscle.

Neurons

There are many distinct types of neurons, but they all broadly follow the same pattern. They have a nucleus and several tentacles, very roughly like an octopus. However, there are two types of tentacles, usually referred to as filaments. Dendrite filaments input messages from the sensory and other organs and from other neurons. There are usually numbers of dendrites feeding information to a nucleus. Axon filaments output messages from the nucleus to muscles, organs and other neurons. Usually there is only one axon, although some axons divide up like a river delta as they near their target.

The nucleus transmits patterns of electrochemical signals along the axons and receives patterns of electrochemical signals along the dendrites in the form of action potentials, or electrical pulses generated by the interaction of sodium and calcium atoms. This electrical activity creates a weak electro-magnetic field around these filaments whenever they are active. All the links to muscles and glands are duplicated. For instance, one axon carries signals down the spine and legs to each toe and a dendrite carries signals from each toe to the brain, at approximately four feet per second. More technical details are listed at Appendix 35 (all appendices are hosted on www.BrainMindForum.org/appendices).

It is observable that if one stubs one's toe, there is a definable time gap before that information reaches the brain. We see the impact but only feel the pain about one and a half a seconds later. As well as carrying instructions and information, the dendrites feedback the performance generated by the instructions transmitted along the axons, providing a form of *quality control*.

At birth the brain can do almost nothing, but it can learn to do almost anything. All the sensory organs are connected to the brain, but that is all. For instance, a baby can hear sounds and make noises, but nothing more. Every human must learn to hear and say every single word.

Power Supply

All neurons have their own individual power generator. Every neuron is connected to the blood supply by astrocyte glia cells. These cells pass nutrients to mitochondria in the nucleus which convert these nutrients to energy. The mitochondria convert more energy than is needed in normal circumstances. This excess energy is stored in adenosine triphosphate, which operates rather like "storage batteries". This stored energy is available in a crisis when the nucleus may need maximum power in a hurry.

All neurons are connected to all organs, muscles, glands, other neurons by very intricate and sophisticated links known as *synapses*. The curious fact is that synapses are not direct connectors but gaps or clefts. None of the signals carried along the axons and dendrites can pass across these gaps. The electrochemical signals travelling along an axon or dendrite stimulate neurotransmitter molecules which swim across the synaptic gap and stimulate an electrochemical signal in the target axon, or dendrite, or reaction if the target is a gland, muscle etc.

Synapses have been something of a "Cinderella interest" in cognitive science circles, as they are very difficult to study; however, recent research has suggested they may play very significant roles that are as complex as their structure and operation. Chapter 18 explores synapses in more detail. For more information and recent research, see Appendix 30 (all appendices are hosted on www.BrainMindForum.org/appendices).

Signal Strength

The nucleus can either send a signal or not, but the influences on that transmission are wide and complex. Whether the nucleus transmits a signal varies widely according to the number of stimuli it receives from its dendrites. Secondly, it depends on the ambient hormone mix. In a perceived crisis, the brain may be bathed in a strong solution of adrenalin, which will tend to amplify the likelihood of signals being received and acted upon, for instance. The length of the signal may depend on the available energy. Over prolonged periods of high activity, stored energy capacity may be run down, and the supply of nutrient and particularly water supplies come under pressure.

The electrochemical signals tend to leak from the sides of the axon and dendrite filaments. Frequently used filaments attract glia cells which coat them with myelin. This has the effect of insulating them. There is a growing body of evidence that synapses are strengthened every time they are activated. Various messenger molecules can attach themselves to the filaments to modulate the strength and length of transmission of signals temporarily and permanently. A great deal of attention has been given recently to accumulations of plaque on neurons, which appears to reduce their efficiency in transmitting signals. Transmission of signals across the synaptic gaps is very variable. Thus, the transmission of information of complete messages from source to destination is both analogue and almost infinitely variable.

Functions of the Background Operating System

The neurons with their axon and dendrite filaments provide the physical communications network. The patterns of electrochemical signals transmit all the instructions over this network. In the womb, the first signals are transmitted from the nascent brain to the proto heart causing it to begin pumping blood to carry nutrients back to the brain, and the whole intricate system builds from there. It is worth emphasising the clearly observable fact that nothing can happen to this whole elaborate machine without this flow of tiny sparks.

The Autonomic Functions of the Central Nervous System

There appear to be three systems that provide a background operating system (OS) that largely operates automatically and only impinges on consciousness if something is significantly wrong and needs attention. It was originally referred to as one single system and named the "autonomic" system, but more recently it is thought the components may be separate.

(1) Current thinking is that the basic autonomic functions are a stream of patterns of electrochemical signals, which in addition to controlling the heart rate, are also responsible for continuously overseeing the digestive system, the lungs, monitoring all the sensory and other organs, sexual competition, arousal and satisfaction; and the waste processing and output systems. It is also responsible for minor reflex actions like coughing, sneezing, swallowing, vomiting, and for major

responses to external circumstances like fighting or fleeing, catching prey or partners, home building and nurturing the young. Some (sympathetic) functions seem to mobilise activity, some (parasympathetic) seem to dampen functions down.

(2) Sometimes thought to be part of this system and sometimes as a separate network, is the somatic nervous system that connects and operates the skeletal muscles. Efferent nerves are responsible for sending commands to stimulate muscle contraction from the central nervous system. Afferent nerves are responsible for relaying sensations back to the central nervous system.

(3) The enteric nervous system governs the functions of the gastrointestinal system. More recently, it appears to have its own independent reflex activity and, therefore, whether it is considered to be part of, or separate from, the autonomic system is the subject of debate.

In short, these sympathetic, somatic and enteric functions, whether called collectively the autonomic system or not, are the agencies that cause the whole body to operate efficiently in coordinated, cooperative, synchronised equilibrium. They continue to operate whether we are asleep or awake.

The Brain Mind

For much of the last century, the brain has been the centre of attention of any research that has been carried out, and any work on its relationship in the holistic body has mostly been left to the medical community.

We have for some time known that the brain — the neurons — do not feel pain or hunger. Recently, we have also begun to realise that the brain is neither intelligent, nor can it remember, nor is it conscious. It is also true that there are no letters, let alone words in the brain. There are no numbers, pictures or music either.

We seem to have gone from the brain doing everything to the brain doing little or nothing all in one sentence. Not so, of course.

How can this be? Our computers can help us unravel this conundrum. Most people nowadays are familiar and comfortable with the concepts of hardware and software. The former are the integrated circuits of semi-conductors — mostly transistors at present — the equipment that we can see and touch. The software is the jargon for the programs of instruction that the processor uses to transmit sequences of patterns of ephemeral electronic signals to activate and control the hardware.

The physical neurons we can see and touch are the hardware, *the brain*. The electrochemical signal patterns that flow over the axon and dendrite filaments are the software, *the mind*. Without this electrochemical activity, there is no life. Just as computer programs are useless without computers to run them on, so the mass of electrochemical signals are useless without the physical network of neurons.

As we have noted above, there are no letters, words, pictures or music in any computer ever manufactured. No one thinks a computer feels pain, is intelligent or conscious. All this must exclusively be the software. Similarly, all these functions and information must be modulated by the mind. The brain transmits all this information around the central nervous system, but the activities and functions are carried out by other organs of the body, with one exception.

The principle role of the brain is to provide, organise, manage, grow and access the memory systems.

The hardware of a computer is fixed. However, the brain can augment its neural networks. We noted that babies are born with a billion neurons in their brains. A mature adult has upwards of an additional trillion new neural links and structures. Babies can only hear and make sounds, but an adult can learn to hear, see, speak and write one hundred thousand words or more, their spelling, syllables and phonemes — and that is just in one language. More significant, we learn to understand the *meaning* of words and phrases. We can puzzle out the implications of this information and we can extrapolate it out to imagine and predict probable future events. We call these functions intelligence, thinking and creativity.

How does the brain "grow" memories? The Canadian, Donald Hebb (see Chapter 7, Appendices 10 and 29) argued that "neurons that fire together, wire together". One hypothesis suggested in 2008, and gaining popularity is that where the electromagnetic fields of two active neuron filaments overlap, their combined magnetism attracts free standing glia cells to form a temporary, speculative link or bridge. More distant active neuron filaments attract messenger molecules to form glia bridges. If these new links begin to be used — they are useful new information or instructions, these glia bridges are strengthened and in due course replaced with conventional neurons. This is a process very similar to how babies grow their first neurons along glia scaffolding in the womb (see Appendix 12, all appendices are hosted on www.BrainMindForum.org/appendices).

Learning System

It is relatively easy to understand how apprentices learn how to carry out crucial skills from their parents and peers. It is largely curiosity, imitation and repetition. We know that there are even specialist neurons — *mirror neurons* — that are active both when we observe someone carry out a task and when we try and imitate them.

Representation of Information in the Brain and Mind

The computing pioneers found a solution in the coding system invented by Morse to transmit signals over telegraph lines. After a few false starts the world standardised on groups of eight binary bits into computer "words". $2^8 = 256$ unique codes for various alphabets, numbers, punctuation and symbols. And these binary codes are also used to digitise images and music.

   One of the most powerful aspects of computing is that a stream of programming instructions appears identical to a string of words, part of a picture or piece of music. In the jargon, data and algorithms are indistinguishable. Thus, programs can be designed to edit programs in hierarchies of complexity in response to experience, thus computers can be programmed to *learn*. Our brain and mind has no such coding system. We can observe that at birth the central nervous system has an impressive range of algorithms in place to operate all the organs of the body. Streams of patterns of electrochemical signals flash along the axons and dendrites coordinating the heart, lungs, liver, kidneys and so on. The whole intestinal tract goes into action, and somewhere in the system a set of instructions causes the muscles of the lips to suck.

At Birth, There is No Information in the Brain

Information is an important subject in its own right and the subject of Chapter 4, but a short summary to set the scene might be:

> *We start from the position that information is as fundamental as energy. When the wave form of a photon collapses a "bit" of information is created. A computer approach is that information is in four states:*
>
> *(1) Passive: memory, or potential information.*
> *(2) Active: processing, doing work, or kinetic information.*
> *(3) Facts and measurements: means things.*
> *(4) Algorithms, formulae, instructions: does things.*

As soon as babies open their eyes, a stream of photons impacts their retinas. The flow of a pattern of photons impacting their retinas generates a reciprocal flow of patterns of electrochemical signals along the dendrites to the brain. As the neurons fire they leave a pattern, say, mother's face. Each time they "see" mother that pattern is strengthened, and perhaps a gland is stimulated to provide an emotional reward. In another part of the brain, a similar activity is growing a pattern of the sound of the word "mother". Baby tries to imitate that sound, and after a while produces a sound that clearly gives pleasure all round and more warm feelings generated by the hormones.

Our baby has now created three codes and learned how to generate a pleasant feeling of achievement.

(1) A neural pattern of the image of a face.
(2) A neural pattern of the sound of hearing the word mother.
(3) A neural pattern of a set of instructions to the muscles of the lung, vocal chords, tongue and lips to make the sound mother. If three responds to one, baby experiences hormonal reward sensations either externally — a warm hug, or food perhaps…and internally as various glands are stimulated.

Watch very young babies and they will endlessly repeat simple movements, simple words. The intestines demand food, so the mind responds by activating a neural network to generate a yell. It works. Repeat the strategy. It works better calling "mother". Another lesson learned — imprinted on the neurons.

There has been much debate over the last 50 years about how babies learn words and language. In parallel baby is learning to control its body functions, and crawl, stand up — wow(!), that is an exciting new perspective, and balance — walk. All these systems seem reasonably congruent.

Sensations

However, we can already see a differentiation of function. Sensations of hunger and thirst come from the intestines amplified by some glandular secretions; soon the first sensations of apprehension and perhaps fear course through the whole body. Then laughter and attraction, as the glands of the endocrine system generate more complex sensations. There is so much to recognise, imitate, repeat, relate together and learn. Words and increasingly combinations of words, give us ever widening sensations, perceptions, impressions, feelings and emotions as the endocrine glands secrete ever more complex combinations of hormones, which reinforce our understanding of the meanings of what we see, hear, touch, taste and feel.

Then come books and reading. We are already able to differentiate between cats in pictures and real ones prowling about. Now they are in books sitting on mats with black squiggles under them. And the squiggles seem to be *ke, ah* and *ter*. Well if you say so. And now we can draw those shapes and people know you mean cats without seeing the picture.

We now have a fast-growing amount of information in our brains and minds. Nearly all the words are cross referenced to other words and representations of images, sounds, tastes, smells and touch, and the sensations the hormones generate. We can break words down into letters and syllables, and build up different words from those letters and syllables, with different meanings. Some words make nice sounds, onomatopoeia. Some groups of words rhyme in time with heart beats generating a pleasant feeling.

The Instructions in the Brain at Birth

At birth, all the autonomic functions are fully operational (whatever titles we give them). In addition, as we noted above, babies can move their arms and legs, and they can hear and make sounds. They can also suck. Whether this is an autonomic ability of the first learned function of the brain is a matter of classification. Again, it is a matter of classification whether learning to carry our functions — learning to walk, swim and ride a bicycle is different from acquiring information. Both are about curiosity, imitation and repetition.

We can note one difference that is much more conspicuous in learning skills, tasks, algorithms. Few people can remember learning to read, write, walk and run. Most people can clearly recall leaning to swim, ride a bicycle or drive a car. To start with we are all over the place, then gradually our arms and legs that appeared to be so clumsy, seem to be doing the job effortlessly.

As with information, we do, quite literally, grow the neural circuits that move our arms, legs, coordinate our breathing: to move the handlebars controlled by the signals from the balance system in our ears to operate the pedals with our feet with unaccustomed precision and so on. We soon find we can do all these tasks with such ease that we hardly notice what we are doing them, and can in fact do other things at the same time. We chat away to the passenger in our car and are almost oblivious of doing the driving. We can call this background mode or foreground mode. People talk about operating below the radar, in autopilot. However, there is a much more interesting alternative.

Background Operating System

Recently, there has been a trend to separate out functions as a way to better understand them. However, it can also sometimes be useful to do the opposite and to think of how various similar functions might converge.

We have discussed how various autonomic functions of the central nervous system operate largely below the radar of our everyday experience — not too different a concept to the many learned functions we do in "background" mode. We concentrate on the text we are writing. We do not need to give any attention whatever to the intricate muscle movements necessary to write each letter.

Observe the history of computing. The great major breakthrough was the development of the standard OS that enabled all programmers to concentrate on the algorithms of applications while the OS looked after all the intricate operations of the system, input, output, allocation of memory, the layout of the screen, etc.

There is a very compelling argument that not only are the sympathetic, somatic and enteric functions all various aspects of one background OS, but the autopilot operation of the brain is also part of the extended autonomic functions of the central nervous system — the OS of the body.

Can This Be?

In the first place, the brain is almost certainly an evolutionary extension of the central nervous system. As the brain has evolved, it is unlikely not to have retained the services of its very efficient messaging system.

Secondly, all the major responses of dealing with predators, partners and prey are all joint functions of the central nervous system and the brain. As all observes down the centuries have agreed, in a crisis, there is no time stop and think of alternative, or more sophisticated responses. Indeed, the foundation of every description of intelligence is the ability to respond to incomplete information as fast as possible. Our survival depended on this policy. It has hardly changed.

There is another much more convincing argument. As we have just noted, as soon as we learn a skill it slips into background mode. We have the impression that our brain has taken over. All those once difficult functions are now effortlessly executed. Logic suggests that our autonomic background OS is taking over the heavy lifting.

There is a third conclusive argument. The world is an ever more complex environment. The instant inherited or learned response worked very well — it is why we are here, but we needed greater sophistication to continue to survive, thus we have learned techniques to enable us to do better: outsmart predators, trap our prey and entice our partners. These are all, ever more clever activities. They are advanced capabilities of our sentient brain, making the maximum use of all the multitude of skills we have learned over the millennia.

We argue that the brain has a duality of capabilities:

(1) A background extended autonomic OS.
(2) A library of continuously new applications.

We argue that all the extended autonomic functions of the central nervous system and this dual capacity of the brain to operate together in unison is the basis of our long sought general intelligence.

We draw two further conclusions:

(1) Information Representation

Everyone learns everything in their own unique way in their own time and sequence. Thus, the coding system that they grow in their individual neural networks of their individual brains and individual minds are as unique as their finger prints and their eye patterns, the sounds of their voices, their handwriting and their personalities.

The corollary is that every person who has passed the same exam may have answered the questions in an identical way, but every single student will have a different perception of what that information means, even if those differences are marginal. Such is the foundation of evolution, and by forcing standard answers on each generation great damage is done, and the advance of our civilisation held back. With the historically scarce resources of the human race in the past, this was probably inevitable, but the situation is changing fast.

At the moment, we only have a symbiotic connection to our computers. When we develop prosthetic brains, and begin to learn to edit DNA the fact that every individual stores every piece of information and every activity and algorithm in a unique way, will present some interesting problems, but at the same time offer opportunities currently outside the imaginations of even the most avant garde science fiction authors and futurologists.

(2) Meaning of Information

Meaning is not a function of the brain. Meaning is the combination of sensations, impressions, perceptions, feelings and emotions we experience generated by the hormones and other neurotransmitters secreted by the glands of the endocrine system, partly by the information flowing from our sensory organs as they monitor the outside world but increasingly by the neural processing of our vocabularies and other activities.

Words have meanings in the dictionary sense but only where the meaning of one word is described in terms of numbers of other words, often many words, and often offering different meaning in different circumstances. In the end, however, all words have only emotional meanings. Almost always the brain can differentiate between the usages of one word to mean different things with ease because of the ambient state of the surrounding neural networks at the time.

The Cardiovascular System

The cardiovascular system primarily controls the heart and lungs and circulation of the blood. It controls the manufacture of the blood then pumps it though the gastrointestinal system to collect nutrients and water, and the lungs to collect oxygen, then transports these nutrients to the whole body through the arteries: returning the blood, less nutrients but plus waste, through the veins. It thus transports the fuel for the generation of energy to the muscles, organs and the brain. Although the brain is around 2% of the weight of the body, it uses more than a quarter of the nutrients and fuel.

One can get just as tired thinking, as running. Equally the water supply is crucial. Among other functions, it maintains tension in all the organs and, again, particularly in the neurons.

The cardiovascular system's other vital role is the transport of the hormones and other secretions of the glands of the endocrine system to all parts of the body in general but crucially to the brain. It is also responsible for the "emergency services" to repair damage to the fabric of the body and remove waste.

The Endocrine System

The endocrine system consists of some 100 known glands. Recently, a new type of gland has been identified, and it is forecast that there are likely to be potentially at least a further 100 of these. These glands produce the neurotransmitters that populate the synapses, messenger molecules that carry instructions around the brain and most important of all the family of hormones. In their deep evolutionary past, they controlled a lot of the reactions of their host that enabled them to be aware of events taking place in their bodies and being part of the environment around them — the sensations of hunger and thirst, anger to repel a predator, fear to retreat, arousal to mate, and satisfaction for any job well done. Similarly, it was these hormones that were responsible for displays of aggression, attraction and so forth.

As their hosts gradually grew in complexity, the numbers of these glands and their hormones increased. Their functions grew more sophisticated, and they generated ever more complex combinations of perceptions, sensations, impressions, feelings and emotions. The development of language stimulated many changes, not the least was the need to express to others the feelings of emotions and opinions about the past, what action to take now, what might happen in the future. Words could be used to replace displays of aggression and so forth. Thus hand in hand, each stimulating the emotions of others, the numbers of words exploded. The perceptions, sensations, impressions, feelings and emotions those words represented followed in turn, causing more glands to generate more hormones, and more sensations, and more words to represent them.

Thanks to the ability of language, the usage of a word produced the same response in the hearer as it did in the speaker. With all these sensations attached to the use of every word and phrase, our ancestors could transmit *meaning* to each other.

Thus, we argue that the source of all meaning is the myriad combination of hormones and other secretions of the glands that generates the perceptions, sensations, impressions, feelings and emotions of words, phrases and other methods of communication.

These functions are stimulated by the electrochemical signal patterns generated by the brain, but the source of meaning is not in the brain, it is provided by the endocrines' glandular system. The ambient state of hormones in the brain also varies the responses of the neurons, and the strength of any new links and structures. We can observe that if someone is getting emotionally involved in, say, an argument, they often say things that they would not otherwise have done.

Immune System

Our knowledge of the immune system is rising fast. There are increasing signs that it is much more closely integrated into the central nervous system and the cardiovascular systems than previously thought.

It seems unlikely that evolution would have favoured developing a separate communications system, when the central nervous system is available to do the job. Similarly, it seems unlikely there is a duplicate means of circulating fluids in addition to the cardiovascular system.

There is mounting evidence that a stimulus from the brain can vary the secretion of a component of the immune system, both to activate it and supress it.

There is some controversy as to whether the immune system is involved in monitoring and controlling the mass of viruses, bacteria and parasites in the body, usually now called the biome.

Gastrointestinal (Enteric) System

The gastrointestinal or enteric nervous system controls the conversion of food into nutrients, regulating the selection, supply and temporary storage according to what is available. If the system is becoming short of food or water, it stimulates the appropriate glands to generate a sensation of hunger or thirst. It has the second highest concentration of neurons, some 500 million. However, while the neuron networks in the brain multiply a thousand fold, there is no evidence of the enteric neurons increasing in number at all. These neurons have a job to do and they carry it out.

It confirms the argument that the brain is the learning system of the body and so is uniquely responsible for growing and managing the memory structures.

The gastrointestinal system is responsible for discarding waste. We are generally not aware of these systems unless something is malfunctioning or otherwise not behaving properly.

Summary

Thus, we can begin to see that each of these six systems has their own functions to carry out. The central nervous system provides the communication infrastructure for all the other systems. The brain coordinates the other systems and is the learning centre of the body, which is responsible for growing and managing the memory systems.

The cardiovascular system circulates the fuel and nutrients supply.

The endocrine system does much more than we used to believe and provides all the perceptions, sensations, impressions, emotions and the myriad other feelings of being alive. It is the source of meaning, not the brain as conventionally believed.

The suspicion is that the immune system and the gastrointestinal systems are also much more closely integrated with the other four.

Perhaps a significant breakthrough is that at birth all these six systems operate automatically to maintain the whole organism in equilibrium, including the brain. We can call it the extended autonomic functions of the central nervous system. However, the brain has developed superior processing capabilities: what we recognise as how we learn new skills, talents and abilities. When these applications are fully learned, and operating efficiently they become part of these background operating autonomic functions, freeing up the brain to do other tasks, observe more, be more alert, learn more, have more time to think, be more creative. For some time, we have called this autopilot mode. We can now give it its rightful designation.

There is a compelling argument that all these extended autonomic functions, including the background processing in the brain is part of our general cognitive abilities, and to the extent they are a candidate for what we call our general intelligence.

CHAPTER THREE

IDEAS, PAST, PRESENT
AND FUTURE

I seem to be like a boy playing on the foreshore, diverting myself with shining pebbles, whilst the great ocean of truth lies all undiscovered before me.

Isaac Newton

Over the millennia, many communities have lived for centuries without experiencing much change. Particularly in agrarian communities, it seemed the path of the seasons rolled by and the life of the grandchildren varied little from the life of the grandparents. From time to time, favourable trends converged to generate peaks and sometimes explosions of knowledge.

Then the renaissance led to the birth of science, the enlightenment and the industrial revolution. Simple tools were replaced with ever-more complex machines and engines. As a race, we could supplement our muscles: move at speed over land and sea and even fly, though we did not enhance our personal individual strength. Microscopes, telescopes and scanners enabled us to see the minute and the very distant, though it did not enhance our personal individual eyesight. Telecommunications enabled us to speak to, hear from and see people at the other side of our planet, though it did not enhance our personal individual vocal chords or ears. Advances in medicine nearly doubled our life expectancy. Then in the second half of the twentieth century, we harnessed atomic power, decoded the mechanisms of heredity, and learned to control our reproduction; discovered antibiotics, explored the physical structures of the body, and, notwithstanding all its faults, began the long path to world government. And then we invented computers.

For a while, computers seemed just bigger and better tools; machines that could organise things rather than make things. However, we are beginning to realise they are far more significant than just clever gadgets. These machines can supplement our brains. And we can go further than ever before in history. Computers enable us to enhance our personal individual mental abilities: to simulate, maybe even augment our intelligence, our ability to learn and comprehend, enhance our ability to discover new knowledge and be creative. Even modify our genetic inheritance. No humans have ever owned a machine with this, almost, unlimited potential before. This is the greatest game changer since the discovery of language. A paradigm shift in the history, not just of science, but of our whole civilisation.

Philosophers have often commented that, as we stride out into the future, we can always look back and see the clear path we have beaten, but in front of us we can see nothing. As we cautiously inch forward, or take a leap into the unknown, will we find a safe footing, or will we tumble off the edge of a precipice?

All too easily we can imagine the results of falling off some cliff edge. The atomic bomb falling into the wrong hands. A mistake in gene editing. Failure of antibiotics. Robots out of control. There will be commercial problems flowing from our inventions. Recasting historical concepts of work and remuneration may cause a rethink of capitalism itself. Economic problems and ethical problems. However, the best way to counter intolerance and misunderstanding is knowledge and informed debate. Let us look back over the path we have taken and try and learn as much as we can from our experience.

Milestones in Human Cognition

The greatest adventure of our span of life is all about the excitement of new experiences, new relationships, exploring our talents and abilities, and pushing out the frontiers of our knowledge — principally our own personal knowledge, but, if we are very fortunate the knowledge of our community.

The history of our discovery of ideas and knowledge is a fascinating subject in its own right, one which should be included in every school curriculum. Roughly this covers a period of some 5,000 years, or approximately 200 generations, since we learned to write and pass on records down the generations. The Lascaux caves suggest sentient ancestors going back far further, but we only have hints and clues and the founding stories, myths and legends originally passed down by word of mouth, like Gilgamesh, the Iliad and Odyssey, and perhaps some of the Old Testament and Upanishad stories and Norse sagas that gave early tribes and nations a sense of stability, confidence and belonging.

Language was the great breakthrough, but the development of writing has given us the records to explore the sources and development of human knowledge. Early pictograms and hieroglyphics in due course were superseded by the abstract symbols that roughly equated to 20 consonants, probably developed by the Phoenicians, and five vowels added later by the Greeks (it is interesting that we can still understand text with these vowels removed). No one has put it better than Galileo: "Of all the stupendous inventions, they who conceived how to communicate their most secret thoughts distant in time and place simply by the arrangement of two dozen signs upon a paper".

The fact that the alphabet was made up of *abstract* symbols to represent abstract sounds is a key attribute in the development of knowledge and the mind.

Early Reliance on Natural Resources

The first natural resource that determined the development of civilisation was fresh water, and thus early linear civilisations developed along the Yangtze, Indus, Tigris & Euphrates and the Nile rivers. Perhaps democracy and philosophy thrived in Greece because no city could grow large enough to conquer all the others. All the rivers in Greece are quite small, and the Aegean enabled everyone to meet, trade and debate with everyone else. The Greeks competed at everything. They had sufficient wealth to educate most of their younger generation, and time for some of their elders to speculate, and from then till now one of the major targets of research has been our world, our bodies and our brains. Galen laid the foundations of Medicine: Plato's cave reminds us to this day to remember that what we experience may all be illusion. Aristotle laid the foundation for physics, and along with many others pondered how we learned, talked and thought and were conscious.

Rome had no rivers and so built the network of arterial roads, which has served as analogies down the centuries for the circulation of the blood and the transmission of signals round the body. They might not have known anything about electricity, but the Romans had several advanced methods of signalling and even encryption. Their communication system was not surpassed for a thousand years. The Muslims kept the flame of Greek knowledge alive and added algebra, the number zero and much astronomy, including the concept of the heliocentric universe.

Gradually we have learned to tame the two great driving forces of all life forms:

(1) Competition: Survival of the fittest — competition for space, food, water, which has led to almost continuous warfare.
(2) The sometimes-uncontrolled desire to reproduce, which some people argue was a contributory reason for the growth of belief system and the development of concepts of law to help curb individual excess. Little changes: The twentieth century witnessed the two most destructive wars in history, and pornography has provided much of the resources to create the internet and the world-wide web!

Birth of Cognitive Neuroscience

Communication Systems in the Body

We touched on the central nervous system in Chapter 2. Let us look more closely. Apart from the Cartesian speculation and some experiments in educating children in novel ways, the beginning of neuroscience started with the Nobel Prize-winning work of Spaniard Santiago Ramón y Cajal in isolating, staining and finding ways to look at individual neurons. By the middle of the twentieth century, we had a pretty good idea of the three communications system in the body:

(1) The central nervous system and the brain are constructed out of neurons, each consisting of a *nucleus* with its own independent mitochondrial power generation and storage system, with input filaments — the *dendrites* — carrying information from everywhere, including all the sensory organs, and the output filaments — the *axons* — carrying information to everywhere, including the glands and muscles, both capable of transmitting patterns of electrochemical signals to and from the brain mind, and generating electromagnetic fields in the process. Neurons connect to everything else and other neurons by a remarkably sophisticated connection system consisting of a gap — the *synapse,* the significance of which, we are just beginning to grasp. In addition, there is a whole family of glia cells which carry out a multitude of different tasks from supplying the neurons with nutrients and clearing away debris to playing a key role in memory formation.

(2) Secondly there are the endocrine, immune, enteric and cardiovascular systems, described in greater detail in Chapter 2. In summary, a mass of hormones, neurotransmitters, chemical messengers and messenger molecules produced by the glands circulate around the body through the blood stream and lymph systems. The taste buds in the mouth react to the food we eat by stimulating the neural networks linked to the various organs that secrete chemicals into the intestines to be prepared to cope with what is about to come down the oesophagus.

(3) Finally there is the physical communication system. Often neglected, body vibrations and whole body movements like laughing, sneezing and yawning carry significant information round the body. For instance, they vary the volume of cerebrospinal fluid being pumped to the brain, varying its operations. Changes in temperature, pressure and pulse rate, and glucose concentration vary pulse rates and generate patterns of electrochemical signals in the dendrites and vary

the signals in the axons. Insulin levels have a direct impact on willpower.

Variable energy levels affect the state of the synapses, which vary the efficiency of thinking and learning. Various glia cells in the brain are sensitive to certain hormones. Inflammation in the body generates peptides that signal astrocyte glia cells in the brain to respond in various ways. We are almost entirely unaware of all this background activity.

Operating Systems

In addition, there is the mass of bacteria in the biome; not to forget the genetic reproduction, inheritance and maintenance system.

Then, arguably there is the most important operating system of all: the continuous stream of patterns of electrochemical signals of the extended autonomic system which controls and organises every organ in the whole body to behave in harmony as one co-operative, co-ordinated and synchronised whole.

Contribution of Computing

The arrival of computers has provided some valuable new ways of thinking about the functioning of the brain.

Computers are driven by a processor unit that executes the instruction in a program. The *brain* does not have a processor. The brain is driven entirely by the information that flows in from the sensory and other organs. Descartes argued that we have a body and a sentient brain, or mind, which did the thinking in his famous statement. It is worth remembering he knew nothing about electricity. He speculated "instructions travelled through the mind as puffs or air". Not a bad analogy.

Computers have integrated circuits (*hardware*) over which flow patterns of electrical signals (*software*). The *brain* is made up of neural networks etc. (hardware) over which flow patterns of electrochemical signals whose activity generates waves of electromagnetic fields — software, which we call the *mind*.

Cognitive neuroscientists have puzzled endlessly how letters, words, phrases, numbers, meaning, music and visual images are represented in the brain. Computers can show exactly how this is accomplished. Equally and oppositely, computer programmers have puzzled how to emulate intelligence. A large part of this book is designed to help answer these questions.

The hardware configuration of a computer is fixed. The brain grows trillions of new neural links and structures, which are the basis of learning and memory. Where two or more neurons are active together, their overlapping magnetic fields attract glia cells to form links. *We grow our memories.* Recently developed *optogenetic* techniques are beginning to demonstrate this happening in laboratories. It is called the Hebb effect as Donald Hebb was the first to coin the phrase "neurons that fire together wire together". Donald Hebb's work is described in Appendix 10 (all appendices are hosted on www.BrainMindForum.org/appendices).

Streams of signal patterns flowing round the brain causing activity is said to be *kinetic* information — doing work. Signal patterns encapsulated in neural structures — memory — is said to be *potential information.*

Software

The concept of software has more to offer. The essence of software is that it enables the same hardware to be continuously re-used to carry out an almost unlimited number of different applications. For instance, one set of neural networks connected to the muscles of the lungs, vocal chords, mouth, lips and tongue can *speak* an unlimited number of sounds. How common is this multi-use capability in the whole brain mind system? It is intriguing to think of the implications of multi-use configuration. Maybe this is part of the fundamental architecture of the whole brain mind.

Systems

The concept of systems is well established but has not been applied to the structure of the mind. Programs are almost always built up from a mass of short lengths of code, which in turn are built into ever larger structures until complete, ever-more complex application systems have been constructed. The significance of this architecture of hierarchies of sub-routines (in computer language) or *neurules* (one of many names invented by neuroscientists and listed in Appendix 12, all appendices are hosted on www.BrainMindForum.org/appendices) is that the use, meaning and value of the whole are greater than the sum of its parts. This is the basis of *emergent properties*. A powerful example is the power of a string of words in, say, a poem, compared to their individual meaning (Appendix 25 goes into this in further detail, all appendices are hosted on www. BrainMindForum.org/appendices). Thus, hierarchies of neural systems (and programs) can carry out ever-more sophisticated and complex tasks far beyond the capabilities of the constituent neurons (or program codes). The concept of fractals comes to mind, although conventional fractals are identical. Maybe neural fractals are a variation.

Emotions, Perceptions and Sensations

We are all aware that computers have neither emotions, nor any of the paraphernalia that is a major component of our bodies. Similarly, the brain does not feel pain. If we damage a leg, for instance, the mind processes the signals that cause the glands to excrete the hormones etc. that give us the sensation of pain in our leg. There is no mechanism for a computer to have any sense of pain in any component.

This helps us understand the very important concept that the brain does not learn or comprehend information. Similarly, the brain cannot think or be creative. Stranger still, the brain is not conscious. Patterns of electrochemical signals in the mind stimulate the glands to produce the hormones that generate all the myriad sensations, perceptions, emotions, impressions, feelings and excitement of knowledge, creativity and being alive and well and conscious.

Synapses

Computing has forced us to think in novel ways. We have had to learn to deconstruct even the simplest tasks down to the most intricate and precise detail before we can construct a system and write a program to emulate that job. We have invented programs to help us write programs almost *ad infinitum*, but in the end an extremely complex program that, for instance, can beat a chess master is only one long stream of plusses, minuses and jumps when it is operating in the processor. As a result, computer system designers and programmers often pursue questions into the minutest detail. Synapses are arguably the most complex structure in the brain mind. This is particularly intriguing. Why is this system of connections so complex? Nature usually takes the simplest road. Why is there a gap? How is the width of this gap determined and controlled? Is this gap fixed or variable? Logic suggests the answer is variable. If so, what causes this variability? What is the effect of this variability? What might the evolutionary benefit of such complexity be? Why? The possible answers to these questions may generate a paradigm shift in our understanding of the brain mind, which we explore in Chapters 16 and 18.

Symbiosis and Prosthetics

We already have cell phones which not only connect us to the whole world but also instantly enable us to consult a store of the entire body of human knowledge, art, culture and commerce. New models are connected to our wristwatches, and gradually the interfaces to them will get symbiotically closer.

Huge advances in prosthetics directly linking, say, a replacement leg to the central nervous system allows the users to *think* walking and move the leg appropriately. The possibility of a direct neural interface, therefore, depends more on matching coding system and compatible wavelengths, than in engineering the physical links.

Convergence

Biogenetics

Studying, mapping and deciphering the human genome would not be possible without computers to plot, register, store and process the vast volume of information in an individual genome. Without computer typesetting, the internet and the world wide web, the research community would not be able so easily to publish research results and for the world community to read them. However, computing concepts also help theorise on how the formation of the double helix of the genome leads to a unique, perfect and complete human being who can speculate how it was conceived and born.

The structure of the 23 pairs of chromosomes, divided into genes, built up from codons consisting of individual base pairs each made up of four nucleotides — adenine, cytosine, guanine and thymine — bears more than a passing similarity to the architecture of the duality of brain mind, and the hardware, software structure of computer system and applications. "We now have entered the digital age of biology in which the domains of computing code and those that program life are beginning to merge and where synergies are emerging that will drive evolution in radical directions" says J Craig Venter on page 1 of his book, *Life at the Speed of Light: From the Double Helix to the Dawn of Digital Life.*

The path from deoxyribonucleic acid (DNA) to ribonucleic acid (RNA) to hierarchies of combinations of amino acids, enzymes, peptides and ribosomes to produce the mass of proteins is well established, but the process at the beginning and end is less clear.

We know that each baby is genetically half mother half father. How? Precisely? A computer programmer would suggest that a piece of gene "software" probably works its way down the genes, comparing the contribution from each parent. Where the two sets of nucleotides match, the new gene goes forward. But what if the parental genes do not match? What is the algorithm for which gene is chosen? RNA is thought to be older and simpler than DNA. Perhaps evolution favoured a system that did more than just reproduce the present generation. How much more flexible and robust if a newborn could inherit genes direct from the four grandparents, eight great grandparents?

The possibility arises that DNA contains not only the current active gene set, but also copies of recessive genes going back over previous generations. Perhaps DNA evolved from RNA to carry a history of individuals and so give them a fast track means to adjust to changing circumstances. Perhaps these "history" genes are part of what has been thought to be "junk". Where the enzyme "gene software" finds a mismatch, the algorithm then compares the genes of previous generations of both parents to see if a match can be found. Hence from time to time, a child will be born with, say, red hair when the only other antecedent of that child with red hair was three generations ago.

Once a complete cell is created, then another complex process — some form of software again — folds the proteins into the appropriate shapes to carry out specific activities. In a sense, paying homage to the fact that once long ago when cells were beginning to come together for mutual help and support all cells were similar. For many millions of generations, cells have been specialising.

Experiments have been successfully carried out to use DNA to process information, but the input and output problems suggest there may be better ways of creating "living" processors.

DNA, Gene Editing, Health?

For millennia, mankind has bred animals and plants to emphasise attractive attributes and exclude undesirable traits. It has been a long, slow, haphazard process but has generated spectacular results. We now have a much more efficient process. We can edit the contents of the genome by using a new technique called clustered regularly-interspaced short palindromic repeats (CRISPR). Before we can do this safely and effectively, we have to be very sure we know what each gene does, and this is proving hard to do. Certain hereditary illnesses do seem to be a failure of one or a few genes, but this appears to be rare. The solution seems to be more like the way words, sounds and images are represented in the brain mind, namely a complex mass of links, relationships and references able to recognise inputs from various different sources and capable of generating a variety of output patterns to various networks.

Synthetic Biology

Even a bacterium has processing capabilities. Within the next few generations, it seems likely that we will be able to grow biological neural storage and processing systems and interface them directly to the nervous system.

Artificial Intelligence: The Tantalising Prospect of Building Intelligent Systems

How far can we go in designing systems that behave intelligently, or are themselves intelligent? Or, potentially more intelligent than us. A great deal of research has gone into this intriguing exploration, but success depends a great deal on our understanding of intelligence. No one so far has been able to produce a computer that has the smallest scintilla of intelligence, whichever way we define it. The brilliant programs that have defeated chess masters, won quiz games and learned to play "Go" are just that: brilliant programs.

Robots

We can design sophisticated operating systems to integrate libraries of brilliant programs installed in machines capable of moving and carrying out tasks — Robots. Robots are lineal descendants of automation, which in turn developed out of mass production techniques. The aim is to design *master algorithms* that control ever-increasing numbers of *superintelligent applications* that can steadily carry out more and more tasks. Drones and automatic cars are travelling along this path. However, this is all software and does not make the hardware intelligent.

Effect of Computing on Economics: Reversing the Industrial Revolution

Energy drove the industrial revolution. Steam engines and electricity enabled the manufacture of a mass of products to enhance the lifestyle of the community and a mass of workers with salaries and wages to buy them. Mass production created mass purchasing power. Many of the theories of economics are postulated on this paradigm. Computers are creating a greater mass of products — and wealth — but as computers do not expect salaries or wages, they are not generating the purchasing power for people to buy their wonderful new products and services. Something will have to give. Capitalism will have to evolve a new paradigm. If some goods and services can be produced by computers at little or no cost, do we give them away free? Pay people irrespective of whether they work or not, perhaps? (A scheme on these lines is being trialled in Utrecht.)

Currently, no one has developed a political solution, and so the majority of human earning will drift lower. This is clearly visible in the USA, usually a leader in these trends, for some 40 years — salaries of the lowest earners have not moved. This started to happen in Japan in the 1990s, in the UK ten years ago, and in Europe the imposition of the euro is exacerbating the problem. As with all these trends they tend to start gradually, but have a habit of suddenly accelerating. There are lots of economic indicators suggesting we are close to that tipping point.

Education

Education is outside the scope of this book. However, it is worth noting that education is closely tied to economics. The teaching profession is likely to experience greater changes to their careers than any other group. On the one hand, the community will need people with ever-more sophisticated skills to drive forward the computing revolution, but the overall numbers involved may be relatively small. On the other hand, *life-long learning* may replace what we currently think of as work. The two obvious trends are away from traditional professions of lawyers, accountants, bankers, bureaucrats and managers towards the creative professions of the future: Inventors, researchers, designers, architects, doctors, engineers, programmers and entrepreneurs. On-line distance-learning systems are in their infancy. They offer lessons in every subject given by the best teachers, with clever algorithms to allow every student to ask questions of the teacher apparently instantaneously mirroring a classroom. The greatest advantage will come from offering every lesson in many different formats to suit each individual, from a conventional classroom style for confident academically minded students to a Disney version, where Mickey helps the less confident students, metaphorically holding their hands and everything in between.

Natural Resource of the Future

As the need for physical and repetitive work is steadily replaced by computers, life-long learning will become the norm. At the beginning of this chapter, we listed fresh water as the key natural resource of the first civilisations. Increasingly the key natural resource of our civilisation will be the rainbow of human aptitudes and abilities. Future progress will depend on how successfully we learn to identify, nurture and develop the talents of every individual.

The more we study biogenetics and cognitive neuroscience, the more we realise the latter is in many ways largely an extension of the former. Up to birth, the system is largely driven by the inherited DNA. Immediately out in the wide world the inputs from the sensory and other organs progressively take over control en route to adulthood, culminating in the climax of puberty. Throughout this period, the brain mind — and much of the body — is a learning machine, starting with the natural skills of eating, walking, running, talking and generally coping with the world and everyone we meet in it. Progressively, we start to learn the skills of our civilisation — reading and writing, numbering, and then all the knowledge, tasks and skills accumulated over the generations. Success will depend on many things, not least on how well we learn how to learn.

Just as every eye and fingerprint is unique, so is every brain. Both nature and nurture powerfully influence which talent, skills and the rainbow of abilities and aptitudes we conceive and whether we can develop them. One thing we can observe for certain is that everyone learns to do everything differently: Whether these variations are slight, subtle or significant depends, again, on many things.

Paradox

All knowledge in the brain is analogue, and is always a matter of probability rather than exactitude. This is built into the architecture of the neurons. All neurons generate their own energy and, indeed, they have many of the attributes we associate with being alive. Thus, the reaction of every neuron is never wholly predictable.

The fact that everyone learns everything differently is a two-edged sword. It makes life very difficult for people who are fixated about the importance, not only of examinations, but also the minutest variations in individual grades. The advantage is, that because everyone has a unique view of everything they learn, everyone can form their own opinions — disagree and argue: hence new ideas and new concepts can be debated and new knowledge created.

The downside is that all human beings make mistakes. In debating economic theories this is beneficial, but concentrating on being an airport flight controller is another matter. Lives are at stake.

Computer programs are often thought of as a form of teaching and learning. Getting them absolutely perfect is challenging work; however, the upside is that once a program is perfected every computer can have an identical copy. Programs do not make gratuitous mistakes. They may not dream up innovative ideas, but they do complex jobs like traffic control extremely efficiently. They don't lose concentration, fall asleep or worry their partners have stopped loving them.

Human beings can learn to do some things better than computers ever will. Computers can be programmed to do some things much better than human beings. We have invented a very useful partner.

Next Steps

Never have so many areas of every type of science, art and craft been so wide open to opportunities. Every science seems to be on the cusp of significant breakthroughs. Everyone working in these fields depends directly or indirectly on their brain minds. How do we learn, remember, understand; are intelligent? How do we think and are creative? Let us stride forward confidently into that future to find these answers: all will be well.

Objectives

The objectives of this book are to explore the potential of computers to achieve far more than any of the other machines invented by mankind, identify the necessary knowledge we need to obtain the maximum benefits from what is becoming possible and take the necessary steps in appropriate time to ward off potential problems and risks.

We have made the case that all our other inventions throughout history have been tools — they have raised the quality of life to levels unimaginable a mere century ago, to those that have embraced them. However, the important fact is that they have not changed, modified or caused any evolutionary change in our bodies.

Computers can and will enhance, change, modify and stimulate evolutionary changes to our brain minds. This is not crystal ball gazing or science fiction. It is already happening. That is why computers are game changing — a paradigm shift. They are already beginning to affect the way we think, what we can learn, and how we learn, how we make decisions, but these advances are no more than a hint of what is possible. We already have the entire body of human knowledge, art, culture, commerce, instructions and training freely available, and early examples of online interactive lessons, instructions and tutorials in many subjects. Both are influencing the whole subject of education, training and life-long learning.

Growing Research Effort

In the seventeenth century, only a tiny minority of wealthy individuals could devote their time and energies to ponder the great scientific issues of the day, and form the Royal Society and other groups like the Lunar Society to discuss and debate these exciting possibilities. Nowadays, many of the most innovative ideas come from the science fiction writers. We have universities overflowing with people devoting their whole lives to research. However, our computers are ultimately democratic. Everyone can publish their ideas, and their research. Everyone can access the latest concepts, theories and conjectures in every field of endeavour. History shows that some of the greatest breakthroughs come from the most unexpected sources. In addition, we have a large and growing cohort of older people, with a lifetime's experience, also free to ponder and explore the frontiers of our knowledge.

The Potential

We have begun to design and build computer programs that have many of the attributes that we have historically attributed to intelligence. Programs that will be able to take over more and more of the repetitive uninspiring jobs currently carried out by humans. We are designing programs that can discover additional information by identifying patterns in very large volumes of data, far beyond the capability of the human brain.

The Risks

Scientists of the highest reputations are seriously suggesting we might soon have in our power the capacity to design and build computer systems and robots that could even challenge the supremacy of the human race and replace our civilisation. Intelligent lawyers suggest we need to begin drafting a code of conduct to rein in the possible excesses of robot behaviour.

And this is just the technology that is already in early prototype in our laboratories.

Connections and Interfaces

Symbiotic Computing

How we connect ourselves to our computing power (and telecommunications), what the computer world calls "interfaces", is becoming increasingly significant. Many people still remember massive computers in dust-sealed "laboratories" that could only communicate through packs of punched cards or reels of paper tape. Screens and keyboards connected to personal computers paved the way to today's pocket computers, with earpieces and microphones to enhance our mental abilities as standard, much as many people wear glasses to enhance their visual abilities.

This is symbiotic computing. But we can go so very much further.

Prosthetics

The technology of connecting prosthetics limbs is already quite well advanced. Physical links between the axons and dendrites of the central neural systems to the electrical circuits of a prosthetic limb are in everyday use. Stimulating a leg movement from a brain impulse is a massive breakthrough, but it is trivial compared to an interface from, say, a prosthetic memory to the neural networks of the brain mind, almost as though we are contemplating designing a "sixth sense". However, the first step is always the most difficult. And the journey has begun.

Gene Editing

Editing genes is already a well-established application. Techniques to help solve fertility problems have been common for some decades. Once the genome had been sequenced, it was only a matter of time before we had a new occupation/industry/business learning to read that code and try to identify the rogue elements that cause hereditary diseases that perhaps could be edited out of existence.

As is so often the case, the discovery of DNA, which must go down as one of the greatest successes of science of all time, has flung open a door to a whole new science to discover the secrets of the coding system and the myriad combinations that generate not only the relatively easy organs of the body — the *hardware*, which at least we can see, feel and touch — but also the ephemeral abstract electrochemical signalling patterns of the various operating and communications systems — the *software*, whose detailed functions we can only deduce by observation.

It may take us longer than we think to isolate the gene patterns that code for, say, hair colouring. However, would parents wish to choose the colour of their offspring's hair?

We realise that there is a vast subject for study to understand the balance of good health; then move on to physical disabilities and then mental disabilities. Only now are we beginning to appreciate that, what we once thought was broadly binary — sexuality — is a wide spectrum of variations. And that does not even begin to touch on skills, abilities, aptitudes and, the greatest prize of them all, intelligence.

Synthetic Biology

We do not even have to edit the DNA of existing life forms, because we can study the biology of viruses and bacteria: of single cells organisms and the earliest multi-celled organisms that have a nucleus: the prokaryotes and eukaryotes. Presently we extract the genome in the nucleus, edit it, and replace it in its host nucleus. It is only a matter of time before we will be able to design and build life forms from scratch: *synthetic Intelligence*, perhaps?

We can already see the path to edit, modify, enhance and initiate changing the course of the evolution of the human brain mind. This is the first time in history that a development of such significance has occurred. This could have untold benefits, but it also raises big technical and scientific questions. There are major commercial considerations. The impact on employment will change many of the basic tenants of economics, but the greatest debates on its impact will be ethical.

Thus, we do indeed stand upon a precipice.

It would only seem prudent to start to widen and deepen our knowledge and understanding of the operations of our brain mind.

The Rainbow of Human Ability

The Greeks speculated about the rainbow of human abilities. If we knew how to allot the marks for every known human skill, doubtless everyone would come out equal, but civilisation has developed in such a way that some skills are considered to be much more valuable to the community than others. These carry such a perceived premium that vast wealth is heaped on the few. "To him that hath shall be given, and to him that hath not, even that which he hath shall be taken from him" is the recruiting slogan of capitalism throughout history: paradoxically, it is also its greatest strength. Many would argue it is the economic version of evolution's survival of the fittest.

Curiously, throughout history there has been little attempt to study, define, categorise, list and understand the rainbow of human ability. The practical problem has largely been solved by the hereditary passage of power and wealth. However, the problem is beginning to be acute, even if only in the field of human intelligence. If we want to design and build systems that have artificial (or machine) intelligence, we need to begin to define what we mean by intelligence.

However, it turns out that intelligence is remarkably difficult to pin down. Like many examples of qualia, everyone feels they know what intelligence is, but if asked to describe or categorise it, let alone define it, the task is remarkably difficult. Fifty of the world's best brains, from over the centuries to today come up with quite different answers. One suspects they are all correct. How can this be? What are we missing? Why are we so shy to study this crucial subject?

Convergence: Guide to Intelligence

The convergence and cross-fertilisation of ideas and massive research into biogenetics, cognitive neuroscience and computing are beginning to offer us solutions, or at least a path to look for answers.

Almost immediately, we realise that all three activities have one common core, or foundation. All three use energy to process information, which is the raw material of all living beings.

Cognitive neuroscience — the brain mind — operates on information in two states:

(1) Memory, which is information encapsulated into neural networks: hardware: mass: *potential* information.
(2) Evolutionary intelligence, which is streams of electrochemical and hormonal signal patterns and waves flowing over and around the neural networks: the extended autonomic functions of the central nervous system: process: software: *kinetic* information.

And our computers are an exact model of this; they operate on information in two states:

(1) Memory stored on various media as magnetic patterns, semi-conductors etc.: hardware: mass: *potential* information.
(2) Machine intelligence: programs, operating systems: software: *kinetic* information.

Biogenetics: As the DNA of the two parents (Memory) come together, maternal hormones (the beginnings of software) process the chromosomes into RNA followed by all the complex stages of development up to protein cells, by which time both electrochemical signal patterns and glandular hormones have developed (software) to fold them into individual specialist cells, and drive the autonomic and other neural operating systems.

Chapter 4 discusses what information is? Where does it come from? How do we manipulate and process it to our benefit?

PART II
INFORMATION

CHAPTER FOUR
SOURCES OF INFORMATION

Tomorrow we will have learned to understand and express all of physics in the language of information.

John Archibald Wheeler

Information is the unifying principle of science.

Claude Shannon

Background

Information is the raw material of our brain. Unless we have a capacity to process and remember information, we cannot recognise anything, respond, learn from experience, be intelligent, think, create or be conscious. But what is information? We are surrounded by a mass of information in the universe. Deoxyribonucleic acid (DNA) is a massive compendium of hereditary information. Our brains are alive with streams of electrochemical signal patterns. Nevertheless, our brain minds do many other things than process information. It can be argued that their primary objective is to coordinate the whole body as one cohesive, cooperating whole and processing information is merely the means it archives this.

On the other hand, the sole purpose of computers is to process information — computers, after all, can do nothing else. Computers are the first machines we have invented that can do this. Our computers are generating megabytes of megabytes of data. Only computers and *Homo sapiens* can process information in the universe as far as we know.

Over centuries, information has just been seen as what we store in books and libraries and write letters to each other about. Scientists studied how things worked without necessarily thinking in terms of uncovering and discovering information. However, information is so ubiquitous and universal it seems obvious, but as soon as we begin to ask this question, we realise that until we fully understand information in its many forms we cannot begin to understand how memory works, let alone how we learn, think and are creative and conscious. As we study information, we realise there is a great deal more to study and research. Greater knowledge of both systems helps each other.

Information is a physical entity that plays a part in everything from how the universe operates, how all living creatures function and how machines work. Information is the indispensable *resource,* or raw material of all our natural and mechanical systems that we learn to recognise, store, retrieve, compare and process in every activity in our daily lives.

Science of Information

We had been using steam engines to pump water out of mines for nigh on a century, before we were able to understand the science of energy and formulate the laws of thermodynamics, from studying how steam engines worked.

The scientific community studied the form and structure of molecules and atoms and explored the contents of the periodic table. It seemed that the world of the very small mirrored the world of the very big — a central proton and neutron, or sun, surrounded by a galaxy of electrons or planets. This attractive theory was soon overturned as we realised the electrons, protons and neutrons all consisted of families of quarks, then in the last couple of years we have confirmed the existence of a particular Boson, stimulating much public interest. Quantum science opened innovative ideas and by the mid-century scientists had identified the smallest measureable unit of energy — photon, the unit of light. Photons exhibit some novel attributes. It seems that photons can either be waves or particles. If two particles are entangled and one is touched or measured the other will react at the exact same moment, however far apart they are, which seems to conflict with all conventional theory. However, this undoubtedly does occur and is being used to build quantum computers and quantum cryptography systems. When the waveform of a photon collapses a "bit" of information is created, we cannot forecast how quantum bits or qbits will react. We can only calculate the probability of their response (this is the basis of the famous Schrödinger cat hypothesis).

Computers have provided us with a new tool to study this subject, and like the steam engine before it, it is helping us understand information.

There are three possible theories being debated. (1) As a cousin to the photon, the smallest measurable unit of information could be a qbit. (2) When a photon is a waveform it is energy and when a particle it is information. This is very attractive because it means one "unit" in structures like DNA and many others can contain both energy and information. It would be very relevant to how neurons in the brain process information to generate meaning and other sensations. It could explain how two atoms of hydrogen and one atom of oxygen know how to behave like water. (3) A third possibility advanced by John Archibald Wheeler is that information is the primary unit of life and energy is part of information. He would argue that qbits are the source and explanation of reality, arising from posing everything as yes/no questions to evoke responses. All things are information.

In thermodynamics, a steam engine works because of the *difference* between the heat (energy) of the gas on either side of a movable piston. Hot steam on one side forces the piston to travel towards cold air on the other. Entropy states that all systems degrade over time. Entropy in thermodynamics expresses disorder. The faster the particles move in a confined space, the hotter they get. The slower they move, the colder. So far, all these insights have been applied to energy.

However, observation suggests that one definitions of information is that it is the means of creating order out of chaos. Another observation is that information (more exactly called *mutual information* in recent experiments stimulated by James Clerk Maxwell's demon) enables the disorder of heat to be converted to do useful work.

Is there a parallel set of laws of infodynamics? Are qbits the smallest measurable units of information? Can information be either in the form of waves or particles? Is information neither wave nor particle, but a *measurement* of a state? Or is information the measurement of the *difference* between two states? Are energy and information different manifestations of the same thing? (See Appendix 27, all appendices are hosted on www.BrainMindForum.org/appendices.)

We have noted that a photon is the smallest measurable unit of energy, and speculated that a qbit could be the smallest measurable unit of information. However, as Richard Feynman commented "there is plenty of space at the bottom", a group of scientists from various parts of the world have started to study if there is another layer of components below the photon and qbit. The Planck constant is not an entity but a measurement. A Planck length is some 17 orders smaller than the size of a photon. Another suggestion is that qbits are made up of tens of thousands of axions.

Is information completely objective? A very different school of thought proposed by Nir Fresco of the University of Jerusalem argues that to make sense of information flow in learning, communication, perception and cognition, it is questionable whether information can be understood completely objectively, that is, independently of any receiver?

In parallel with the deep science, in the early days of the telegraph, pioneers like Samuel F. B. Morse used the waveform that could be transmitted to create two states — the birth of binary systems, and as described above created a 5-bit code still used today; however, there was essentially no understanding of how to turn a message into a transmitted waveform.

In 1948, Claude Shannon showed how information could be quantified with absolute precision and demonstrated the essential unity of all information media. Telephone signals, text, radio waves and pictures, essentially every mode of communication, could be encoded in bits.

Information: Indispensable Resource

Whatever form information does indeed take in the universe, we can argue that it has three components: difference, measurement and patterns.

If nothing changes in a situation, event, state of affairs or behaviour, then there is nothing to report. However, if and when something measurable changes, then a unit of information is generated. If this unit is the smallest quanta of information we can observe, we can call it a qbit.

We can define a qbit as the smallest measurable unit of *difference*.

One qbit is of limited value, but a stream can tell us a great deal. If the position of an object or living entity is recorded regularly over a period, differences in its position enables the observer to compute if the entity is stationary or moving, and, if the latter, its direction and speed. Patterns in a mass of qbits enable us to identify how things work, and ultimately how we operate.

Working Definition of Information

We can identify information, therefore as regular and repeatable patterns of the smallest measurable units of difference — that means things, articles, artifacts, events; and that do things, activities, instructions or behaviours over a fixed or determinable period of time, which can be described, measured and titled sufficiently accurately so that others who observe the same phenomenon can obtain similar patterns.

We can argue that different types of information are made up of different combinations or patterns of qbits — not dissimilar to the architecture of patterns of proteins combining in different ways to create different cells.

Information exists in the same way that energy exists. How does the natural world store and access it? How is it accumulated and processed? How do we humans make it work for us? How do we make our machines take advantage of information? How do we extrapolate information into meaning?

Categories of Information

Once we have tied down patterns of qbits that provide us with manageable information, we find it divides into three main categories:

(1) There is the information that we have discovered about our universe — all the fields of science — the operations of our planet. Our distant ancestors studied the heavens, kept records, worked out the lengths of the years, when to sow, when to harvest and learned to

forecast eclipses. We refer to the laws of physics, the laws of thermodynamics and the laws of gravity. These are "laws" that after centuries of observation, we are reasonably sure are the way things work. For instance, how two atoms of hydrogen and one atom of oxygen know how to come together in a molecule and behave as water, steam or ice; and the attributes of all the elements in the periodic table and their behaviour together in various combinations. There are the streams of energy that enable us to see patterns of photons impacting our eyes, sound waves that enable us to hear and speak to each other and, of course, so much more.

(2)   Secondly there is the biological information of living things — plants and animals; how they and we reproduce, grow and behave — biogenetics — DNA, the raw material of life. There is a vast body of information about how plants and animals are nourished; for example, photosynthesis and how it generates the energy that ultimately feeds all living things.

(3a)   Thirdly there is human information, which divides again into how the neural networks in our brain process the information that our eyes, ears and other sensory organs monitor in the outside world — cognitive *neuroscience*.

(3b)   Then there are the information systems that we have developed and are unique to us — language, speech, writing, literature, music and the arts.

(3c)   Finally, there is the whole information panoply we have invented to drive our computers.

There is another dimension again. Information can be just a list of the sequence and frequency of events, records, features, facts or values, which we can describe loosely by the term "data". If we can identify form, consistency and meaning in data, then we have information that means things — what we can call knowledge. Alternatively, and quite separately, there is the mass of information that describes how things work — information that does things, which we describe as functions, instructions, procedures, processes, activities, recipes, algorithms and formulae. They do not directly provide information but instruct us how to find information, or carry out tasks. By way of analogy, there are the neural networks of instructions that manipulate our muscles to ride a bicycle, and the neural networks that describe a bicycle and its features. We can use the word *competence* to describe our ability to ride a bicycle. We can use the word *comprehension* to explain our understanding and use of bicycles — how they are manufactured; how, why and by whom they were invented; how they might develop in the future and so forth.

Two States

A neural network that is the algorithm for carrying out a function — riding that bicycle, for instance, can be in two states. When we are not using that function, it is still present in the brain. It is *potential information*, or memory. When it is being used — activating our leg muscles and adjusting our hand movements in response to signals from the balance mechanism in our ears, it is *kinetic information*. It is a contributor to our intelligence. This is true whether it is a physical or a mental or an intellectual activity.

Meaning of Information

There is a wider implication to this definition of information. From our point of view, the importance of information is the meaning it conveys and the knowledge that it develops. Having once identified and isolated items of information, we can begin to process volumes of related items. The interpretation of volumes of information — the implications of the data, perhaps we can use the term patterns of information, contributes to the *meaning* that information has for us? This use of meaning suggests the understanding of the *significance* of information. How that information relates to, and may affect and be affected by other information. *Knowledge* suggests the accumulation and relationship of meanings that enable us to *extrapolate* multiple patterns of information to predict *the* future course of events.

In turn, this suggests that not only have we evolved the capacity to identify, discover, compare, capture, store, recognise, recall, modify and develop knowledge but also presumes parallel mechanisms and skills capable of absorbing, acknowledging and benefitting from that knowledge.

We examine meaning in greater detail in Chapter 8 and explore some alternative sources of meaning, but before analysing some of these aspects of information, there is something we have learned, or perhaps discovered, in the process of inventing computing.

Attributes of the Structure of Information

We have noted that some information can be of two types — facts and functions, but further study suggests information is more sophisticated and that a great deal of information encapsulates both fact and function and that both are necessary for us to gain any useful knowledge.

Information as Hardware and Software

Let us return to the way two atoms of hydrogen and one atom of oxygen know how to get together and behave like water. The *fact* that we know the form and structure and proportions of atoms is essential but not sufficient. We need to know the *process* of how they interact to form molecules. And the patterns of the interaction of the ions between these molecules determine whether they behave like water, steam or ice. We can draw two conclusions. The facts about the component atoms are rather like *hardware* — we can see, touch and identify them. The instructions — the sequence and patterns of their relationships — are abstract. We cannot see these sequences and patterns but only the reactions they generate. These sequences and patterns are rather like *software*. Both hardware and software are indispensable to each other.

Thus, the concept of "software" that we thought we had invented to drive our computers, appears to be a fundamental attribute of most, if not all information in the natural world. We can see a seed, which might be dormant for centuries, but, give it water and warmth (energy) and it will grow. We can only see the result of that growth but not the driving process. Similarly, two strands of DNA are inert until they come together and start to react. The genes both grow the fabric of the organism, which we can see, and determine how each cell is expressed, which we cannot! The neurons in the brain can do nothing until a stream of electrochemical signals flows over them. Every computer is useless without a program. No programmer has ever seen their program working, only the results.

Information as Catalyst

There is another aspect common to all information, not so ubiquitous but equally significant. Information exists. It does not suffer wear, no matter how much it is used. In this sense, it is like a catalyst — necessary to every process but unaffected by that process. For instance, words do not wear out, no matter how many times we speak or write them. DNA remains the same, no matter how much it is used to produce, maintain and mend an organism throughout its lifetime.

Information is not used up like energy. When energy is used, it changes its form. If information is processed does it change its state?

This raises the question. If information does not wear out how is it possible to remove it, if we should wish to do so?

Evolution of Information in Humans (Cognitive Neuroscience)

Natural selection has optimised the brain mind to respond as fast as possible to incomplete information. At the slightest hint of a predator, we were running as quickly as we could. The speed of processing information from our eyes to the muscles of our legs was, and still is paramount. To increase our chances of survival above and beyond pure speed of reaction, we needed to learn from experience. Next time we encountered a predator was there a better way of responding? Firstly, that involves the ability to tease out the significance and implications of the information we obtain; and secondly, the capacity to store that information in a form that we can access it in the future and so respond to events not only faster, but better. Thus information is very closely linked to memory.

All the earliest civilizations had realised that careful observation and meticulous record keeping of natural phenomena made it possible to identify patterns that repeated over time, and thus it became possible to make ever more accurate predictions. To be able to forecast an eclipse was power. The first computer, or at least calculator, was the Antikythera, probably made at the time of Archimedes. It calculated the eclipses. *Knowledge* is to do with repeatable and predictable *patterns* in information.

The ancient Greeks pondered these questions, and the great triumvirate of Socrates, Aristotle and Plato suggested that we can tease out the meanings of information by deduction, induction and by asking questions. Pythagoras observed the repetitive pattern of the eight sounds in the octave, arguably opening the door to the manipulation of numbers — arithmetic, and with his famous theorem of the proof of right angles enabled architects to build buildings and surveyors make plans and maps. Euclid identified the pattern of shapes opening the door to geometry. Eratosthenes calculated the diameter of the earth. It had to wait until Persian mathematician Muhammad ibn Musa al-Khwarizmi developed the processing of relationships to develop algebra — the third element of mathematics.

The logical next step is to explore how information is transferred or communicated. And that takes us straight into the development of language. Language is arguably the greatest game changer — paradigm shift, in human evolution and is one of the three fundamental attributes that makes *Homo sapiens* sentient and unique.

CHAPTER FIVE
LANGUAGE

The first massive game changer or paradigm shift in the evolution of life forms on earth was when early organisms of simple cells, but with a nucleus and basic deoxyribonucleic acid (DNA), began to come together for mutual help and support. As these eukaryotic creatures attracted more and more participants, they became more complex allowing individual cells to begin to specialise — the first example of the division of labour. All skin cells can register light, but eyes developed a very specific faculty.

Millions of years later, some animals began to group together in families and packs. For communities to work and cooperate together, they needed efficient communications. While the young adults were out hunting, the older adults looked after the babies. All animals could make simple sounds, but the vocal chords of *Homo sapiens* developed a very specific faculty — the emergence of speech, then language, writing and printing.

This second massive game changer enabled specialisation and the division of labour that we have today. Most research on speech has concentrated on its crucial role in providing a very accurate and nuanced means of communication; however, we are also concerned here with the specific role of language in transferring and expanding information processing in the brain.

Our closest ancestors, the monkeys, even today, have very little need to represent information. It has been pointed out that the animals used for neural research — mice and rats equally have a very limited range of information representation. Language dynamically effected the representation and processing of information. Most adults can easily learn around 100,000 words, and that is in one language. Then there are phrases, and we have not even mentioned numbers. We are also concerned with its effect on memory, the transfer of information involved in teaching and learning; the meaning of information and the impact on our ability to think, and be creative, which have been at least as profound.

The roots of speech may lie 100,000 years in the past or even double that, which seems a long time to us but is very short in evolutionary terms. Speech has not evolved into a hereditary skill — it is not part of "nature". At birth, not one single child has been able to say one single word, let alone be able to write one! The brain has adapted to many of the ever-increasing demands of speech, but essentially speech has had to be accommodated by the plasticity of the brain and the nurture of each succeeding generation by their parents and community.

Speech has had to be mapped onto the neural structures that had evolved very slowly over eons; and writing has had to be mapped onto speech.

The benefits have been nothing less than spectacular, but these two successive mapping processes have left some problems and difficulties which are becoming increasingly apparent as we strive to educate our whole community for the first time in history.

Arrival of Speech

Like most mammals, birds and fishes, the first humans could make, hear and differentiate between quite complex sounds: mating songs and several types of warnings. One theory is that the first means of communication were extended whistles. Some 70 versions still exist. Whistling can carry sound over several kilometres. It conveys meanings by compressing the air at the edges of the lips in different ways, but it lacks the harmonics of the voice and has a very narrow band of frequencies. Maybe this was the starting point.

The more conventional theory is that when our distant ancestors started to reach up, stand, walk and run upright the muscles in the throat developed to ensure food and liquid did not accidently enter the lungs. These extended throat muscles widened the repertoire of sounds and evolved into the vocal cords. Gradually, gradually sensations of fragments of song became associated with visual, sound, taste, smell and feel sensations of objects and activities. Steven Mithen has described these early manifestations of what we recognise as speech as holistic, multi-model, manipulative and musical, or "Hmmmm", while the ears and eyes became adept at identifying statistical regularities — patterns — in these multimedia communications.

What today we recognise as words probably started out as fragments of music and parts of songs. We have learned to separate individual words out, but if you look at a phrase on an oscilloscope, it is still one long sound. Poetry, alliteration, onomatopoeia, rhythm, rhyme, metre, cadence, jingles, music and song still play directly to our emotions to this day. Orators move crowds by the impression they give just as much as the individual words they speak.

Our best guess is that when our distant ancestors started to widen their repertoire of sounds, the first sounds — or proto words — were patterns of sound that were accepted by everyone in the group as referring to specific individual things or actions. This facility proved extremely useful so a number of neural patterns evolved to activate the muscles of the lungs, vocal chords, lips, tongue and mouth to produce ever wider patterns of sound waves, while the hearing system of the ears evolved to analyse these patterns of sound waves into recognisable streams of neural activity, and these were passed on to each succeeding generation. Those initial sounds were probably random or made up of the phonemes of syllables and were unique to each group. Indeed, there might have been a benefit for adjacent groups specifically to choose different sounds — the dawn of the Tower of Babel.

There is the intriguing hypothesis that our earliest ancestors made the first sounds that evolved into words, as a result of frustration at wishing to express their emotions, their sensations, perceptions and feelings. In other words, the beginnings of consciousness drove the development of language — the opposite of the generally held belief.

It is not too difficult to conceive of words, even in all their complexity being representations of things and activities — words being, in effect, labels for artefacts like trees, or actions like running. Thus, the neural networks are linked to visual images, sounds, smells, taste and touch.

Then there is the status of words that are abstract: concepts like freedom, beauty, leadership, design and attraction — the family of conceptions we call qualia. To what are abstract words anchored?

Abstract words have enabled us to reminisce about the past, discuss alternative actions now and imagine possible future events, and find alternative solutions to potential problems and make decisions.

Neural Precision

The biggest change has been in precision. The brain was, and is, an entirely analogue system; it evolved to process generalisations and simplifications. For the first time, the brain had to make and deconstruct extremely accurate sounds. The memory system has had to accommodate not only this step change in precision but also an ever-increasing volume of words, phrases and their meaning. Understanding this system is central to our understanding of a great deal of neural information processing.

Our distant ancestors adapted the primeval ability to recognise words — primary memory. Variations in sounds stimulate different neural combinations and the experience causes new neural networks to grow. Similarly, variant output combinations stimulate new networks to generate new sounds — secondary memory. Thus, new words flow down the new neural paths they have created to the new neural structures that enable that person to speak that unfamiliar word. Therefore, words are recognised because they pass along their own neural networks while the memory of a word is the whole neural network plus the networks that control the vocal chords etc. It could be said that these memories are sets of instructions or algorithms. Appendix 12 lists some 20 examples (all appendices are hosted on www.BrainMindForum.org/appendices).

Tertiary memory — the ability to process several incoming signals together was adapted into coping with phrases.

Cross References: Relationships

Similarly, the whole neural network from the ears to the speech system was linked up and cross referenced to and from the neural structures of all the sensory and other organs. The image of a mother was associated with the word mother, as also was her scent, taste and feel. Similarly, the sensation of hunger, thirst, fear etc. also generated the cry of mother. This is being called the relational frame theory. Thus, these new-fangled words were mapped onto the whole existing system. Words were so useful they proliferated and so the brain had to accommodate a massive increase in its recording capacity. As sound became ever more sophisticated, more and more neural capacity was generated and sound started to take up as much space in the brain as eyesight.

Parents and peers taught their young to speak the language of their tribe by mapping these sounds directly to the sensations, impressions, feelings and emotions that flowed from their sensory and other organs. Thus, everyone developed a sense of the meanings of those words.

Abstract Words

The speaking brain, therefore, became significantly more sophisticated, but still words were only effectively labels to identify the information from the sensory organs. Then a very small innovation caused a very big advance. People started to use words like a "big" tree, or a "fast" deer. This was a very useful addition but with enormous consequences. All nouns and verbs were neurally anchored to objects or activities. The humble adjective and adverb are not. They are abstract. The neural structures for abstract words are only anchored to other neuron structures — other words.

One adjective can apply to many nouns — the beginning of phrases, where the meaning of the pair is greater than the sum of the two words individually. This is an early example of the powerful concept of "emergence". More significantly these abstract words can only be described or defined in terms of other words. Their existence is entirely cerebral.

Thus, was opened Pandora's Box of *abstract* thought, which only exists in terms of neural patterns. We think about ideas and concepts. We endlessly imagine possible events. We create infinite plots of complex novels. We remember vividly events that have *not* happened. The way was open to speculate, to think, to be creative.

We have developed abstract information, which can only exist in a human head.

Abstract language made it possible to discuss concepts and ideas — to ask questions, discuss past experience and, crucially, speculate about better ways of behaving in the future. This gave us, uniquely among all living things, the ability to envisage the future course of events and make provision for eventualities. We had the tool to influence our environment.

First Major Expansion (1)

Words expanded the existing memory systems and structures, but abstract words created a major extension of information-processing capability: arguably the first neural systems expansion of memory. One adjective can be applied to any number of nouns. Quite a wiring problem! These word pairings heralded the birth of phrases and sentences. Abstract words, ideas and concepts only have meaning because we chose to give them meaning, and we can only do this in terms of other words. We need language to use language. Language is a curiously compound skill.

The meanings of abstract words, like concepts, ideas, aspirations, speculations and ambitions were not fixed or anchored to things and actions. They could not be pointed at, but they could be debated.

Gradually, the early civilisations teased out by endless observation, measurement recording and speculation how the world about them worked, but the only way of transmitting this burgeoning volume of knowledge to succeeding generations was through the medium of memory. If not strictly an evolutionary benefit, verbal memory was a very valuable social benefit. The Greeks built up and passed on the founding concepts of their race by reciting the Iliad and the Odyssey. The Jews still recite the Torah; the Hindus, the Upanishads. The story of Gilgamesh is remarkably like the narrative of the New Testament.

Writing: The Second Expansion (2)

Some 5,000 years ago people started making marks on clay tablets as an aide memoir, of which cuneiform is one example. The Egyptians developed symbols, or hieroglyphs, initially stylised pictures. Modern Chinese is an example of the latter. They all experienced difficulties coping with the expansion of the vocabulary but more significantly they could not express abstract ideas. Thus, alphabets were born that represent the sounds we make as we speak words. Twenty-seven symbols can encapsulate all the ideas of all mankind, or nearly all. We struggle with representing abstract ideas and we still cannot adequately describe things like beauty, leadership, charisma — what we generically call qualia. We look at this again in Chapter 13. We all experience and recognise qualia, but as yet we have not created the words that reproduce those sensations, impressions and feelings. However, to a great extent sounds and poems gave way to prose and arithmetic.

Writing and reading arrived rather more gradually than we realise today. Punctuation did not arrive for nearly a millennium. Writing was the preserve of a tiny minority and for a long time remained a supplement to memory. Its principal use was to transmit messages and to store knowledge, rather than be a part of the daily life of the vast majority. Socrates was famously horrified that it would herald the demise of human memory. Fortunately, he was wrong; however, it certainly changed the structure of human information processing.

However, the invention of coding systems like the alphabet had an immense impact on information. This was the first of many notations that enabled scholars to communicate and encapsulate knowledge and witnessed the beginning of artificial or machine information. The numerals 0–9, which arrived in the thirteenth century, musical notation and scientific notations are just three of many. In the twentieth century, all these notations have themselves been subject to the further coding of the ubiquitous binary Morse-based machine information (further explored in Chapter 6).

Drafting Skills

Writing and reading made new demands on the brain. Human beings had been able to manipulate tools from the far distant past — many claim it was the very first skill — but only the most expert craftsmen had needed to manipulate a pen or stylus with the precision needed to draw the symbols of the alphabet. Now anyone who wished to write had to be proficient to an unrivalled degree, putting further pressure on the controlling neural networks. Similarly, the vision system had to be able to decode these symbols and convert them to words.

Writing can be defined as the conversion of speech to symbols and reading the conversation of symbols to speech. For a millennium that is exactly what people did. They talked as they wrote and they recited out loud what they were reading. The arrival of printing accelerated all these trends.

Spelling

The completely novel skill of being able to spell had to be mapped on to the entire neural structure of human speech. Words started as one single sound. Multi-syllable or compound words began to be made up of two or more sounds or phonemes, much as two or more words made up phrases. Spelling was a step change. Linked to every neural word structure the writer and reader had to append or access a string of characters.

Complexity

So the "memory structures" of words had to include its access path, for quick recognition; all the relationship and cross references to other relevant media, and other word structures to establish aspects of the "meaning" of that word to provide access and recall; the output instructions to speak that word. Now, added to all that, was a string of letters and the instructions to the fingers to write them, and decoding structures to read them.

First Schools

Writing and reading gradually modified the structure of memory and learning. Both these skills needed different teaching. People could not pick up these skills by imitation and repetition largely unconsciously. They needed conscious effort. As a rule, parents no longer felt competent to teach their young, and the concept of schools and the profession of teaching came into being. (Some records suggest the first schools in the Tigres river basin around 3,000 BC.)

Role of Text

The relationship between external, written and later printed information and internal, neural information changed. Broadly, until the invention of printing and the renaissance, the neural memory remained in the ascendancy. Memory was the prime source of information. Writing was steadily more important for transmitting information and storing accumulated knowledge, but it remained a way of assembling data and triggering information recall and rather than supplementing it. The age of enlightenment, the scientific and then the industrial revolution began to change that.

Firstly, there was increasingly more to learn. In the seventeenth century Roger Bacon suggested it would take adults 30 years to acquire the knowledge that 14-year-olds today would take in their stride. Dictionaries, encyclopaedias, newspapers and magazines flourished as the appetite for knowledge spread throughout the community. Merchants and Guilds set up schools to provide literate employees to staff their growing businesses. One of the demands of the Council of Oliver Cromwell's new Model Army (c. 1650) was that all freeborn citizens should be taught to read, write and number. Information became international and competitive with translations and patents.

The Information Stored in Memories

Secondly, external artificial information became increasingly part of the memory system. Nobody was expected, or was able, to memorise all the available knowledge. People had to cooperate and individuals specialised, enabling the division of labour propelling civilisation forward.

The arrival of telecommunications and computing has taken this trend further. The invention of binary coding of words, numbers, sounds and pictures has exacerbated the difference between artificial or machine information, and biological or neural information. Now in the twenty-first century, we are on the cusp of having the entire body of human knowledge, art, culture and commerce, teaching, training and emotions instantly available. Binary codes map to visual words. Written words map to sounds of words and map to multimedia and multi-sensory sensations, impressions and feelings, which are still the unchanged basis of biological, neural information.

Plasticity

Evolution has not had time to respond to change at this speed, but the phenomenal plasticity of the brain can respond, does respond and continues to respond. The evolutionary systems still ably support all these new developments. The basic algorithms do not appear to have changed.

From the far distant past, the ability to record experience has been a key building block in the operation and ascendency of the brain. Even the simplest organisms evolved the ability to build memories. Additional information from the sensory organs generates electrochemical signals and electromagnetic fields in the neural networks. This activity automatically stimulates active neurons to grow links — neurons that fire together wire together. New temporary links and networks create new neural structures — new memories, over which successive electrochemical signals can carry out novel tasks in the future. This is explored further in Chapter 7.

The Third Expansion (3) of Neural Information Processing: Thinking and Creativity

So far, we have concentrated on the history of the evolution and development of the creation of biological neural information processing and memory. At the dawn of civilisation, language gave us the means to communicate with each other, but in addition, as if that was not enough, it also gave us the means to speculate. We could exchange experiences and debate innovative ideas, alternative ways of behaviour. We could bring many brains together to cooperate to tease out an innovative new way of doing things, solutions to problems and answers to why things happened as they did. It gave us the *tool to think*.

If we experience a problem, and we have the luxury of time, we can interrupt the automatic conditioned response while we evaluate alternatives. We can predict potential future events, then can select and execute our preferred choice.

This ability to extrapolate the past then project our experiences into the future is of immense importance. Some people call these memories of the future. Lowenstein has suggested "forecognition". The literate world calls this activity imagination. One indication of its importance is the large numbers of words that are associated with imagination. Appendix 13 lists the many words associated with "imagination" (all appendices are hosted on www.BrainMindForum.org/appendices).

More significantly, we have developed the skill to express problems as an adventure in the exploration of everything we know about this issue. In doing this, we stimulate masses of neural structures which automatically grow links: the epithet "firing together, wiring together" again! Only a very small number of these innovative new structures prove to be breakthroughs. Of these, a tiny minority are "eureka" moments and the majority are formed by gradual empirical elucidation.

Tertiary memory, the ability to hold information in limbo, while we worked out the speed of an object, was first adapted to deal with strings of words, but it was also pressed into use to evaluate alternatives then expanded again to enable us to assemble ideas and innovative concepts. As we stimulated all the neural networks involved, they automatically grew links creating whole new memory structures made up of many components of other structures. We could create *neur*al mod*ules*, or *neurules*, for short. Conceptually, neurules bear many similarities to the sub-routines of computer programs. Both enable simple small units to be built up into hierarchies of ever more sophisticated structures that create complex systems. Many neuroscientists have studied this facility and come up with a variety of words to describe it, which are listed in Appendix 12 (all appendices are hosted on www.BrainMindForum.org/appendices).

Computer scientists have suggested practical solutions proposing that these programming concepts are very like the universal processing "engine" described by Alan Turing in his famous paper in 1936, which arguably launched the computer revolution. He described this as an abstract procedure to use the minimum instruction set to compute complex functions. Thus, was born the concept of a "software" program that could operate the hardware of the circuits and semi-conductors of electronic digital computers. There is a remarkable similarity with the neurons and synapses. Electrochemical signals or software operate over the hardware of the neuron networks of the brain. Synapses are a form of biological analogue semi-conductor. It is then only one step to suggest that this neural software is what generates the mind from the hardware of the brain. But that is discussed at length elsewhere.

The first and second waves of memory expansion were driven by external stimulations — unfamiliar words, writing and spelling and increases in the volume of information to be stored. The third expansion has been driven from internal activity — our own abstract thoughts. For instance, the entire structure of string theory is abstract. It is completely a human creation, yet it is debated and discussed worldwide. That raises many questions — another debate.

The First Steps in Transferring Information to the Brain

The process of acquiring information or learning is illuminating. We know from several experiments, some at the Royal Institute in London in 2013 that all the information that we see for at least 20 seconds is recorded in the brain (see Appendix 28, all appendices are hosted on www. BrainMindForum.org/appendices). These images cannot always be recalled, but we can prove they are present because they always enable us to recognise an image if we see it again: the first step to forming memory. Every repetition strengthens existing structures and adds additional cross references and relationships. All knowledge is built up by tiny incremental steps. Innovative ideas can be assimilated more easily, if they are explained as extensions of accepted concepts. Leaps forward are difficult to appreciate as there may be little or nothing to which the new neural links and structures can be anchored.

We can now move on to the representation of words, numbers, images and music in the brain and in our computers.

CHAPTER SIX

REPRESENTATION OF INFORMATION

Representation (Form) of Information

Over the centuries, some of the greatest brains have puzzled over how information is represented in the brain. In particular, how words are recognised, stored and accessed. Children learn to speak the language of their community, parents and peers. One of the early Holy Roman Emperors, Ferdinand, took several children from various parts of his empire and brought them up so they heard no speech, so that he could determine which language was the basic one. He was confounded to find that none spoke any words at all.

The Greeks were aware that if children were separated from their parents at birth they would speak the language of those who oversaw them and their peers irrespective of the language of their parents. Thus, they concluded language was not hereditary. In addition, individuals could learn more than one language and act as interpreters.

Much more recently, we have learned that sounds not used are pruned. Japanese children at birth, and if brought up in the west, can make the "r" sound, but if brought up in Japan lose this and can only make an "l" sound by puberty.

With the beginning of writing and then printing, the first dictionaries were produced. Greek, Roman, Phoenician and Aramaic were all spoken around the Mediterranean, and there is some evidence that there were early dictionaries in the library in Alexandria.

We can learn from the development of writing. The first characters we attempted to write were images, thus Egyptian Hieroglyphs and Chinese characters. The first writings represented roughly what we see. As the lexicon grew this was soon obsolescent. Even the Priests could not keep up, and how does one draw abstract words? Rather than represent what we see, better to represent the sound. Thus, was born the alphabet and Galileo's famous comment that "Of all the stupendous inventions, they who conceived how to communicate their most secret thoughts distant in time and place simply by the arrangement of two dozen signs upon a paper".

We think of words as being autonomous, but they are conglomerates made up of letters: spelling. Then phonemes are sounds of groups of letters, while syllables are similarly groups of letters, which can be put together to make different words.

Representation of Words

We suggested in the last chapter that words originated and developed to enable individuals to be able to indicate things (nouns) or actions (verbs). Thus, the objective was to make a unique sound to represent, say, a tree. If this conjecture is correct, the neural pattern of the "word" for a tree started as an extension to the neural patterns for the visual image of trees, the feeling of trees, the smell of trees and the taste of trees. Every experience associated with any aspect of trees symbiotically extended the neural networks of both trees and all new experiences associated with trees, all cross referenced against each other. There was not, neither is there now, a specific neural network just for a specific word. There is a massive cluster of all the associations and cross references to our perceptions, impressions and sensations associated with our experiences of that word, which includes sending to the muscles streams of signals that are the patterns of instructions, the algorithm, to speak that word, and later to write that word and think that word.

Writing, reading and printing added another dimension. The brain had to evolve the ability to manipulate the muscles of the fingers to move a writing instrument with a degree of precision never previously needed by any living thing, while the eyes had to decode shapes with a new degree of accuracy. Writing involved expanding words into alphabets and spelling, and reading into phonemes and syllables. The brain had to evolve massive new neural structures to cope with storing, cross referencing, editing, reinforcing, recognising and retrieving 100,000 words or more, and that is just in one language. Then there is the meaning of each word and the meaning of strings of words, where the position and sequence is as significant as the words themselves. Then there is the emphasis placed on words. Actors are especially skilled at being able to say a phrase with many different emphases such that one identical phrase can even mean the opposite of another.

In short order — over less than 4,000 years and less than 200 generations — the brain has had to respond to the invention of writing, and every child must cope over the first decade of their lives with a mass of interleaved, interrelated, associated and connected hierarchies of neural network patterns. We have one verbal input system, ears, and one verbal output system, speech. Another input system is the recognition of visual patterns and reading. Blind people can "feel" braille. We have another output system making precision images with our fingers, writing or sequencing characters and more recently, keyboarding.

Silent Speech

In addition, we can talk silently and hear things we have not spoken, and speak without making a sound, suggesting that we have a short-cut mechanism connecting the output systems directly to the input systems, perhaps across the corpus colloquium. Our best guess is that writing was an evolution of the speech networks and reading an evolution of the hearing networks. Many people used to speak what they were reading. Young children that are learning to read still do. Only in the last millennium have we learned to read and write silently. We still hear words as we read them. We assemble words and phrases silently in our heads as we speak, write or keyboard them. Famously Augustine of Hippo expressed amazement at witnessing that Bishop Ambrose of Milan could read without speaking — around 400 AD.

Some people argue that this "silent speech" has become the medium we use to consciously think, to speculate, to predict, to imagine and to create — to initiate neural activity. However, the opposite may be true that silently sorting our ideas in our heads developed silent thinking. In other words, it was not thinking that led to silent speech, but silent speech helped us learn to think. More of the implications of silent speech are discussed in Chapters 10 and 11.

Structure of Every Word

So, the neural structure of just one word contains a neural monitoring facility to visually recognise a pattern of images of that word in various formats, and neural algorithms to write those symbols of the letters that spell that word. We have the structures to decode the incoming sounds of the phonemes, and the algorithms to operate the muscles both exquisitely accurately and with precise timing, and with modifying facilities to emphasise the sound to add to, and vary the meaning. Then there are all the links to other word structures and multimedia images associated with this word, phrase, and relationships which form part of the meaning, and rules which circumscribe the usage and positioning of many words — grammar and syntax. In addition, there are the phrases and sentences and other conglomerate uses of this word. If this were not enough, there are records of when we used that word, when, why, what was the occasion and what was the outcome?

With such a vast array of neural involvement it seemed to early cognitive neuroscience explorers that it should be reasonably easy to locate well-used words. But, try as they might they found there none.

Once again, our experience of computing comes to our aid. It comes as something as a surprise to many that there is not one single letter, let alone any words, no numbers, no pictures nor sounds in any computer ever made.

It comes to many as an even bigger surprise that there are no letters, numbers, pictures or sounds, let alone words in our heads. Evolution did not have the benefit of Morse's inventive brain, so there is no binary code in the brain! There is no coding system, as such, at all. Nor is the brain digital. Information is transmitted by the mind and stored by the brain in analogue patterns — that is, the strength of each part of every pattern is as significant as its form and position.

We can understand this concept more easily by looking again at the development of language that we discussed in the last chapter. We noted that when our distant ancestors starting to walk upright this new activity stretched their necks and vocal chords, enabling them to widen their repertoire of sounds. The first sounds — or proto words, were patterns of sound that were accepted by everyone as referring to specific individual things or actions. Neural patterns evolved to activate the muscles of the lungs, vocal chords, lips, tongue and mouth to produce patterns of sound waves, while the hearing system of the ears evolved to analyse these patterns of sound waves into recognisable streams of neural activity.

There is absolutely no reason why these neural patterns of sounds should be identical in each person's brain. On the contrary, it would seem to be extraordinary surprising if they were even similar. The occasions that people hear a word for the first time are bound to be very diverse. Completely different circumstances will modify the current brain activity, often by a great deal, and almost always strongly affected by the ambient hormone mix — state of our emotions. What counts is that everyone recognises their neural pattern generates the same reactions as everyone else's. It is not the neural structure of words that needs to be identical but their meaning to each person.

Thus, precisely like our thumb print or retina pattern, every piece of information in our brain and mind is unique.

We can say that a word, phrase or larger structure is a concept. It is a conception, an idea, a meaning (and we study *meaning* in Chapter 8). Even just one word can also be said to be *emergent*. All the mass of neural structures, cross references and relationships taken together generate the conception of an idea — just one word. And that word is more powerful by far than the sum of all the constituent neural structures added together — a good example of the power of emergence.

Language Translation

It also explains how people can learn to speak multiple languages. They do not swop one English word, for, say, one Latin word. They add the Latin algorithms to hear, say, read, write and think to the conglomerate concept of that word they already have in their brain and mind. Thus, when they think the English word, they can, in principle, output the Latin equivalent. The syntax and grammar of the target language is often quite different, but that is a metaprogram as the constituents of the sentences that are being assembled. The more the languages people learn, the more they can learn. It also explains the phenomenon that people who learn a second language find they begin to think in that new language.

We can observe a very useful attribute of language, starting with the native language we first use. When we assemble a sentence or more to speak, write or think, it is fairly clear that we assemble all the words we need and then output them through an output metaprogram to include the grammar and syntax. Observe children and adults learning a new language. They start with simple sentences and all the words in the present tense. Different tenses and sophisticated structures come later.

There has been much debate over the last few decades by Naom Chomsky and others about the possibility of a language instinct, suggesting that grammar is, at least to some extent, hereditary.

If we learn our first language, let alone any others, with the words first and the grammar and syntax second, this hypothesis is likely to be wrong, or at least incomplete. Similarly, the syntax and grammar of two languages can often be very different. It seems likely that we have evolved a predisposition to acquire lexicons — just the processing of such a large number would seem to be proof, however, as grammar follows lexicons, this would seem to negate this hypothesis.

Computer language engineering systems nowadays do not try to convert words for words, but they analyse a mass of speech to try and ascertain the identity of a word, to understand an instruction or generate speech (speech recognition) or output in another language (translation).

The Poetry Effect

We can learn a lot more by using the example of learning a piece of text. This might be a speech, or the part in a play or the best answers to give at a viva, but reciting poetry is more fun to discuss.

In all computing, every time a word is used, whether to include in an article, report or whatever, the program collects words from a file or from the keyboard and places them in a new special file for each job. One word may be repeated hundreds of times in just one work. Computers have limitless memory capacity. If one unit is full, install another. The brain cannot afford such profligacy, and for the time being we only have one. If we wish to recite "Out of the night that covers me, black as the pit from pole to pole", then our task is to grow a neural network that visits each word network in turn, stimulating the algorithm in each to move the vocal cord muscles to say each word. Or alternatively draw the words, or think them. Thus, the "memory" to recite the first line of "Invictus" is not actually the 15 words, but the infinitely simpler single neural network that visits and activates each of the word networks in sequence. However, a reference to the fact that the word has been included in the reciting will be stored in the word complex. The whole of the poem "Invictus" is set out in Appendix 25 as poetry also demonstrates how the position of words in a sequence affects their meaning (all appendices are hosted on www. BrainMindForum.org/appendices).

This poetry effect is a key piece of the jigsaw of our understanding and is explored in Chapter 7 on memory formation, Chapter 8 on meaning, and in Chapter 14 to demonstrate the phenomenon of emergence.

Representation of Abstract Ideas, Concepts, Thoughts, Imagination and Prediction

It is one thing to conceive how we represent things and actions. We can point to a tree and draw attention to someone running but discussing freedom or democracy is a completely different problem.

We have discussed above the role of adjectives and adverbs, modifying nouns and adverbs and the beginnings of phrases, and this early example of emergence, where the two words together mean so much more than the sum of the two words separately.

Abstract concepts take this further and by linking up a number of phrases into, say, a paragraph, and then numbers of paragraphs into a chapter, and numbers of chapters into a book, we can build up complex ideas. We have the means to store unlimited amounts of information in this format, and we can discuss these concepts with others. We can change individual paragraphs in the light of discussion.

Thus, we developed one of the most powerful attributes *Homo sapiens* has evolved. We can predict the possible course of future events.

Arguably this is one of the key attributes that make us sentient. The ability to predict, enables us to prepare for possible eventualities. Thus, we can influence our environment. No other life form has this ability. Everything else in nature are self-organising systems, they can only react to events. That is true of physical events in the universe, or here on earth. Many animals store food for the winter and build simple shelters, but none have our ability to change the course of nature, thus we are beginning to rule the world.

An adjective is abstract. As we noted above you cannot see, hear, feel smell or touch one. Thus, we can only describe, debate and discuss them with others through the medium of language. It is an interesting system engineering problem to consider how the brain stores words that can apply to, and be attached to, many others. It is a similar conundrum to the poetry problem. It would not help if every adjective was individually connected to every noun, let alone the volume problem. Store a new noun and how would it automatically be linked to every adjective? If we meet a new adjective, it is not automatically connected to every noun, and yet it is immediately possible to relate them together. Logic suggests that, just as we have one neural representation of a word in every possible format, so we have one adjective with multiple connections. It seems likely that the families of modifying words operate like indexes. Just as we have a neural network of all the words in the poem, we have a neural net of all the words that can be modified by the word in the index. This architecture has the advantage that it supports that aspect of where certain combinations of words are not allowed.

Few people can compose an entire article, let alone novel in their heads without, at least, making notes. However, Solzhenitsyn is reported not to have access to paper and pencil in the gulag, thus he composed a whole novel in his head, then, on being released, typed it straight out. Authors who write novels, or to a more limited extent computer systems analysts who write about intelligence and consciousness, have to try and do something similar. The writing is the less difficult part. The invention of the plot or the development of the theory is a more difficult subject and is explored in Chapter 17.

This growing knowledge of how we learn will be of very great importance as computing replaces ever more repetitive jobs and lifelong learning becomes the norm. We have for a long time been aware that every child has a unique brain, and we are now learning that every child has a unique representation of every single word, let alone every concept they are taught. Classrooms with a number of students with different thinking systems all being taught together has been out of date for half a century, but the education profession has been curiously backward in adopting, even researching, new knowledge and new technologies. At the moment, on-line distance learning systems are rudimentary and just use existing computer technology to deliver more or less conventional lessons. As we learn more about intelligence and the learning processes, innovative learning systems will be developed. Massive open online courses (MOOCs) will be developed far ahead of present teaching techniques (see Chapter 19).

Representation and Computation of Numbers

It seems that a very great deal of more time and efforts over the centuries have been devoted to understanding how numbers, counting and arithmetic are accommodated in the brain and mind, than the aspects of literature discussed above. This probably has a lot to do with the fact that numbers and the brain are both associated with science, whereas words and literature are seen as somehow different. In particular, words and literature are associated with emotion, whereas numbers are most definitely not.

This is misguided and probably says more about fashions and prejudices than about knowledge. There are many similarities. Numeracy, literacy and computing have a remarkable amount in common.

Pythagoras identified eight sounds in the octave, arguably the dawn of both music and arithmetic. Interestingly, he is reported to have insisted on keeping this knowledge secret as he feared that "in the hands of the common people all sorts of trouble would ensue!"

Children and many animals can differentiate between, "one", "two", "three" and "more", and can count in threes. Older children can expand these quantifiers to phrases like "about a dozen" and "around a hundred". Conventional thinking suggests that semantics determines how place varies the value of a number. A one with three noughts is rather greater than a one with no noughts. Numbers can be represented symbolically in language, thus "seven", or iconically, like a picture, thus "7" (see Appendix 54, all appendices are hosted on www.BrainMindForum.org/appendices).

Some people think there is an "innate perceptual input analyser". Dehaene in his excellent book *The Number Sense* suggests a numerosity detector.

John Locke, who might be described as the Descartes of arithmetic, in *An Essay Concerning Human Understanding*, published in 1690, suggests that "our ideas of numbers resemble the numbers of which they are ideas". And he had never seen a computer!

Learning to Count — Early Numbers

In the beginnings of civilization, our ancestors observed that using the fingers and thumbs of both hands provided a useful counting system. They recorded that there were roughly 360 days in a year. There were roughly 30 days in a moon cycle; 12 months in a year and 4 weeks in a month; 52 weeks in a year; $52 \times 7 = 364$. And that turned out to be more accurate. It has taken us to the nineteenth century to measure the length of a year accurately.

Observation suggested that 364 was more accurate than 365, but 360 had a considerable benefit. If you counted out 360 stones, you could parcel them out in a wide variety of piles. Thus, the concept of multiplication and division:

$2 \times 180 = 360$
$3 \times 120 = 360$
$4 \times 90 = 360$
$5 \times 60 = 360$
7? No not seven
$8 \times 45 = 360$
$9 \times 40 = 360$
$10 \times 36 = 360$

So, 360 degrees was an excellent number to use for measuring circles. Cut out a circle of papyrus and fold it in half and half again and the angle is 90°, a right angle, and 7 was the days of the week. Pythagoras's eight sounds seems not to fit. Had the gods slipped up?

One of the great curiosities of life is that the Greeks, for all their genius, could not get their heads around the concept of zero. Equally they did not have numbers and used the letters of their alphabet with a tag.

Roman Numerals

The Romans were not overly interested in numbers or at least mathematics, but adopted a thousand paces, "mille passus" as a useful measure of distance; roughly our miles; and a centurion for a unit of soldiers. Why 10? Apart from 10 fingers and thumbs, if numbers were displayed, they were often carved, and straight lines are easier to carve than curves. Also, slaves, soldiers and farm labourers could only count in threes. Hence I, II, III, then IV and so on. One finger = I or one. One thumb = V or five. Cross hands = X or 10. This system lasted Rome for 2,000 years. Arithmetic is impossible. Even computers find it hard to add IX to IV and get XIII. And as for multiplication, one can see why the Romans closed the Academy in Athens. However, this problem helps us understand how our brain manipulates numbers.

It took a group of monks in the monastery of Ripoll north of Barcelona till the fourteenth century to design a notation which could be carved, read and counted by everyone. A set of 10 numbers from one to zero made up of right angles that could be counted, so if an artisan or proto clerk forgot the shape of a number he could work it out (see Appendix 54, all appendices are hosted on www.BrainMindForum.org/appendices). Almost immediately Gutenberg came up with moveable type and the stylised characters were rounded off so that they could be written more easily, and so gave us our familiar European number set.

So how does the brain and mind cope with the representation of numbers, and with counting, addition and multiplication? Computers to the rescue again. It comes as a considerable shock, especially to scientists, that there are only two numbers in all computing — 0 and 1. There is only one formula and that is for addition:

$0 + 0 = 0$, $1 + 0 = 1$, $0 + 1 = 1$ and $1 + 1 = 0$ and, if appropriate, carry 1. With 2 bits we can represent four alternatives: $2^2 = 4$ — the foundation of binary, the foundation of computing; and very probably the basis of neural processing (00 is the first number, 01 the second, 10 the third and 11 the forth: we need 3 bits for four). This is similar to our decimal system based on 0–9 (0 is the first number, 1 the second, 2 the third... and 9 the tenth number: we need two digits for 10).

There is also collate or the logical add formula: $0 + 0 = 0$, $1 + 0 = 0$, $0 + 1 = 0$ and $1 + 1 = 1$ *and no carr*y, used to isolate bits.

There are no other formulae in any computer. Are there any more in the brain, mind?

Children first learn to count: one, two, three.... The neural structures created are going to be similar to any other string of words. They will learn to associate the sound of one with the image of a "1", and so forth. Composite numbers like 21, 101, 121 economise on thinking time. Thirty-six *feels* smaller than 54, but this is not a strongly held emotional view. Two sweets + eight sweets = 10 sweets. "Please may I pick my favourites?" Similarly, children chant their tables till they can recite them in the same way they sing a song. "Six eights are forty-eight" is smaller than "seven nines are sixty-three" — neither are exactly exciting. Every one of these counting numbers, additions or multiplications is a statement no different to "the tree is green", "the river is blue". No computation is involved whatever.

As computers use a fixed stylised coding system every "three" in binary is represented by the same pattern of bits 00000011 out of the 8 bits in each byte. Numbers can be programmed in three forms. For historical technical reasons, numbers start in the Morse alphabet at code 48 in every byte. So, six is code 54. Letters start at Morse code 65 so J is code 75, S is code 80 and X is code 89.

Keyboarding "6" will input code 54 to the processor which will generate a 6 on the screen and everything printed out. Alternatively keyboarding S I X will input codes 80, 74 and 89 and will display and print SIX.

If the program calls for *computation*, the processor will generate the 6 in Morse code binary of 00000110.

All computers have adding circuits that can compute

$$\begin{array}{ll} \text{six} + & 00000110 + \\ \text{four} = & 00000100 = \\ \text{ten} & 00001010 \end{array}$$

If the program calls for the *multiplication* of six times four, then it has to run a subroutine that adds six to six four times. An example is set out in Appendix 32-H (all appendices are hosted on www.BrainMindForum. org/appendices).

There is no neural structure in the brain and mind that can do anything like this in any way.

If accidently Morse code for "B" is added to Morse code "D", it will generate Morse code "F". The computer has no idea what it is doing. Every computer program multiplying, dividing or any other formula is a combination of neural algorithms. It is similar to the metaprogram that assembles the sounds of a "group of words" to recite a poem. There is one difference. Words generate sensations, feelings, emotions and meanings. Numbers generate a sense of relative size but a little more. No one gets excited using the world's best-known formula to calculate the energy needed to move a given amount of mass. Mental arithmetic, and indeed the panoply of mathematics, is neurally rather like an author putting together a long string of words for the plot of a novel.

There Are No Numbers in the Brain, Mind

Interestingly the brain is in the same position as a Roman citizen. Nine is a random network pattern. Just like the other numbers. At least the Romans were consistent amongst themselves but humans are not even that. The neural image pattern for, say "nine" is different in every human brain.

There is no way that a pattern of neurons can be processed next to another pattern of neurons and by some neural process add them together. There is no equivalent neural adding circuit.

We do not learn a *process* to add three to seven, we learn the *fact* that three plus seven equals 10. Thus, we add as the Romans did.

The pattern for III.

+ the pattern for VII.

= the pattern for X.

Multiplication is similar. We learn *three sevens are 21*, like we learn *trees are blue*.

Long division and long multiplication are ways of assembling these statements and processing them in a particular way to give a value, just as we assemble words to give an impression. The genius of logarithms is that it enables us to multiply two complex numbers only using the facility of addition.

Thus, the entire structure of mathematical formulae, which is such an important part of science, is a series of images and algorithms much like language — stringing words together. Formulae are much like grammar.

Visual Arts

The ability to see our surroundings proved so valuable that evolution selected ever more complex and sophisticated visual systems. The neural visual processing system takes up a hugely disproportionate amount of the brain.

How the brain mind perceives the images we see with our eyes, has understandably been on the 'far too difficult' heap until very recently.

We open our eyes and instantly see our surroundings in minute detail. We recognise familiar sights, so we must have a sophisticated memory system. We recognise images whether they are close at hand or distant, from the front or back, or any other angle or context, background, environment and even images specially disguised.

Over the last century, we have learned a great deal about the spectrum of light and energy waves from the very short to the very long. We have learned that the smallest measurable unit of energy is a *photon*, which is also the basic unit of light. It is the streams of photons in the spectrum between ultraviolet and infrared which enables us to see. That is about 10% of the total known spectrum. We know that some animals can see a larger amount of this spectrum than we can, although not much more.

When our eyes are open, they are bombarded with a stream of photons that have bounced off everything around us. The front of the eyeball acts as a lens to focus this stream of light onto the back of the eyeball, sending a stream of electrochemical signal patterns along the optic nerve to the brain.

To recognise that image, or its parts, there must be an existing image in the brain with which to compare it. As we move our heads, even slightly, the photon pattern hitting the retina jumps about all over the place, yet the image we perceive remains quite stable. Thus, we can draw the conclusion that we store very sophisticated images in our brain. But how? For once our computers and telecommunication technologies do not really help, except, perhaps, to rule some solutions out. We can store complex images in our computers and transmit them to television screens as a stream of dots. TV screens have ever more pixels of chrome dots which cathode rays or similar technology light up. All TV screens can only display fixed immovable images. The illusion of movement is achieved by frequently refreshing the screen with a slightly different image — the more often, the sharper the picture.

What this suggests is that, while we do not have a digitised system, we are able to store images. In fact, it is likely that the images we perceive in our brain mind are always the heavily processed image we store, not the raw image that flows in from the eyes.

There is quite a lot of supporting evidence for this hypothesis.

The most obvious is that if we are looking at some image, it is obvious that this must be to do with the flow of information from our eyes. However, if we close our eyes and cut off that stream of signals, we still "see" that image. We must be accessing a stored image. It is not as sharp, but all the detail is present. We can zoom in to scrutinise those details. Open our eyes and the image is the same, but much sharper.

Another very useful example to use is how we respond as fast as possible to incomplete information and so avoid predators and live to reproduce our more efficient genes. Avoiding predators galloping towards one not only involved seeing them, but also being able to compute their direction of travel; to see which way they were running and whether they were running faster or slower. To do this involves the ability to compare successive images — the *Zeno* effect. Thus, the ability to store an image began to develop — temporarily to begin with, but the capability was there to improve.

This ability to interrupt the automatic response, pause and compare the pattern of signals with a previous pattern, opens the door to the ability to store and refresh images, and even further to be able to pause and evaluate alternative courses of action — the beginning of thinking, which we refer to often.

Recognising Differences

If we see a familiar image, we immediately see whatever is different. The image from the eyes activates the stored image and a quick scan highlights differences. One can begin to see how analogue patterns could do this better than digital ones. Analogue always works with general approximations as opposed to digital precision. Neuroscientist, Professor Howard Poizner, and his team at the University of California at San Diego, have recently demonstrated this ability to recognise a difference, something new and our brain knows it before our mind can compute the implications. Thus, we have the illusion of reacting *before* we consciously see the event. They argue that the images we store are more like spacial maps than TV pictures. This timing difference is useful evidence in Chapter 16.

Transmitting Thoughts

Chantel Prat, an Associate Professor of Psychology at the University of Washington, has been using functional magnetic resonance imaging (*f*MRI) scans to identify the thoughts people are concentrating on at any one moment. Many researchers in many laboratories are developing prosthetic limbs controlled by a person's thoughts — by transmitting patterns of electrochemical neural signals along dendrites and then over interfaces to activate electric motors in the prosthetic limb. Going further, it is possible to replace this physical interface and use transcranial magnetic stimulation to modify the brain waves, in other words, downloading thoughts — information from one brain to another.

This is remarkable in its own right but the implications go far. *By transferring an image to someone else's brain, they are seeing that image with their brain, not with their eyes.*

Orienteering

We can better understand these concepts of analogue spacial patterns by reference to orienteering and conventional map reading, using our Ordnance Survey maps as an example. By using a series of icons and conventions, we can look at a two-dimensional map and transpose it into a three-dimensional panorama. For instance, looking at a map and standing on a hill, we can see a valley falling away to our left towards a village with a church with a steeple. To the right, we catch a glimpse of a dual carriageway main road leading up to a station with a railway crossing a river and into a tunnel in quite a high mountain....

We can turn around to look at the landscape behind us. Twist the map round and it promptly re-orientates in our heads to this new perspective.

The history of the representation of art arguably mirrors the development of intelligence. Only in the middle ages did artists learn to draw in perspective, then to frame an image. Artists moved from telling stories to finding ways to express emotions directly. Just as poetry and literary art began to move from describing events and facts to represent emotions, the verisimilitude of a Constable gradually gave way to the impressionism of a Turner. Photographs replaced pictorial art and opened the gates to abstract art across the board.

Sound of Music

For many millennia, sound was a long away behind sight, but once the language revolution got underway, it has played an ever increasingly significant role. Sound is unique in the senses that we can both hear and speak, both read and write. In computer speak, both input and output. Sound is also unique in that it operates at a distance. Many animals mark their territory by leaving their aroma, but they must be present to do that. Telescopes and microscopes have extended our visual abilities. Telephones have extended our ability to hold a two-way conversation with someone across the globe. We have discussed the impact of language, but we also have another sound system — music. We can endlessly discuss which came first, music and song or language and their impact on each other, but we do have detailed knowledge of how music came to be understood.

Pythagoras

Famously, Pythagoras identified the eight notes in the octave. One of the best and earliest examples of how careful observation and recording of masses of, in this case sound, enabled the identification, description, classification and definition of a crucial piece of information. The same process, in principle, to every baby recognising the image of its mother and to the recent computer programs to play chess, is learn "go" and identify the beginnings of an epidemic.

Of all the senses, music plays powerfully and in some cases instantly to our emotions. Hear the first few bars of a piece of music and it can change one's mood in a moment. Another tune can send a community off to war, and another, sober a nation to remember their dead. A poem can do the same. Put together in song and the effect can be compelling.

Aristotle's description cannot be bettered: "Emotions of any kind are produced by melody and rhythm; therefore, by music a man becomes accustomed to feeling emotion".

Arguably, a well-remembered tune plays directly from the ears to stimulate the hormones of the endocrine system, without needing to be modulated extensively by the brain on the way: arousal, elation, anger, rebellion, passion. All music is a combination of those original eight notes, in different sequences and combinations, different wave lengths, with some notes sounding for longer than others, some quieter, others louder, thus generating an infinite number of combinations.

The emphasis of one note repeated rhythmically — the beat, directly impacts on the heartbeat, and if synchronised, impacts on the cardiovascular system, which in turn can impact on the extended autonomic system. In so far as well-loved tunes can clearly have a calming effect, it is likely that hearing a favourite tune can impact the immune system and digestive systems, at least indirectly. Thus, a tune is a hierarchy of patterns of sounds.

Looking at the history of music, we can see a parallel to the development of the other arts and much more.

Simple plain song and chords developed into harmony. A greater variety of musical instruments capable of greater range and accuracy, of which the piano is probably the best example, enabled orchestral music. Peasant music and dancing was commonplace far into the distant past, but formal choirs, orchestras, opera and ballet are inventions of the renaissance, the enlightenment and the industrial revolution, that, like so much else, provided both the time and the resources for a larger and growing part of the community to participate.

Up to the twentieth century, the majority of the population only heard music or danced on high days or holidays. Few were familiar with classical music. The radio and the phonograph, gramophone then the tape recorders and now the on-line libraries of every piece of music ever composed play endlessly. At one point, you could pay for a juke box to be silent for one session!

We can observe that all the arts have moved forward over the last half millennium fundamentally widening and extending the lexicons and capabilities of the human brain. Children today have at least 10 times the amount of information that was available to their grandparents and, in addition, have a plethora of skills open to them, which suggests that they have a much wider intelligence than has generally been appreciated. Not necessarily better at any one talent, although that is at least possible, but a much wider palette to paint from.

Bandwidth

We have explored the visual range of eyesight and the audio range of sound, but we know we are only able to access some 10% of light/energy waves and soundwaves. We know dogs can here sounds we cannot and bats can navigate in the dark using a form of radar.

We all have experience of meeting people and instantly feeling attracted or repelled. Often it is mutual and specific and not broadcast. It is rare but it unquestionably exists. Certainly, some people can impose their will on others. Orators can raise crowds to mayhem.

Maybe there is a form of communication we have not discovered yet.

Drama, Analogy, Story and Parable

We should not overlook another important method of communication — the communication of ideas, concepts, politics, morality, ethics and behaviour, and in particular the likely effects of certain behaviours.

Human societies have discovered that it is possible to enforce certain sets of rules by force of arms, or by persuasion, or by mutual agreement. Charlemagne famously invited the Saxons to convert to Christianity or be murdered. The Saxons considered this to be force of arms, Charlemagne considered this to be persuasion and the Vatican considered this to be mutual agreement.

The Greeks came up with the idea of *drama*. They invented plots where the Gods did terrible things and got everyone in a mess. By transposing oneself into the character of the misbehaving God, one could readily appreciate what could go alarmingly wrong. Best to avoid that mistake.

The secular law and the belief systems have tended to make lists: the Ten Commandments, sermons on mounts, all the way to the Code Napoleon. Belief systems must try and cope with a changing scene and parables, or stories, are much the best way of setting out a rule in such a way that it can be applied to new circumstances.

Novels, plays, opera explored human experience. Television "soap operas" have largely taken over the role of moral and ethical doorkeepers to many communities. Arguably the greatest advance in the twentieth century is our ability to control our own reproduction. Knowledge of the natural diversity of human nature has advanced in the last half century by leaps and bounds, and while belief systems have been almost completely unable to keep up, soap operas have explained and educated the population, thus we have one of the most tolerant, generous and wealthy communities in history. Yet in many ways, we are just discovering how complex some subjects are, but at least we are better equipped to understand how we operate. The first steps to identifying problems and the path to find solutions.

It is a valuable truism that it is almost impossible for anyone to understand a solution until they understand the problem.

This phenomenon teaches us a useful lesson. Learning a list of rules is not very interesting. Rules do not generate much emotion. However, a delightful story can be very emotional and excellent entertainment.

We should learn from this that for education to be successful it must be entertaining. The Royal Society of Arts is carrying out some valuable research into the use of learning techniques used by the arts. This is amplified in Chapter 19.

The community suffered a major shock with the arrival of printing, opening up knowledge to everyone who could read. Another jolt was the discovery of a complete new continent; we were not unique. Another, with the advances of science, and in particular, Darwin's theory of evolution, contradicting many long-held beliefs. The Internet is administering another massive shock with the instant communication world-wide of everyone's views on everything. Some will retreat, some will adapt, survive, prosper and advance.

CHAPTER SEVEN

MEMORY & LEARNING

The palest ink is more reliable than the most powerful memory.

Confucius

In the Beginning...

As soon as living organisms started to move around, they began to develop sensory and neural systems to alert them to danger and opportunities. To be able to take advantage of the information that the sensory organs obtain from monitoring the environment, the neural system had to adapt to provide two functions. To recognise a threat, some form of memory is required. Apart from the inherited skills of the species, memories can only be acquired by learning from experience. Only by accessing that experience can threats be avoided or opportunities embraced.

Evolution by the survival of the fittest is a hard regime. Speed is of the essence, so the recognition of incomplete information was lifesaving. There was less value in a detailed memory. An impression was sufficient to enable recognition capable of stimulating the muscles to move towards the opportunity, or away from the threat; and of exciting the glands to generate sensations like fear, hunger and arousal.

All our vastly more complex memory systems have evolved from these basic abilities — minimum information, maximum speed, relationships and the simple recognition of impressions, while the generation of sensations sowed the earliest seeds of conscious awareness.

We have clear evidence of this. One of the simplest life forms is the sea snail or *Aplysia* and, remarkably, it does not appear to have evolved over many millions of years. It only has the primary sensory capability of feeling. Eric Kandel has shown in his Nobel Prize work with *Aplysia*, that, simple as they may be, they can grow and modify their neurons in response to changing situations and so can learn to react differently as external events change. We need to define this with care. The evidence suggests they can recognise the repetition of an event; however, there is no suggestion that they have any facility of recall. They are capable of the basic building block of learning and can grow memories, the barest glimmerings of latent intelligence, but no more.

Five Senses

Taste and smell followed touch, then sound and finally sight evolved. Sight made the greatest demands on the neural system. Only very recently, thanks to our expanding knowledge of quantum physics, have the neurophysicists been able to tease out how the brain processes the patterns of energy (photons) that impact the retinas. Some species use more of the light spectrum than we do, but essentially the original model did not change down the millennia. Vision brought its own advantages. Sight operates over long distances, and so brains had to evolve ways of recognising distance and orientation. Sight could register movement. Survival could depend on the speed and direction of a threat or an opportunity.

Initial Processing Needs Memory

These survival mechanisms involved a new type of memory processing — the beginnings of computation. To determine the speed of a moving object it is necessary to hold a succession of images of that object in a form they can be compared, followed by a rudimentary prediction of where that moving object may be in the next few seconds or so. That is a very far cry from simple "recognition". Nevertheless, some of the primeval rules were still adequate. There was no imperative for the images to be particularly detailed. Impressions were still adequate, but there were advantages for memory structures to be more sophisticated than just be able to support simple recognition. In addition to memory structures to support the processing of movement, association to other information began to blossom — being able to associate different types of flora with food sources, for instance. Memory formats might stay the same, but memory processes began to expand.

The Brain Has Evolved as a Learning System

When we are born, we can do little more than suck, but we can learn to do a quite remarkably wide range of things. As we have commented before, we are born with a central nervous system that connects every organ. We use the example of speech and language. When we are born, we can make and hear sounds and nothing more, yet we learn to hear, see, speak, write and think hundreds of thousands of words, phrases, songs, ideas and concepts.

The trick is that all learning and knowledge acquisition is incremental. With enormous effort, babies produce their first word and the second is a little easier. Soon they are inventing new words.

There is an important lesson here. Learning to extend an existing subject is easier than starting on a completely new subject. When starting to learn a new field, the best way forward is to build a framework, including why this subject is important, how we discovered it and some interesting general background of how it fits into the general scheme of things, and why it might be interesting and useful to learn. With this outline architecture in place, it becomes increasingly easier to fit in ever more detail.

The more we know about something, the more neural connections, relationships and cross references we grow, and the more paths are open for us to recall that information.

Many people find learning the proof of Pythagoras' famous theorem interesting even enjoyable, especially if they are told its importance. Very few are taught why being able to form a right angle is so very important. Quite a lot of adults, including a remarkable number of teachers appear never to find out.

Recent Research

Minimal Memory

It is easy to demonstrate that our twenty-first century brains still continue to store automatically neural structure, impressions, memories every time they experience seeing a visual image, even if those images are exposed for only 2 seconds. However, this neural memory is only sufficient to enable the participants to recognise those images and no more.

Thus, the modern brain still operates to the age-old principle to automatically store the minimum information in a form that it can be recognised at maximum speed.

A recent experiment demonstrated the automatic formation of the *smallest stable measurable unit of memory* in the brain. Minimalistic primary memory, perhaps we could identify them as *Neurands*, see Appendix 28 (all appendices are hosted on www.BrainMindForum.org/appendices).

More Sophisticated Memory

Secondary memory introduces interconnection and cross references to other memory structures, thus information can be accessed, retrieved and recalled from these other references.

More complex brains evolved more complex memory systems. In mammals, and particularly early humans with longer and longer periods of adolescence, the brains became a learning engine. The young acquire new skills by curiosity, imitation, and endless repetition. Every time a neural structure — a memory — is accessed it is strengthened and made more efficient. Neurons and particularly the synapses are reinforced and the axons and dendrites insulated (myelinated).

Notwithstanding these major advances, the basic underlying systems stayed much the same. Minimum information, maximum speed, even though the volume of information steadily expanded, if not its structure and form. Underlying this evolving panoply was another force. Rapid repetition of stimuli can cause sensory processing to uncouple. Such systems enable organisms to reflectively respond to fast changing environments. Neural systems respond to transients not to the status quo. Neurophysiologists call this *sensory receptor adaption*. Adapt or perish.

Growing Neural Memories

Eric Kandel's *Aplysia*, can grow new neural links and structures and so learn to respond in different ways to varying stimuli. They can "grow" memories of alternative responses — and so can every life form that followed them, including ourselves who have made by far the most use of this facility.

Whereas the hardware of every computer is fixed, the hardware of the brain is volatile, plastic and grows. Every time two neural networks are stimulated by electrochemical signals they grow connecting links, or as Donald Hebb put it very succinctly "Neurons that fire together wire together". Thus, the activity of the *software mind* grows new neural links and structures — stimulating the growth of new memories — in the *hardware brain*. Every time that, subsequently, these new links and structures are activated they can generate a similar pattern of neural activity to that which created them in the first place. Where a similar event occurs — is repeated — existing networks and their synapses are edited, modified and strengthened and in due course insulated (myelinated). New born babies have about a billion neurons in their brain.

A mature brain has grown some trillion new neural links and structures solely created by the neural activity of the mind. Thus we learn to walk, talk, read, write, swim, drive, and learn algebra and quantum physics. Travelling electrochemical signals have been converted into fixed memory.

This is the best theory of how those new synapses and new linking axons and dendrites are formed.

Description of the Formation of Memory

Chapter 2 describes how signals transmitted along axon and dendrite filaments generate electromagnetic fields. When two filaments transmit signals concurrently and are close enough for their electromagnetic fields to overlap, glia cells are attracted and form a temporary link, or *glia bridge*. These temporary, speculative glia bridges are capable to transmitting a signal from one filament to the other linking the two neurons together, and, therefore forming a new link in the structure of a neural network.

Where active neurons are further apart, messenger molecules carry out a similar task and provide a path along which glia cells can form a temporary speculative glia bridge.

Some glia cells appear to be double synapses. The function of these glia bridges is to provide a scaffolding along which neurons can grow to form new permanent neural links and structures, much like the process by which the first neurons grow in the foetus.

Whenever these glia bridges are activated, they are proving useful — they strengthen the link either by re-enforcing an existing or a new synapse linking two filaments or by fortifying the glia scaffolding or the new neural link that has grown up that scaffolding.

If the new link or structure is not used — does not appear to be proving useful, the glia bridge or scaffolding may gradually dissolve, and no long-term memory is created.

Forming these new links and structures uses a considerable amount of energy. If someone is in a high state of emotion — the ambient hormone mix is strong amid a high level of neural activity providing a high level of energy for each activity, these bridge building functions can be foreshortened and complete new neural links or whole structures are built quickly. Similarly, if the energy level is low, then these bridge building functions may never be completed.

The former is an example of a very intense experience — a first emotional experience for a young person, perhaps, while an example of the latter is a trivial event perhaps in an older person and maybe associated with dementia.

Statistics

The numbers of neurons in the central nervous system and in an average brain at birth and in maturity are, of necessity, just estimates. However, if the forecast of approximately a trillion new neuron links and structures in a mature brain is anywhere near right we can do one illuminating calculation. In every year, there are some 30 million seconds; in 30 years, therefore, nearly a billion seconds. This arithmetic suggests we grow an average of some 1,000 new neural links and structures every second of our lives.

In youth, probably more, while asleep probably less. Perhaps teenagers are growing a couple of thousand new neural links and structures each second of every day. Even if the over 70s are achieving quarter the rate, their brains are trying to cope with some 250 new or attempted new links and structures. Logic suggests it is quite possible that this generates the overload and confusion that is a major contributor to all the forms of dementia and Alzheimer's problems.

Two Types of Information

Patterns of electrochemical signals flowing over the neural networks processing instructions can be said to be *kinetic information*. It is doing work. It is activating muscles, glands or other neurons. Similar information encapsulated in new neural links and structures is fixed, at least temporarily dormant, and can be aid to be *potential information*. This is what we call *memory*.

In many circumstances, information and memory are the same knowledge in two different states. Information can grow memory, and memory can reproduce information.

Neural software grows neural hardware, and neural hardware replicates neural software.

In biology, a seed can be dormant for years, centuries even. It is potential information — memory. Add water and heat (energy) and it goes into action to create a plant — kinetic information. In biogenetics, the sperm and egg are potential information — inert. When they come together, plus energy, they build a human being — kinetic information.

Facts and Actions

We can observe two quite distinct types of memory. One group records previous experiences and events. They are usually called *episodic* memory. The other groups store records, facts, measurements and values, including instructions and is usually called *semantic* memory.

There is much discussion about whether these two classifications of memory are similar or different. Clear instructions activate the muscles and so forth, and episodic memories supply information for other purposes; however, the brain may not know on the arrival of patterns of electrochemical signals what they are and has no filter to separate them. It seems likely that they are constructually similar but just carry out different tasks.

Short-term Memory?

There is also much debate over long-term and short-term memories. Very short-term memory — the second or two keeping a telephone number in one's head as one writes it down, can probably be accommodated by the refresh function. However, the brain mind has no way of knowing whether information that starts to flow in is important or trivial. Whether it will be the centre of attention continuously or not used again for a year or more. Equally, the former may be soon discarded and the latter needed over the decades. It seems likely that whatever information arrives, the brain mind will initially give it equal prominence and grow glia bridges to integrate it into the existing structures. Where memories are used frequently, the dendrites and axons will get insulated (myelinated) to increase the efficiency of signal transmission, similarly the synapses will be strengthened.

There is just one memory, starting simply and gradually being improved. It is difficult to see how it could be otherwise. A computer system would normally be designed quite differently. Processors have a relatively small bank of immediate access memory to hold current data. Programs obtain records from databases of long-term memory, then process and return them. There are no such facilities like this in the brain mind. The brain mind has no immediate access memory and no databases; there is just memory. Equally, it is unlikely that information in some form of short-term memory is transferred to some form of long-term memory — people suggest this might be a function of sleep — to tidy up the files. The problem with this hypothesis is that it supposes some form of central processor and some form of program to do this "filing", and there is neither. We have learned that all brain processes are driven by the flow of information. At this *input* level, the brain is a self-organising system. It reacts to events. It has no means of forecasting.

This important factor draws attention to the significance of our *sentient* ability to extrapolate the implications of the meaning of information and imagine the potential future course of events.

Other Factors

However, this is not the whole story. The ambient hormone state has a major influence on how information is stored — and recalled. If a person is suffering stress or in a state of very high alert, then new neural links and structures will be created with far more energy than if that person is in a passive state, thus the first network may be laid down very strongly. Similarly, if we search for some information, in a crisis for instance, there has been an accident and we badly need to recall a telephone number, the rush of hormones will give the search function maximum strength and that telephone number that is not in our mobile directory and has not been used for years immediately comes to mind.

There is another clear example of this that has probably affected every one of us sometime in our lives. We can observe that a bunch of children, who, for whatever reason are bored at school and are the bane of the life of their teachers, and who, perhaps, compete against each other to be the class dunce, nevertheless often behave quite differently when following up their hobby. Should this be, for instance, the local premier football team, all those recalcitrant children will almost certainly be able to recite every detail of every player and every incident in every match.

The ability *to want to learn* something cannot be overemphasised. It is a major problem for educationalists. However inspiring a teacher, if students do not wish to learn, they will not!

Information Recall is a Subject on Its Own

Database system in information technology is almost a sub-industry of its own. Everyone discovers that a filling system is as good as its design and very dependent of the discipline of the users. Finding a record depends entirely on how carefully it is filed.

Early memory equipment was very expensive so databases were designed to take up minimum space. Also, almost all processing was mathematical, or at least accounting. For instance, in an order-processing system the database would be designed showing a customer number, then product number, then quantity and price, per item. Fixed fields would be assigned for each. Thus, the product number would be assigned, say, six digits, the quantity four digits and the price per item 5. The item record would be 15 digits long. The programmer would isolate out the seventh to tenth digits to obtain a quantity. With the arrival of word processes, this was not appropriate so *variable length records with floating fields* were designed and that is the architecture of databases to today.

To simplify access, early systems were designed to hold records in alphabetical sequence, but that involves indexes and the brain quite clearly does neither have, nor could it support, an index. Library systems often become inefficient because, information not known when they were designed came into use, and the system did not know where to file it or search for it.

Relational Databases

The solution for computer systems has been to copy how we think the brain works, namely relational databases. In the brain mind, new information forms links and cross references to all other information with which it has any affinity. This is part of its *meaning* process. To recall information where we do not know exactly how we filed that information is a matter of imagining what information might have been considered similar when the record was created, or last updated, go there and see if a link or cross reference leads us to the data we want.

Observe how we search for the answer to some question — an everyday event or the stylised environment of some quiz game, perhaps. We recognise four results:

(1) No idea.
(2) We know the answer, but we cannot pin point it.

(3) We respond with what we think might be the answer.

(4) We respond with absolute confidence.

This everyday experience demonstrates how the brain mind grows memories and why we sometimes struggle to find answers. In example two, the general word network is activated, but the signal to speak or write the answer is not strong enough to activate the muscles. We know we have found — know — the answer, but no sound comes. Diagnosis: not enough energy.

In example three, the instructions to speak or write the answer are activated successfully. The difference between three and four is that in the former we have only one, perhaps not very substantial, access point to the answer, whereas in four we are receiving the answer from multiple sources. Diagnosis: low-energy signal, or multiple signals deliver high energy.

We have both direct and indirect access to memories. If the question is "what is the capital of Britain?" then we can access "Britain" and "capital" and the cross references will take us to "London".

If the question is "How did New York get its name?" we first have to think how to approach this problem. If the information we have on New York does not produce the answer, we might have to think about access through "history".

Multimedia

We have five senses. If we only use one sense to store some information it may be hard work, but if we find a way of using two or more, then we learn more easily. If we hear someone tell us something, then we start to build a network on that sound input. Did we hear everything?

If we read something, it often helps with recall if we note any associated links, even that, for instance, the information was at the top of a left-hand page. That tiny extra piece of context may work as a trigger.

The great advantage of encyclopaedias is the pictures. Hearing something, reading the words and seeing an image build much stronger neural structures and increase the means of access.

Many people report a sudden strong smell or powerful taste immediately recalling a powerful memory.

Synaesthesia

People report "hearing" colours and "seeing" sounds. Fairly obviously, this would suggest that the "wires get crossed" somewhere in the system. This may be genetic, or some events very early in life.

Of particular interest, is the possibility that this supports the theory that the five senses are one system with five variants, as opposed to five different independent systems. Touch is thought to be the first sense. Each sense has an input, transmission link to the brain, and associated recognition, memory formation and recall processes. Synaesthesia suggests that the other four senses built on "touch architecture", expanding and adding sophistication, but nevertheless the same basic structure. Observation would suggest that this would be the most likely method of evolution.

If this is indeed true, then it helps us understand how complex visual images and complex musical tunes are represented in the brain. They are just immensely more complex variations of the simple neural patterns of the sensations of our skin being touched in different ways.

Physical Memory, Synaptic Timing

When we watch a great gymnast, it is impossible not to be impressed by the exquisite timing of some of the moves. Maybe this is one of the many advantages of variable width synapses. If neural links were fixed, then, when the neural network to perform an activity — move legs, arms etc. — was laid down, the time that action took would also be fixed.

However, a *floating synaptic link* could, in effect, enable an axon carrying a signal to slide along the receiving dendrite. Thus, the timing of any particular action could be infinitely variable, and precise. The implications are explored in Chapter 18.

Learning and Teaching

It is observable that every human brain is unique. The way in which people learn and the neural structures in which we learn are all variable. Some of these variations are likely to be genetic and some the result of the way we are taught.

These variations are clearly observable in educational environments. Some teachers who are immensely inspirational to some students may have little or no impact or empathy with others.

Historically, limited economic resources have required that 10, 20, 30 or more students are taught by one teacher. This is especially true of the very early years, although this is the most sensitive time for growing brains.

Inevitably, some students react faster than others, come from different places, and are interested in different destinations. One teacher can only go at one pace in one way. Statistics suggest it is unlikely any student will experience an optimal lesson.

Universal education has exacerbated this problem. Politicians have seen education as a means of social engineering and arguments over equality of opportunity and equalities of outcome have muddied the waters. This is no place to stir up the hornets' nest of education theory and practice, but there does seem to be a strong argument that students who are broadly within a similar neural group are likely to gain the most from being taught together. Trying to teach children of completely different aptitudes and expectations together surely maximises all the problems?

Help is on the way, and it offers us a useful window on the processes of learning.

Massive Open Online Courses (MOOCS)

A lot of work is going into designing online lessons to facilitate distance learning. At present, these MOOCs are very good for some subjects but less good for the majority. As with many innovative technologies, new media is merely replicating traditional procedures. Soon, however, designers will start to use the innovative media in innovative ways, and the teaching profession will be obsolescent.

The education community have been some of the least keen professions to embrace computing. Some education authorities have tried to ban computers in classrooms. Others wanted to have spellcheckers disconnected. Even university professors tried to ban students using the internet. It took continued lobbying for 50 years to get *coding* into the national curriculum, eventually in 2015. Coding or more accurately *programming* is only one piece of the process of creating a computer application. The substantive part is the design of the system and particularly the user interface. They are two separate disciplines requiring quite different skills. Extraordinarily, just when coding was included, design was downgraded.

Throughout history, those who have resisted gradual change tend to suffer the most when it becomes inevitable. We are on the cusp of having the entire body of human knowledge, art, culture and commerce, craft, skill and emotion instantly available together with lessons in the meaning and application of every single item, given by the world's most competent teachers. In addition, techniques and algorithms are being devised to allow students to ask questions online and in most cases, receive an immediate personal answer from the lecturer, be they ever so famous.

Technology and Psychology

This is the technical breakthrough. The psychological breakthrough is far greater. We commented above that students learn best if they empathise with their teachers. Future MOOCs will be designed in families of methods of presentation. Thus, particularly younger students will be able to choose the style of teaching that suits them best. Some will prefer a more traditional style. At the opposite extreme, some will learn best from their own private personalised guru, even possibly a Disney type tutor. Shy students will be able to learn from their very own bespoke *Pooh Bear* tutor. Students will be able to flip though what they comprehend quickly and repeat less obvious lessons as often as necessary, but privately, without risking the derision of their peer hood and their teachers. Better still, if something is obscure it will be easy to visit an alternative "teacher" to see if an unfamiliar perspective solves the conundrum. How many students in Britain can pop along the corridor and sit in another teacher's class, to get a different perspective to solve a problem?

Computing and Languages

This is important because it has been well established that learning a foreign language is a very valuable tool to help general education. The reason is that it helps students to see subjects in a different perspective. It operates like multimedia we discussed above. The neural structures are enriched.

As robots become common place, stylised languages will be designed to instruct them. Thus, very soon it will be essential to be proficient in the language of computing (as distinct from programming languages which are programming tools). Learning these languages will be much more like learning a static stylised language like Latin or Greek. Adults without this facility will progressively find it hard to get high value employment.

Function of Education

The primary function of education will change, gradually to start with, and then it will suddenly become a flood. Historically, education was about passing on the accumulated wisdom of our civilisation to succeeding generations. That role is already being taken over by the computing world.

There is already little point in teenagers cramming a very small percentage of the available facts in a very narrow range of subjects. The more important skill is to practice finding and applying the particular information needed and understanding its implications.

The new function of education is to identify, nurture, expand and support the individual talents of every single individual and to help and encourage them to explore the world and every type of skill and activity to pick the best careers suited to their abilities and personalities. For these functions, skilled *Mentors* will be needed. Some existing teachers will be able to train to fill these posts although it may be that the best recruits will come from the older generations. Members of their grandparent's generation often have better relationships with young people, and evidently more experience. Some of the more flexible teachers will be very useful as *Tutors* to act as backstops for problems even the most sophisticated MOOCS cannot solve, and also to support the mentors to continuously broaden the interests and abilities of students. These tutors will need very broad educations themselves to be really useful role models.

The community seems to have accepted that within a couple of decades there will be no need for car, lorry and train drivers. No one seems to have thought what to do to help those drivers, especially the particularly skilful drivers of very large lorries. No one seems to be giving any thought at all to the future careers of schoolteachers and lecturers.

Learning and Being Taught

We have talked about the wide diversity of brain types and the difficulties where teachers and students happen to come from opposite ends of the spectrums.

There is another group altogether who simply do not fit into the existing conventional classical education structure, and have not down all the ages.

Broadly, these people are quite able to learn almost anything if they want to, *really want to*, but they find great difficulty in being taught.

In the conventional environment, they become bored, some are mischievous, some tease weaker teachers, some become the class joker, some do exactly the minimum necessary to keep out of trouble, while they do their own thing. Interestingly many teachers recognise this last group, yet curiously, it does not occur to these teachers that it might be their fault.

Prize

The great prize of the computing age is that it will become possible to help everyone to learn, whatever their background and skills, so that they can maximise their contribution to themselves and their community.

It would be a massive breakthrough, if we could help every young person discover how best to use the particular type of memory system they happen to have been born with; how best to learn given the particular type of neural structures they have; how to channel and control their natural concentration and how to think.

Methods of Supporting Memory Formation

All down the centuries, people have tried to discover ways of helping themselves remember. How to deliver an important speech without notes, from Cicero to Churchill. How to commit the lines of a play by many actors. How to retain and recall information for examinations. Appendix 5 lists some 20 such systems (all appendices are hosted on www.BrainMindForum.org/appendices).

The oldest known is from the fifth century BC. Simonides of Ceos had invited many guests to a dinner. The building collapsed killing all his guests. He could recall the names of everyone present by recalling where they were seated. Try it. It works. Next time you are at some event that involves numbers of people sitting around a table, recall later who was sitting in which sequence round that table. It is an example of the multimedia effect.

Many people have marketed full-proof systems! The curious fact is that these systems genuinely work for their inventors and also for their fervent believers, although probably for few others.

This phenomenon strengthens the hypothesis that *need* or emotional importance of both memory formation and recall can play a significant part. In this case, belief or absolute belief helps stimulate the hormones to strengthen memory formation and memory recall — the strength of will power. The reason for this may be that the brain is better at spaces and places, which are skills that have evolved over many millennia, than at words and names that are a relatively recent invention.

A variation on this background, emotional attitude at the time of memory formation is the age-old problem of whether a student is interested in learning, is curious and wants to learn, or not.

Osmosis

People of all ages but particularly the very young learn a very great deal passively. Present generations know vastly more about the natural world than their grandparents simply because they have watched a mass of fascinating TV documentaries. The grandparents knew a lot more about the outside world and about other people's ideas and beliefs than their grandparents simply because of the invention of the cinema. Social media makes the world its playground.

The logic of this observation is that education should be a branch of entertainment.

Learning versus Creativity

There is one contradiction and conundrum in the theory and practice of learning.

All the above emphasise the importance of repetition and the building of ever stronger links, relationships, cross references. Repeated use of neural links strengthens these links and in due course insulates them (myelination). Synapses are routinely strengthened and new links are continually created.

The gradient of stasis can turn possibilities into ideas, ideas into opinions, opinions into theories, theories into facts, facts into prejudices and prejudices into belief systems.

Yet creativity is about coming up with new innovative solutions to existing problems. How, then, if the entire system is geared to maintain the status quo, do we come up with alternative solutions, compose new music, write new novels, invent new machines and promote new ideas and concepts?

Creativity and thinking are some of the attributes that make us sentient and set us apart from the rest of the natural world.

The best answer, as so often, comes from the Greeks. Socrates' admission that "the only thing he knew for certain was that he knew nothing for certain". It is rare indeed for us to be able to improve on the words of Socrates, but quantum physics would say this is *creative uncertainty.*

Civilisation is about the tolerance of innovative ideas. How does this work?

We have used the analogy of poetry before, and we can use it again. We used the example of learning poetry — linking up the sequence of words. Composing poetry, songs or ideas is about assembling words into a sequence where the whole is greater than the sum of the parts: using the power of emergence.

Logic is about assembling all the relevant known information, ideas and concepts and arranging them in a rational structure to give the maximum opportunity for a solution or decision to *emerge*, where the solution to the problem or the decision is greater than the sum of the information gathered together.

Thinking is about assembling new innovative information, ideas and concepts, then iterating the arrangements of them till a better solution or decision *emerges*.

Thinking is the poetry of information.

Sequence of Events

Only the present is reality; what happened in the past no longer exists and the future is unknown.

We think we have a clear idea of past events and can often reminisce about them endlessly, but are we sure they are what really happened? It is well known that a dozen people witnessing an event may come up with more than a dozen descriptions of what they think they saw. Over the passage of time, people's memories of events slowly migrate from what actually happened to what they wish *might* have happened.

Many people inhabit parallel imaginary worlds. One of the most valuable ways of thinking about complex problems is to explain the difficulty to an imaginary friend and discuss possible solutions with this alter ego. Young children often have imaginary friends. Adults create completely imaginary worlds and put them into novels which are hugely popular. The behaviour of the hero of a teenage adventure is a far better way of expressing ideals and how to cope with problems, than by repeating abstract rules.

Energy

We have outlined above the processes by which the mitochondria in every individual neuron independently generate power from the flow of nutrients in the blood stream, and how the mitochondria generate more energy than the nucleus needs in normal working and stores this excess so that it can deliver extra energy quickly to cope with an emergency. We have noted how the ambient hormone state varies the energy needed and available in various circumstances. We have a working understanding of how memory is formed and the various processes of recall.

For example, in principle, if we initiate speaking a sentence, we must start by activating one, or probably a pattern of neurons. Individually, or more probably, the group of nuclei initiates a pattern of electrochemical signals along their axons to the synapses that connect them to some dendrites that connect to the muscles of the vocal cords. We can see in simple outline how we assemble a group of words and speak them.

We need energy at each step along the way — the initiating neuron nuclei firing patterns of signals along their axons. Energy to pass the synapses to maintain tension across the synaptic gaps or clefts or a more expressive word might be "gates"? The synapses also use energy to transmit the neurotransmitter signals to the corresponding dendrites. More energy is needed when the same process is repeated to instruct the muscles.

Observably, any weakness, let alone malfunction, along this route (and this is only a simplistic description) may result in no word, let alone sentence, being said correctly. If no word "comes to mind" we think we have forgotten that word or cannot recall the sentence. We are not conscious of either saying it or thinking it.

Dementia

As people grow older, they hold an ever-greater volume of information in their mass of neural networks. As the formation of cross references and connections are automatic, the neural structures for all information continue and expand creating ever more complex structures. Failed new links clutter up the already restricted space, and the glial cells responsible for clearing away debris are less efficient.

The energy needed to activate the successful recall of a word or fact tends to increase. The nutrients and oxygen along the whole length of the nutrient path from the digestive system via the cardiovascular system to the brain are pumped by the astrocyte glia cells into the neurons and then processed via adenosine triphosphate ATP "batteries", which is a very robust system, but it naturally comes under increasing pressure over time.

Much research has gone into dementia in all its forms; however, it seems likely that diet, volume, regularity and quality of food, plus a continuingly improving nutrient supply may be fertile areas to study.

Senior Moment Syndrome

One well-known experience supports this conjecture. Everyone is from time to time irritated when a particular word is temporarily forgotten. Older people call this *a senior moment* and start to worry. Young people often do not even notice it happening. At school, it happens all the time. Teacher asks a question; few hands are raised! Hardly a senior moment.

The answer is present and the neural group around the word is activated, but the signal sent to the vocal cord system is not strong enough to penetrate all the way through the system, so no sound comes forth.

However, and this is the key evidence, a short while later up pops the word. The latest thinking is that when a synapse discharges its neurotransmitters, it promptly clears away any that have not been used. The logic is that the signal has been sent and the whole system would become hopelessly cluttered if that signal was continuously retransmitted, so the synaptic "gate" is temporarily closed.

A while later, perhaps when pressure on the whole system has abated, the energy in the whole circuit and in the synapses involved is restored, the signal is resent and we suddenly recall the missing word(s). Alleluia!

This supports the hypothesis that the more we use our brains, the more efficient they get, or on the "use it or lose it" presumption, if our brains deteriorate it may be through lack of use. We should also take into consideration the confidence — or lack of confidence factor. If we worry something is going wrong, it will increase the chance that it does go wrong.

It is quite possible that the brain mind and all the associated systems do suffer degeneration for other reasons. Lack of sufficient water to maintain pressure is a likely candidate. Other liquid intakes may have the opposite effect. However, the nutrient conjecture deserves careful study.

New research at the University of Southern California has shown that if the mitochondria in the neurons are short of nutrients, the myelin around the axons and dendrites begins to be canibilised, weakening the strength of the electrochemical signals.

Forgetting

The whole of this chapter is about remembering — memory formation and memory recall. It is worth a postscript that forgetting is also possible, and in many cases a useful ability. It was, of course, the foundation of a large part of the Freudian school, but that is another subject.

[Author's note: In the children's classic book *Black Beauty* by Anna Sewell, Jerry the cab driver encourages his family with the words "Do your best and shame the rest. T'will all come right some day or night". It was my family's motto. Seemed good to me. At eighteen I found myself at Officer Cadet School in the Army doing National Service. The instructors would say to us. "Are you doing that as well as you can, Soldier?" "Yes, sir". "Then, Officer Cadet, do it better". Different perspective. Useful lesson.]

CHAPTER EIGHT

MEANING

There is nothing in the intellect that was not first in the senses.

Aristotle, c. 400 BC

The meaning of information, particularly words, tends to be a Cinderella subject that everyone takes for granted, "that is what dictionaries and encyclopaedias are for" we might say. The whole object of language is that words enable us to communicate the meaning of things, and how to do things. The whole of science is about trying to work out what the natural phenomena we observe can mean.

We can argue that meaning came first and we "invented" words to allow us to communicate that meaning. So, what is the problem?

If we use a dictionary, encyclopaedia, google or wikipedia to look up an unfamiliar word, we are usually looking for more information than just the meaning of that one word. We are interested in the implications of the meaning of that word, or how we can extrapolate the meaning and, therefore, additional uses of that word.

Whether we have learned a word to identify something we have observed with our sensory and other organs, or met a word for the first time and wish to know what it represents — generally speaking we know what things mean or know where to look to find out. But how do we "know"? What is the mechanism?

Our first observation is that meaning appears to be essentially an extension of language. Clouds in the sky mean rain; a bad taste, spit it out; a strong smell may mean a competitor's territory or a potential mate, but for *Homo sapiens*, 99% of meaning is about words and combinations of words. We learn words as a means of increasing our knowledge. But look more closely, and it is the meaning of information that we want to learn. This seems an obvious truism, but what value to us is a word; being able to say it, spell it, write it or think it if we do not know what it means? There is no point in going to a great deal of trouble to input and store a string of random letters or a string of random sounds, sights, tastes or smells unless they generate some sort of reaction, impression, sensation or feeling; some sort of information that is useful to us.

There is no reason why a class of 10-year-olds — or 50-year-olds for that matter — should know that the word epistemology means the science of knowledge, if neither class has ever seen that word, heard that word or ever had it described or explained to them. The 50-year-olds might make a stab at a meaning. "-ology" suggests a science. "Epistle" is close, therefore, perhaps epistemology might be the science of letter writing or the science of communication. "Epitaph" is not that far away. Science of inscription? Science of eulogies?

When we learn about this new word, how do we store it? We have studied the representation of words in the brain and mind — how we learn to hear it, speak it, see it, write it and think it, but how do we store its meaning?

Flow of Information

One thing we have learned is that the brain and mind are driven by the flow of information from all the sensory and other organs. Language allowed us to attach words to all those sensations, so that, for instance, in our preferred example, when we "hear" the word tree, we experience all the sensations associated with trees — probably a fleeting image. The pair of words "oak tree" might also generate the sensation of the image of an oak leaf; the word leaf, the sensation of leaves rustling in the wind. So, it is easy to see how the meanings of words and phrases used as labels are generated by impressions, feelings and sensations from the five senses and our internal systems and organs. The intestines of the enteric system generate feelings of hunger and thirst. The hormones generate a wide range of sensations; so, for example, words of warning set off sensations of fear.

Dictionary Meaning of Words

If we encounter a word we have not met before, we can consult a dictionary or encyclopaedia online or offline. If the word is, say, elephant, we can see a picture of an elephant and we have the meaning instantly, but if the unfamiliar word is not easily depicted or is abstract, then a reference work or dictionary will only describe that idea, concept or whatever in terms of other words. If we do not know the meaning of these other words, we are no further forward. Dictionary descriptions only solve our problem, if we can work back to words that are anchored in labels we can recognise.

Abstract Words

Abstract words of which there might now be a majority in any lexicon, and in particular words for what we call qualia — beauty, leadership, the redness of a rose ... present a different problem. Take the two words, house and home. The former is relatively easy to describe and define, but we could write a paragraph, an essay or even a whole book to describe the latter and not cover every aspect. However, we have a very strong sensation of a home, and what a home means to us, nearly instantly. How?

Evolution of Meaning

The answer is in our evolution. Long before we had words we experienced hunger, thirst, fear, attraction, arousal, pleasure, reward, guilt etc. The glands of the endocrine system pumped out adrenalin to put the whole body's systems onto full alert, rushing oxygen and nutrients to the muscles and putting the mind into overdrive. Words like "freedom" can generate similarly powerful emotions which give them very specific meaning.

Much less dramatic words generate similar meanings — hearing the word "filthy" or reading the letters f i l t h y generates an immediate sensation of unease or even disgust — that word has meaning alright — and far more accurate and effective than any dictionary entry, however lengthy.

Hormones

We have been able to identify some 100 glands and hormones, neurotransmitters and messenger molecules, and the specialists think they have identified another class of hormones, perhaps another 100, forming the endocrine system. Given they can flood the body in any combination and any volume, they can begin to compete with the alphabet to match the number of alternatives. 75% adrenalin, 20% testosterone, plus a dash of others, would be a recipe of some power with no doubt about its meaning. And all the sensory organs generate meaningful sensations: beautiful sights, inspiring music, glorious wine, enjoyable massage, heavenly scent etc. Words are digital; senses are analogue. There is no limit to their sophistication and complexity.

Language of the Endocrine System

As we developed our dictionaries of words and phrases, the endocrine system developed a parallel language of cocktails of hormones that each and every word and phrase generates, which in turn give us the sensations, impressions, feelings and emotions of the meanings of every word and phrase.

Definition of Meaning

The sensory organs, the cardiovascular and enteric systems, and the glands of the endocrine system generate the sensations, impressions, perceptions, feelings and emotions that provide meaning to all our experiences and to the individual words and phrases of our languages. Meaning is a whole-body experience.

Four Types of Meaning

A word or phrase can:

(1) Have an immediate one-to-one meaning.
(2) Have implications of the present meaning.

(3) Mean an instruction or algorithm to do something.
(4) Be extrapolated to stimulate the prediction of possible future meanings.

In everyone's favourite example of our ancestors on the savannah, recognising that the grass waving was one level of meaning, but realising that the implications of the pattern of waving grass meant a predator is why we survived. If teenagers fail to do their homework, the immediate meaning is likely to be trouble tomorrow. The implications mean they may not get the grades they want next year.

Immediate meaning suggests the present. Implication introduces an element of time and suggests drawing a conclusion.

Meanings that enable the solution of problems are a very powerful tool in the armoury, particularly in mathematics. This is the meaning of how to do things. For instance, the single word 'multiply' has a very precise and powerful meaning.

Extrapolation goes further and also introduces an element of time to predict the possible course of events in the future. The extrapolation of meanings is the basis of imagination and creativity.

Other Aspects of Meanings

As soon as we move away from one-to-one relationships, we begin to realise we have a much more complex problem to solve. Abstract words, ideas and concepts are one thing, but how do we experience the meaning of music, art and so forth, as we most assureably do. And we need to look more closely at the meaning of qualia.

One key observation we can make is that two or more words together bring into play the powerful effect of *emergence*. Two words often mean much more together that the sum of the two separately. Phrases often mean significantly more than the sum of the meanings of the individual words. In discussing the representation of information, we have called this the *poetry effect*, described in Appendix 25 (all appendices are hosted on www.BrainMindForum.org/appendices).

Meaning is an extension of information, and we can emphasise this point with references to our computers. For once their only value to us is a negative. We can download onto a screen a complex string of words — even a very well loved and emotional poem. We know there is a binary pattern of those words in the processor. All the information is complete, but the computer has no sense of the meaning of that information whatever. No computer has any sense of perception, emotion, sensation or feeling at all. If we want computers to emulate sensations, we will have to design simulation programs. That opens Pandora's box of ethical problems.

When we go further and begin to bring words and phrases together into patterns we begin the process of building knowledge. We have explored how the recognition, identification and recoding of patterns enables us to create useful information out of an apparent unorganised mass of chaos.

Patterns of Information

Patterns of information enable us to create meaning. Patterns of meaning enable us to create knowledge.

We observe the natural phenomena around us, we record what we see, we measure what we can, we categorise and describe what we witness over time, and we search for patterns: *consistent and reproducible patterns*.

We have noted that 5,000 years ago the Egyptians recorded the annual floods of the Nile. Appreciating the meaning of this information enabled them to forecast when to plant and when to harvest. The first thing every child learns to do is to recognise the pattern of light of its mother's face and the pattern of sound of her voice. Today's most powerful computers analyse vast databases to search for patterns to forecast the weather, and identify epidemics and economic trends. This ability to identify patterns is so important to us that it is one of the basic sections of our Intelligence Quotient (IQ) tests.

The brain is optimised to expand simple patterns of information to build ever more complex patterns of meanings by working out the implications of stored and new information and coming up with the best available response to every developing circumstance. Computer programmers design *subroutines*, then build ever more complex hierarchies of subroutines into fully developed applications, which can beat chess masters, navigate to the moon, analyse a genome and infinitely more.

Cognitive neuroscientists have recognised this close similarity to the way we build up neural information into consistent and reproducible patterns, patterns into meaning, meaning into hypotheses, hypotheses into theories, and theories into knowledge. Donald Hebb suggested calling these neural modules "engrams". Richard Dawkins suggests "memes". Computer programmers call these building blocks "subroutines". Another alternative to describe these mental subroutines or bioprograms is to call them *neur*al mod*ules* or "neurules". The suggestions of many other cognitive neuroscientists, philosophers and observers are listed in Appendix 12 (all appendices are hosted on www.BrainMindForum.org/appendices).

We can learn something very useful from mathematics. In the same way that the position of a number in a sequence is as important as its value, the position of a word in a phrase often varies its meaning. Hence we have developed syntax, grammar and the other tools like onomatopoeia, alliteration, rhythm and rhyme, of the writer to convey ever more sophisticated meanings.

Meaning as Part of the Process of Learning

Indexes

Let us look again more closely at the process of how a mass on neurons in the brain understand the meaning of individual words and combinations of words, and how it is possible to work out the implications of their meaning and then go on to extrapolate their meaning to solve other seemingly unconnected conundrums.

The initial components are the evolution of words as labels to represent the sensations of things and actions; then words to represent the more complex sensations of abstract concepts and ideas; then the ability to link words together to form patterns and the ability to link patterns together to make meta patterns which we can call engrams, memes or neurules. And we cannot stress too strongly the power of two or more words meaning more than the sum of the individual words. The power of emergence is amplified in Chapter 17.

The next major step was the ability to invent single innovative words to act as indexes to these structures, thus saying, reading, or thinking one word conveyed a mass of detail. This was much more efficient, but at a stroke expanded the breadth of meaning. In reverse, this mass of detail was the meaning of the innovative word. New portmanteau words can be built up into hierarchies of ever more complex grammatical and sensual structures.

Mapping the neural patterns to hear and say words onto the representation of information coming directly from the senses appears to be straightforward. However, almost everything seen by the eyes is part of a group. For instance, there are many types of trees. These arguments equally apply to all the senses, but using sight is the easiest to describe. Immediately there is the problem of the association of ash, beech all the way down the alphabet to willow, which in many ways all look quite different, but are nevertheless equally recognisable as trees. Then there are all the other attributes of trees like leaves, bark, reproduction habitat, diseases, uses of their timber etc., the list goes on and on.

One possibility is that the neural representations of words like oak and elm are cross referenced by axon and dendrite links to words (and their sense representations) like trees, leaves and so forth. The brain may grow a trillion new neural links in a lifetime, but even this immense number would not be nearly enough to provide links from everything to everything, and the result would be so unwieldy, ever slower and increasingly inefficient. It is more likely that the neural patterns for all the members of each grouping are connected to one meta pattern for that category. Thus "trees" becomes a logical or category generalisation which, over time and usage, develops its own neural patterns that have agreed and defined boundaries and defined combinations and relationships that are acceptable and excluded. Thus, for example, "trees" includes bonsai, but excludes bushes. Thus, the word "tree" is not associated with any one specific meaning but with many meanings of specific types of trees. In neural terms this is very efficient, because whether a representation — memory — is being accessed or added to there is always only a one-to-one link either from "oak" to "trees" or from "tree" to "beech".

Icons and Symbols

We can use the word "icon" to describe the way we use words and concepts like "tree". Icons represent attributes and experiences and the relationships between associated members in that category. They also define limits. Trees produce seeds, but trees cannot walk or move about. We can deduce knowledge from these limitations. All the members of this category can be a source of food, and they will always be in the same place if we wish to find them again. This meta information needs only be represented neurally once and not wastefully repeated for each constituent, similarly it is only necessary to update the knowledge bank of trees for some new discovery, and not the knowledge bank of every individual tree.

Thus, iconic words like "tree" have a meaning in the context of all the other words and phrases. The reference and meaning of such words are distributed amongst all the words involved. When a person hears such a word, all the relevant sensual information associated with all the members of that category are alerted — all the multimedia representations of oaks, cedars etc. All the associated information is available, which cumulatively contributes to a sense of understanding, provides the basis for any reaction or associated activity, provides the raw material to appreciate any implications and further provides the foundation to extrapolate this meaning to establish or add to a higher order neural pattern or create links to existing category patterns.

Trees are part of the whole natural plant world. Trees are constituents of rainforests; they are similar but different to bushes. Neurally this creates another level in the hierarchy of neural patterns. At this level, it is possible to develop relationships between groups. Similar rules for inclusion and exclusion apply but on a much broader basis. Thus, all the information known about trees can be compared with all the known information about bushes without having to think about a single type of tree or a single type of bush, yet the outcome of such contemplation will apply to every tree and every bush.

We can go one step further. All the examples to date are grounded in one-to-one object relationships — the word oak and all the multimedia representations of oaks. There are visual images of trees. There are visual images of rainforests, plants and so forth. We noted above that abstract words pose a different problem and we used the difference between "house" and "home" to illustrate this. However, we can go further. No one has seen, heard, smelled, tasted or felt a "home". Words like "home" are abstract, but they are also symbolic. They are the manifestation of a concept. They are both the sum total of all their constituent parts, yet they are more than that. They are an impression, a feeling, a sensation. A multitude of individual objects contribute to a home, and many iconic groups of things and attributes contribute to a home. There are many groups of groups, but the concept of a home has a life of its own which can stir the deepest emotional responses. This concept of *a life of its own* independent of its constituent parts is itself a symbolic representation of a series of concepts. They are represented in the brain by their own neural networks that are grown as a result of thinking about the underlying concepts. They are grown as connectors to all the networks that contribute to their conception, level by level right back to the initial one-to-one representation of an artefact or action matched to a word. Nevertheless, such symbolic concepts exist only in the neurons; however, they have very strong meanings and very powerful influences over behaviour.

Evolution of Neurons?

As the human brain evolved, the ability to associate patterns together from the direct mapping of words to objects, all the way up to symbolic conceptual representations, it seems likely that more sophisticated neurons, perhaps with many more axons, dendrites and synaptic links evolved to carry out these tasks. This suggests that the pressure to acquire and understand the meaning of knowledge was equally responsible for the evolution of the brain as the evolution of the brain facilitated the ability to acquire knowledge. At the very least the development was symbiotic.

This structure of hierarchies of nested neural networks has many implications. The creation of meta patterns is a sophisticated extrusion of the basic neural ability to recognise, respond to and emulate statistical regularities. Higher order patterns are stimulated every time lower order patterns that conform to a category are accessed. Over time, the lower order pattern activity becomes so ubiquitous that is drops into the background, and the conscious activity fades across the boundary of consciousness.

Unlearning: Forgetting

Similarly, relationships fade into redundancy below the conscious horizon. The neural networks are still in place and active, but they no longer operate within the conscious domain. Thus, the sensations of knowledge, meaning and understanding all are present. Only if it is necessary to investigate why a person holds a particular belief, it is possible to activate these underlying lower order patterns. Hence it is often difficult for people to un-learn something, as these underlying lower order patterns have to be consciously activated and then amended — not always an easy task. For example, people who were brought up before the adoption of metric and centigrade can sense the length of a yard but not a meter. They are more comfortable with the number of miles their car can do to the gallon. They know exactly what 80°F feels like, while 27°C does not have any meaning to them.

Cumulative Learning

Learning is all about discovering relationships — linking something new to something already known. For instance, it is much easier to learn about a new tree, if a lot is known about trees already. It is only necessary to slot in the new species at the lowest level and the structures already in place provide further information. This demonstrates the great importance of learning some new subject by first establishing the outline structure into which increasing levels of detail can be slotted. Establishing the meta pattern then adding in lower order detail appears to be reversing the natural order for the acquisition of knowledge. However, this is just a manifestation of how greater knowledge of the brain operates, which can help us improve the whole process of teaching, learning and education. Higher order meta structures can be established in many subjects by first studying the purpose of learning this subject. Once the framework is in place, it is progressively easier to work through how these objectives can be answered.

The more symbols are in place, the easier it is to create more. Conversely it is difficult to relate symbols until some are in place — a chicken and egg problem. Hence, it is much easier for adults to learn new subject than it is for teenagers. Similarly, adults are more likely to appreciate the implications of some new piece of knowledge and be able to extrapolate knowledge of one subject to expand their understanding of another. Equally and oppositely young people often come up with more novel solutions to problems than adults, because they have not been taught the "correct" answer — the current accepted wisdom. Adults have in place structures that generate the learned response to some situation and quite often that solution becomes apparent without conscious effort, so it is not apparent to that person that their answer could, should or can be queried.

The greater the variety of structures that can be assembled to establish some new relationship or pattern, the more effective the new knowledge, hence the value of multimedia input from as many sources as possible. This also explains why it is easier to understand something from a second source especially, if the second source approaches the subject from a different perspective, style or structure. The part constructed pattern is completed and made more robust with the new input from the different source.

Diverse Ways of Learning

A great deal of this processing happens automatically as more about the subject is discovered. If a person is learning something that is of great interest to them, this process will be easy and efficient. If that person is learning something of little interest, perhaps only part of that person's attention is in play and so the stimulus to establish a meta pattern is weak. What we can observe is that meta patterns are built on existing knowledge structures. If one group of people are growing pattern structures in a different way to others, their experiences will be different and they will frequently draw different conclusions from the addition of similar information. Similarly, people learn with different goals. The obvious example is where people are learning something in a particular way to answer certain types of questions, for instance, for the purpose of satisfying the format and structure of sets of questions like an examination. It follows that the meta pattern structures of, say, one group of students learning something for their own edification will be different, possibly substantially different, to another group of students concerned with passing an examination. The two groups may well have a quite different understanding of the implications from their activities.

Location

These masses of hierarchical neural patterns are not region specific in the brain as they link so much together. This geographical spread is already surprising the researchers who are studying brain activity related to various stimuli. As meta patterns are developed, individual items of knowledge are less position specific. This makes knowledge increasingly robust, as the volume of cross referencing is ever increasing and there is huge overlap. Any one item can be accessed from many different levels facilitating recall. Similarly, any neuron wear or damage is less serious as alternative means of access to specific neural structures are available while replacement networks can be grown.

Statistical Regularities

The facility to recognise and neurally replicate statistical regularities helps identify new rules of combination of lower order neural patterns into higher order structures. Such rules are inclusive and exclusive, and from these structures have grown syntax, semantics and grammar. It is also the process by which the patterns of behaviour of people have been worked out, rules devised and the laws of behaviour amongst the members of communities developed. It is the same process whereby the statistical regularities we observe in the universe are promulgated into what we call the laws of nature and the laws of physics.

Programming

It is interesting to note that programming computers is a similar process involving the construction of hierarchies of patterns within an overall structure designed to achieve specific objectives. Lower order patterns, or subroutines, are repeated frequently in various parts of the system. Similarly, programs sit conceptually on top of each other. At the bottom are the machine code instructions, which nowadays few programmers know much, if anything about — they have disappeared below the conscious horizon. Above this sits the operating systems like the various versions and successors of MS-DOS and Windows. Above this sits various applications, constructed in a series of micro subroutines, or patterns known as a programming language. Each micro subroutine is indexed by a words or words that have carefully prescribed meanings. Often an application will have a higher order method of varying the application to tailor the general system to fit the detailed needs of the final user.

Systems Design

Systems analysis is about designing the overall framework and architecture of an application. Programming is about filling in the detailed instructions to execute that application, and it involves designing, building and integrating a plethora of patterns into an elegantly constructed whole. It is a task whose complexity is on the extreme edge of human capability and requires a degree of accuracy that human beings have never needed to deploy at any previous time in history. A computer has no common sense or consciousness of what it is doing in the way that all humans do, so these instructions must be designed to respond to every conceivable eventuality and combination of events, with a precision never before even contemplated. Designers and programmers commit their plans to paper but no one ever sees a program working: only the results. The design of a program is entirely cerebral and as such is pushing out the frontiers of human knowledge and, arguably, modifying the structure of human thought in the same way that the invention of writing which similarly required human beings to be far more precise in the way they described things to avoid ambiguity. Thus, like the invention of words, then writing and printing, computing is a key-driving force in the continuing evolution of the brain.

Meaning of Space, Time and Orientation

An analysis of meaning would not be complete without addressing space, time and orientation. Long before the beginnings of speech and language, humans shared another dimension of meaning with other living forms — mammals and possible others. We know that when the senses register an event, a considerable amount of processing takes place as this information enters the brain and alerts the representations of similar events in the past. Thanks, in part, to two ears it is possible to identify from which direction a sound comes from. Having two eyes helps indicate the distance away some object is and its position and direction of movement relevant to other objects. The brain has a sense of the sequence of events in the procession of time. Animals, like the insects and birds, have a sense of orientation. They can all find their way to their nests, while many species migrate over immense distances. Bees can describe to other bees where to go to find honey, or select a site for a new hive. These are all essential contributors to our understanding of events happening in the context of the surrounding world.

Words have multiplied these latent skills because it is possible to describe them and so help people to make the most use of their latent talent. Similarly, human beings have a sense of harmony and balance. To a limited extent, we can describe these attributes in words, not so well as to be able to define them, but well enough to teach people how to recognise and develop their own latent abilities.

Another critical component of conscious awareness is the ability to imagine. It is possible to engage the full range of our attributes into imagination. Imagination encompasses all the emotions: space and time, but above all imagination is dependent on words — the whole massive vocabulary. Without words imagination would probably still exist, if in a much-reduced form, but it would not be possible to communicate imaginings and so they would lose a large part of their influence. Imagination makes it possible to experiment with alternative meanings. Words give imaginations meaning, and, in turn, the ability to imagine greatly supplements the ability to understand the meaning of everything that happens.

The ability to associate seeing fruit to recognising food, and hearing water to recognise a source of water to drink, contributed to the beginnings of awareness. Being able to understand the meaning and implications of what our senses register, through the medium of language, and then go on to be able to extrapolate one set of solutions and map them on to another set of problems and so invent some novel solutions, has expanded the boundaries of awareness onto the plane where we find ourselves today. It is not going too far to say that without this sense of meaning, understanding, implication and extrapolation, we would have very little awareness. We would be not much more than ambulatory computers.

The ever-richer panoply of words and their meaning is an index of our level of awareness.

Dreaming and Imagination

The ability to string words together and build meta patterns suggests a degree of control, or at least initiation. We do it all the time, stringing words together to prepare a speech, or write an essay. Thus, human beings learned to take control of their propensity to dream and build it in to the quite extraordinary and apparently unique ability to imagine. Imagination makes it possible to speculate about the future course of events in a very constructive way. To be able to imagine what might happen if certain events developed and what might happen if one course of action was followed as opposed to others is, perhaps the most powerful weapon in the human intellectual armoury.

It is possible to live in the existing world and at the same time disappear into a fantastical imaginary world. It suggests a very sophisticated processing capable of developing hierarchies of priorities. In neural terms, it suggests further layers of ever more sophisticated neuron networks that can prioritise the activities of masses of neural networks almost as if they were in competition with other masses of neural activity. On top of such a pyramid of abilities must be neuron structures that enable each individual to direct the activities of other neurons.

The great breakthrough in computing was the ability to store programs, which meant that a master operating system could control what work was done in what sequence. This is a hugely powerful attribute but we can go further. This means that one set of programs can be designed to edit, update and enhance another set of programs in the light of the results of yet a third or more sets of programs. Hence the conclusion that systems can be designed to learn from experience.

Summary

This analysis helps us understand the 'mechanical' and neural processing of information and meaning. In microseconds, neural signals to the endocrine system can generate an almost unlimited mixture of sensations, impressions perceptions and motions. Not only can we mix and match various hormones but the quantity of each as well. Just as we have a *verbal language* of almost unlimited combination of words, thoughts ideas and concepts so we have a *hormonal language* of almost unlimited capacity to match them with meanings, simple, direct and also endlessly nuanced. Hence the sensations, perceptions, impressions, feelings and the wide range of emotions: the surges of fear, elation, depression, euphoria, horror, delight, discovery and achievement, which bring all this information to life and make such an exciting adventure of every experience.

We are beginning to learn a great deal more about the source of these sensations which are generated by the endocrine system — the glandular system. We have long experience of a piece of music generating an instant impression, changing people's mood in a second — art and drama the same.

Now we can understand how the poetry effect we have referred to a number of times is so powerful. Each word may generate a hormone secretion, but word after word builds up that output. But there is more. The strength of the accumulation influences the subsequent output, thus the emotion level after each word doubles the normal output of each subsequent word, and hence the power of *emergence,* where the whole is greater by far than the sum of the parts. Now we have a much better understanding of how this operates in everything that involves communication.

Patterns of words and phrases are very similar to the patterns of notes in the octave. Tunes are patterns that can be recognised and so sound both striking and familiar. The process of recognition directly stimulates the glands so, often immediately, changing mood, sometimes dramatically. Laughter is often generated because an expected pattern is interrupted causing sudden surprise. Poetry and song overlap the domains of words and music. Rhyme, rhythm, metre, onomatopoeia and alliteration enable phrases to convey meaning substantially greater than the sum of the individual words. They convey such ephemeral impressions as beauty and attraction by stimulating emotional responses that add so much to the understanding and meaning of things, which otherwise are so difficult to describe, define and measure, and which are often classified as qualia.

Meaning, therefore, is one of the most important keys to our understanding of the way our brain, mind and body operate, and a major contributor to the debate about intelligence, thinking, creativity and consciousness.

PART III

INTELLIGENCE

CHAPTER NINE

SUMMARY OF THE EVOLUTION OF INTELLIGENCE

Ah! But mankind's reach should exceed his grasp,
Or what's a heaven for?

Browning (apologies to)

We live at one of the most exciting periods in all history. In almost every field of science, medicine and even politics, new discoveries are being made at an ever-faster rate. The established order is having to adjust to the effects and results of innovative ideas and new technologies. New ways of working that have not changed much over the millennia are moving like tectonic plates, slowly but unstoppable. The whole study of employment, economics, education and ethics created largely by the industrial revolution needs radical re-evaluation as our computers impinge on ever more aspects of everyday life. All these changes reflect back onto how we help prepare the next generations to prosper, ride these storms and are equipped as well as possible to succeed in an ever more competitive world.

At the centre of all this flux are, as it always has been, our brains, minds, bodies, our intellect and our intelligence. It is the mechanism that has helped us create our civilisation — that alone has brought us to where we are today. It is by far the most important natural resource we have. Notwithstanding its central role in almost all our endeavours we know remarkably little about how we function, how we acquire and expand our information, how we learn, how we concentrate, how we think, how we forget, how we create, how and why things can go wrong. More curiously still, we devote a remarkably low priority and a relatively minor amount of resources to expanding our knowledge.

Whichever way we approach the subject of our human abilities and how to best use and develop them, how we make decisions, how we push out the frontiers of our knowledge, the focus always returns to our *intelligence* — how to identify, nurture and develop it to the maximum benefit of each individual and the whole community.

Alternative Approaches to the Problem

There are three major ways that leaders in this field have contributed to this debate over the last few decades, led off and stimulated by Howard Gardner's multiple intelligence theory. This carefully associated intelligence with specific activities, linguists, maths, music, body movement, special visual, interpersonal and self-awareness. This broadened the scope of the debate about intelligence to include more than just the brain, which had been the centre of attention since the famous Dartmouth initiative of 1956. Later, he added naturalist, spiritualist and moral intelligence.

This can be argued to be the output approach — associating intelligence with our external activities. In 1996, Daniel Goleman suggested the addition of *emotional intelligence*.

Another school of thought is that there is a branch of intelligence associated with each sensory organ. The brain is driven by the input signals from the sensory and other organs monitoring the external and internal worlds, so associating intelligent abilities with this inflow of information has its attractions — the input approach.

In between these input and output concepts, Guy Claxton's *Hare Brain, Tortoise Mind: Why Intelligence Increases When You Think Less* published in 1997 and Daniel Kahneman's *Thinking Fast and Flow* published in 2011 explored the concept that *intelligence* is to do with speed of reaction, while *thinking* is to do with reflection and evaluation.

This book explores another approach, from the perspective of a computer systems analyst who must design a *system*, perhaps for a robot, or perhaps a cyborg. The first task is to observe all the existing processes in the most meticulous and intricate detail, so that the resulting programs can carry out all the observed tasks.

In these pages, we have explored the present state of the art of our knowledge and understanding of cognitive neuroscience, of the contribution of computing to understanding the way both systems operate, where they are the same, where they are so very different. We have looked carefully at the raw material of intelligence, namely information, and how we garner it, store it and bend it to our will. We have a growing knowledge of how we convert pure information into the sensations of meaning and knowledge. One way to approach this subject is from the philosophical perspective on induction and deduction handed down to us from the sages of ancient Greece. Time to pull all these threads together. What is intelligence? How can we use it to the best of our ability?

Etymology

The meaning of intelligence, used as a noun, has not changed over the centuries. "Say from whence do you owe this strange intelligence?" Macbeth asks the witches. Today we have the National Criminal *Intelligence* Service. In both examples, intelligence is nearly synonymous with information. The important difference is that this is more than just information; it presumes high-quality information — good, significant, important and better information. This is useful because it draws our attention to every usage of intelligence in all its forms — the presumption is that it is good, better and faster than anything comparable. it always has a qualitative meaning.

Intelligent and Intelligently

Used as an adjective or adverb, it is a qualifier or modifier, it is not an entity in its own right. For example, it is possible to have a big tree.

But there is no such thing as a big. It is possible to have an intelligent program or application. But there is no such thing as an intelligent. A program can be said to be intelligent, but then it is the function that the program is executing that is better than alternatives, or achieves its objectives more efficiently, that is displaying this intelligence. It is the process not the function that is being described as intelligent. Individuals can be said to behave intelligently when they carry out a task efficiently, quickly, competantly and accurately, or more particularly more efficient, quicker and more accurately than their peers. In both cases, it is the outcome that is measured.

Relative and Abstract

A person can be said to be tall. A person can be said to be intelligent. A program can be said to be intelligent. However, in every case this measurement is only relative to others, not an absolute.

Observably it is quite possible to see, touch, smell, hear the rustle of the leaves and taste the fruit of a big tree, as opposed to a little tree. Similarly, we recognise an intelligent computer program is better than a poor program; intelligent behaviour is more attractive than stupid behaviour. We recognise, assess and measure the program and the behaviour. The *intelligent* component is an abstract concept. We can rewrite a more efficient — more intelligent — program, but there are no sub-routines available that we can just insert. You cannot pop into a shop (or even go online) and buy an errant friend some intelligence!

A Selection of Current Definitions

One of the most curious aspects of intelligence is that nearly everyone who has directly or indirectly studied the subject has their own definition of what it is. The Greeks linked the concept of intelligence to theories of the immortality of the soul. Bacon, Hobbes, Locke and Hume strongly objected and preferred the word "understanding". The arrival of computing and the potential of artificial or machine intelligence have stimulated a new dimension to the debate.

Leaders in the field admit that hampering our ability to design general artificial intelligence (AI) is the embarrassing fact that we don't understand what we mean by "intelligence". This lack of knowledge makes any predictions of when we will achieve strong AI fraught with uncertainty.

This book contains an anthology of about 30 of the most disparate current definitions and listed them, together with some dictionary definitions in Appendix 2. (The importance or significance of a word describing a concept can sometimes be gauged by the number of synonyms there are. Imagination is a case in point. Appendix 13 gives some examples of these lexicons, and Appendix 47 lists some of the synonyms of the word intelligent all appendices are hosted on www.BrainMindForum.org/appendices).

We would argue that this very diversity gives us some useful clues. We can look at intelligence as something of a chameleon. It takes on the attributes of what it is associated with.

An Alternative Perspective

Some philosophers go further and argue that intelligence is only an evaluative concept and is not a scientific one and, because the underlying value and belief systems vary so much, no description or definition of intelligence is possible. The best we can say is that *intelligence is mind at its best*, and that depends on what society considers "mind" and "best" to be at any one time.

This is very helpful because it sharpens our dilemma.

We have noted that you cannot buy a kilo of intelligence but you can design an intelligent program. John Stuart Mill insisted that everything must be open to question. Can we open our minds to the possibility that intelligence can be both a *fact* and a *measurement* of that fact? That it can be both actual and abstract. That intelligence combines both a process and the relative quality of that process. It is a system.

We can define this question as:

Is intelligence an abstract evaluation concept, or a measurable neural process, or can it be both?

This may be a very novel, innovative, inventive concept, but that does not mean it is impossible. We will spend the rest of this book arguing that we can describe, design and build intelligent computer systems, and we can learn to behave more intelligently. We can define intelligence.

Intelligence is a System

We can observably draw the conclusion that "intelligence" means different things to different people in different circumstances at different times.

Most things can be in either a state or a process. A state is passive, a process active; however, arguably, intelligence is neither (or both) at different times. Intelligence is a system. A system contains components that can be both states and processes. The essence of a system is that a structure, pattern, combination and sequence of these states and processes, which, in turn, can be interchangeable.

All the definitions, therefore, can be said to be *correct,* within the limits of their individual circumstances. The problem with all these definitions is that they are *incomplete.*

We can go further and observe that intelligence has an element of duality. We will discuss this further when we consider the measurement of intelligence, but for now we can note that this duality appears to be that all systems tend to have a specific foreground application and a generalised background. The application may display one specific type of intelligence. The background is a generic facility. We can only measure the outcome of the duality. So in most cases we can only identify and measure the visible foreground application. This application is powerfully influenced for good or bad by the efficiency of the background general processes, but we have no direct access to these.

All the Myriad Definitions Proposed Have One Thing in Common

Every definition and description is about quality — executing some task better, faster or more efficiently. We have noted above that every manifestation of intelligence or intelligent behaviour is comparative not absolute.

Even where we use the word to describe information, we mean good information, even special information.

Source and Foundation of Intelligence

The sea slug *Aplysia* can grow neurons to respond in different ways according to circumstances. It is just possible to argue that this is the first glimmering of intelligence — the mechanism to respond to events.

Thus, the earliest expression of intelligence is *coping with the unexpected*.

Fast forward to that favourite example of all cognitive neuroscientists, describing how our distant ancestors caught prey or partners and lived to reproduce their successful genes.

The Source, Foundation and Evolution of Survival Intelligence.

Thus, we can argue that the source of all intelligence is for the whole body to operate ever more efficiently and survive, and therefore the first modern definition is

"the ability to respond to incomplete information as fast as possible".

All subsequent evolutions and developments of intelligence are derivatives of these basic skills.

Ability to Respond...

Response depends on being aware of events, so all intelligence begins with, and depends on, the continuous and efficient monitoring of the external world by the sensory organs and the brain being alert to assess risk and process what is recorded. This includes concentration and the allocation of resources in prolonged crises. It also alludes to the ability to do more than one thing at a time — multi-tasking. While just coping with the problem before us, nevertheless we still notice the arrival of an assailant out of the corner of our eye. This is one source of foreground and background neural processing.

...To Incomplete Information...

This is an extremely important attribute, because at some level all information is incomplete. The usual example is noticing the grass waving as the invisible predator approaches. At the other end of the scale, we are reasonably sure, at least for the past 500 years, that the sun is the centre of our solar system and planet earth revolves around it, but there is still a very great deal of other information about the sun we do not know. We are far from certain we fully understand gravity. The entire economic fraternity are freely admitting that their whole corpus of knowledge is incomplete.

Socrates' aphorism that "the only thing he knew for certain was that he knew nothing for certain", or "constructive uncertainty" in today's quantum speak, is a key foundation of intelligence.

Intelligence is bound up with the acquisition of knowledge. If we do not know anything about a particular corpus of knowledge, we cannot behave intelligently about it. The wider our knowledge and the greater our experience — fluent in a second language, learning to play a musical instrument, the widest possible curriculum while preparing for life-long learning, the identification of talents — all generate a wider intelligence: not necessarily faster, but deeper, which is a fertile ground for intuition.

...As Fast as Possible

Speed has always been of the essence, and still is to this day. It is still a crucial element of IQ and all other similar tests: how many questions can be answered correctly in a *defined time*?

When the group, herd, or tribe were escaping predators, it was not good enough for individuals just to be fast to survive to reproduce their efficient genes. The winners were the ancestors who were *faster than their peers.*

In the controversial IQ and similar tests, the absolute performance is less significance. The only mark that counts is not just how fast, but how *much faster and better* you are than the average of your peerhood.

Speed in the acquisition of knowledge is ever more important in an ever more complex world.

Perhaps the most important attribute of all is that *Intelligence is all about competition*. Doing things better than the crowd. Evolution is based on, and only works thanks to the principle of competition. We can, therefore, say that one of the primary definitions is that:

Intelligence is the competitive driving mechanism and force of evolution.

Intelligence is the essential ingredient of all human activity, thus:

THE EQUATION OF INTELLIGENCE

SPEED OF PROCESSING	ABILITY		THINKING, PROBLEM
ACQUISITION OF KNOWLEDGE =	AND	=	SOLVING, DECISION MAKING,
BREADTH OF EXPERIENCE	APTITUDE		CREATIVITY, WISDOM

History

Intelligence has been a driver of improvement, not only on the evolutionary scale but also within recorded history as tribe and nation fought for space, food and scarce resources.

Our present interest in intelligence has been driven by the renaissance and the age of enlightenment generally, and then particularly by Charles Darwin's *On the Origin of the Species*, and the beginnings of universal education stimulated by the needs of the Industrial Revolution. The genesis of the IQ tests was to identify students who were falling behind, so that they could be given extra tuition. Then, largely for political reasons, IQ tests, and therefore concepts of intelligence have been tied to the academic agenda of teenage education.

Quite understandably the leaders of the academic world who found that they scored well on these tests, promoted them, generating a feedback system, thus intelligence is now almost exclusively associated with academia to the exclusion of all other abilities.

The Mind at Its Best: A Greek View

Prior to the renaissance, the situation was very different. To take the extreme case, all the male citizens of Sparta served in the army till they were 30 or so. Had boys of 11 taken national tests, alertness in monitoring the surroundings, response to possible movements of an enemy force and quick reactions to support one's brother soldiers on either side in battle would have been by far the most sought-after skills.

The Olympic Games were a centrepiece of Greek civilisation. However, the first plays and some of the first poetry dates from the time of Aristotle and Plato, who both argued in favour of a good education including both physical and mental excellence. We are seeing this returning again as sports of all types become full-time professions.

All down through history, personal skills have always been recognised and rewarded. The ability to lead has been most prized, with empathy, tolerance and cooperation similarly at a premium.

Our ancestors who survived the ice age, around 10,000 years ago, had speech, but their mental equipment was aligned to survival. Gradually, gradually our mental equipment improved, but very unevenly across the community. Reading and writing and then printing generated a major advance. Arguably, 500 years ago intellectual strength was drawing even with physical strength.

Mind at Its Best: The Industrial Revolution

The Industrial Revolution provided both the need and the resources to educate, at least minimally, the whole population. It also generated a mass of largely manual employment. A conscientious labourer could earn a reasonable income. Since the Second World War, the number of people earning a good living from their intellectual skills has risen exponentially. Now that the industrial revolution is almost over, we are facing the imminent prospect that people will only be able to earn any income at all if they can develop their intellectual attributes.

Mind at Its Best: Late Twentieth Century

We can learn a lot about the state of the art of intelligence in the twenty-first century if we plot, as best we can, how we have adapted our inherited survival intelligence to meet today's demands.

In the twentieth century, (1) intellectual intelligence has grown to be the leader.

Increasingly, dexterity and (2) physical intelligence, most obviously in sport has been catching up. The intelligence of the five senses. The ability to craft beautiful things, from architecture to cabinet making, and fine china has been present throughout civilisation, but more recently design as well as fabrication has been gaining ground especially in manufactured goods and fashion. This includes all the visual and performing arts.

(3) Personal intelligence, emotional, behavioural and relationship intelligence — empathy, leadership and charisma — have always been important but have tended only to have been given serious attention in recent decades.

In addition, what we might call medical, or (4) health intelligence is in its infancy — the symbiotic relationship with the immune, cardiovascular, endocrine and enteric systems.

We can explore how these different facets of intelligence map onto and extend and amplify the three phases of survival intelligence:

Ability to Respond   Incomplete Information   As Fast as Possible

Has expanded and been refined to:

Reactive intelligence   Acquisitive intelligence,   Creative intelligence,

or learning   driving improvement

Reactive Intelligence depends on the most efficient usage of the monitoring of the five senses of the external world and the organs of the body. The endocrine system generates both meaning and alerts the system, feeds energy to the muscles and alerts the appropriate application(s) in the brain. It raises the concentration level, and in changing situations changes tactics.

Acquisitive Intelligence. In almost all circumstances information is incomplete, thus stimulating, prediction and imagination to attempt to fill in the gaps. This has developed into the driver of all the learning systems.

Creative Intelligence. The ability to respond as fast as possible has always been a key attribute. However, the battle over seconds has developed into the battle for quality. Even in modern IQ and similar tests, speed is still of the essence. How many questions can be answered correctly *in a given time*? But whenever the luxury of time allows, the ability to pause and evaluate alternatives is the foundation of thinking — prepare better physical reactions, mental responses, new solutions and better decisions. In the long run, quality always trumps quantity.

All three - reactive, aquisitive and creative intelligence contribute to the acquisition of experience, to learn from others and observe, and look for patterns in the flow of facts and actions to build up a library of ever better, ever more complex specific applications. This learning starts in the foreground and, as it becomes familiar, slips partly into the ever more flexible background. Some are always either states or processes. Some can be either or both, according to circumstances. Both build into systems with the duality to operate as specific intelligent activities, or as components of the background or general intelligence that provides the facility to do more than one task in parallel; for instance, monitor the background while executing some application. In a crisis, the whole focus can be directed at just one specific task — what we call *concentration*.

Executing that far more complex operation faster and more efficiently than our competitors is how we survive and prosper in the modern world.

We can observe the eight great drivers of Intelligence are:

(1) The development of language to communicate with others, cooperate together and discuss future plans. Every manifestation of intelligence puts a premium on the manipulation of words, the ability to listen and learn and the ability to express ideas coherently.

(2) The endocrine system to alert the whole body if a risk is identified, generate hormones to prepare the brain for crisis processing, prime the muscles for possible action and cause the cardiovascular system to go into overdrive.

(3) The extended autonomic functions that operates across the whole central nervous system. This is the background operating system that continually monitors all the sensory organs that observe the external world and the internal organs that enable the body to operate in optimal conditions. It selects the most appropriate application system to

be activated in the foreground at maximum efficiency. In particular, it enables the whole system to carry out more than one task at a time by enabling foreground and background actions to operate in parallel.

(4) The ability to identify coherent patterns of information in bodies of data or events that are happening.

(5) The feedback system which confirms that the various muscles, glands and all the other organs have performed the tasks requested, plus the responses are generated internally and externally.

(6) The ability to extrapolate all the information available to predict the possible future courses of events and so be able to make contingency plans to cope with any potential emergency.

(7) To gather all the appropriate pieces of information together and arrange them in various sequences and patterns to try and identify alternative activities to produce better decisions, and creative new ways of doing things and solving problems.

(8) Last but not least, when all other activities are exhausted, to cope with the unexpected.

Summary

The first glimmerings of intelligence are about a mechanism to respond to events. Thus, the earliest expression of intelligence is a means of

Coping with the unexpected.

However, we can fast forward to describe how our distant ancestors caught prey and partners, operated ever more efficiently and lived to reproduce their successful genes. Therefore, the first modern definition is the ability to

Respond to incomplete information fast.

All subsequent evolutions and developments of intelligence are derivatives of these basic skills.

CHAPTER TEN

GENERAL AND RESPONSIVE INTELLIGENCE

Give us a definition and we will program the world.

With apologies to Archimedes

We have observed in the previous chapter something of the history of intelligence. How *survival intelligence* developed and how various modern intelligences have developed from this distant base.

Now let us study how the brain grows in the womb and develops into the staggeringly sophisticated adult organ that is so central to all our lives.

Growing the Modern Brain Mind

The growth of the neurons that create the modern nascent brain mind in the foetus is a two-stage process. Initially, the DNA blueprint uses a mass of specialised glia cells to construct a series of fibres which extend radially within the developing cortex to create a scaffolding. Once this framework is in place, neurons begin to develop a nucleus and grow axon filaments which find their way along the scaffolding to connect up all the sensory and other organs, muscles and systems of the body, and in turn, all the sensory and other organs, muscles and systems grow a parallel set of dendrites which are attracted back along the scaffolding to the neuron nucleus. Time delay photographs show neural cell adhesive proteins tentatively finding their way to, and then building synaptic connectors to their individual destinations. As early as the 1950s, Rita Levi-Montalcini won a Nobel Prize for the discovery of the first of a family of nerve growth factors that drives this entire process.

At birth, this framework is thought to consist of about one billion neurons and networks making up the central nervous system and, in addition to connecting up all the sensory and other organs, muscles and glands, it also links up the immune, cardiovascular, digestive, energy, enteric and other systems. Over this infrastructure — these neural pathways, a continuous stream of patterns of electrochemical signals flow throughout life, enabling the whole body to operate as one coordinated, cooperative and synchronised whole. These patterns of instructions are known as the extended autonomic functions.

In addition, a further billion neurons are concentrated in the brain mind — whose primary functions are to execute the coordination instructions, continuously monitor the sensory and other organs and organise appropriate reactions — which is the body's learning centre.

Learning

As noted above, when a baby is born it can do almost nothing, but it can learn to do almost anything. For instance, the initial framework of neural networks enables babies to hear and make sounds, but no baby ever born can speak one single word. A vocabulary must be learned. In the same way, the precise functions of eating, crawling, walking, running and so forth have to be learned. The brain mind has evolved to grow a mass of additional neural networks to extend and then fine tune the original basic framework. The brain mind is a massive learning system optimised to acquire, remember and retrieve a mass of functions, processes and information from simple things like saying one word to complex functions like driving a car. A mature brain mind is thought to grow of the order of a *trillion* new links and structures, which encapsulates a lifetime's experience, building a vast library of applications all controlled by the extended autonomic functions of the central nervous system, operating unobtrusively in the background.

In Chapter 7, simple arithmetic suggests that growing a trillion new links and structures in a mature brain involves growing an average of some thousand new memory units per second.

It is useful to observe and note that, like so much in the body, the neural system is duplicated. Every neural link to every organ consists of an axon transmitting signal patterns from the neural nucleus to each distant organ, and a dendrite transmitting signals from the distant organs to each nucleus. The brain mind consists of two ventricles connected by the corpus collosom. Electrochemical signals can only travel in one direction along axons and dendrites, much as blood can only flow one way along arteries and veins.

We have a fairly clear idea of the learning process of the brain mind. The sensory organs continuously monitor the world and transmit information to the brain mind. If an event is familiar, we respond with the best response we have learned as fast as possible. If this event is different, we automatically *grow* new neural links and structures to enable us to respond in new innovative ways. Thus, we learn to strengthen successful reactions and grow alternative solutions by imitation and endless repetition, as we enhance and construct our memories.

We have observed over the centuries that some people are better at some groups of tasks than others. Some people are better at abstract academic subjects, while others are better at more physical occupations like the art and crafts. There is a strongly held opinion that some people are naturally better at logical matters like maths and science, while others are better at more emotional themes like languages and literature. Some are more imaginative, some practical and pragmatic. And some seem to be better at everything!

We have devised ever more tests to see how successfully we have been able to build the neural networks — learn — to read and write and manipulate numbers; learn another verbal language; cope with the unexpected; acquire information and appreciate its implications and meaning; extrapolate this knowledge to solve problems, predict the future and make decisions. We pack all these attributes and skills into libraries of applications grown as a result of all the experiences of our upbringing, education and subsequent lives. And we try and identify and measure this illusive ability that seems to underlie everything, which we call intelligence.

The Autonomic Functions of the Central Nervous System

What we call general intelligence is to do with the efficiency of this general background operating system that makes all these applications possible — the extended autonomic functions of the central nervous system. We have experienced great difficulty in identifying boundaries, describing categories and defining intelligence, because it is not a specific function or process in itself. The autonomic system is an overall *facilitator* that enables and supports all the many other abilities, which we can more easily categorise, describe, define and most importantly measure.

To understand this concept more easily, we can again make use the analogy of our computers. In the early days, the programmer had to organise and manage the input of information, usually on punched cards or paper tape (no nice easy keyboards and screens), organise where the program resided and if it was large, where the active part was and how to store, obtain and switch over to other sections when needed. Standard subroutines could be brought together to help. In particular, Microsoft built a very efficient way of managing data that was stored on disks, and so the disc operating system (DOS) was born. Massive programs were needed to organise, monitor and manage screens and keyboards as they were invented. MS-DOS developed into *Windows*. All modern applications use the ever-growing facilities of these operating systems. Many people are unaware they exist. For them, the applications they use are all they need to know about.

Examples

Let us take an accounting application as an example. This program may input payments from a keyboard and the present state of an account from memory, then adds, subtracts and all the other maths, updates the account and prints a statement — all that is in the application program. The background operating system does not process one single number. It looks after the keyboard and sends whatever is keyboarded to the processor. The operating system does not do any maths. It manages the memory system — collecting the account file and later returning it. It sends one stream of signals to the screen and another to the printer. The operating system would do exactly the same tasks if the next application was a word processor.

Thus, we can clearly separate the Windows (or similar) operating system from the individual applications programs. The latter is entirely dependent on the former. The former carries out no obvious activities visible to the operator. However, if the former is old and slow, the application program is likely to appear to be inefficient and vice versa. Generally speaking, few end users have any access to the programs of the operating system. Many application's designers know how to use the interfaces, but they have no need to know more.

Duality

Similarly, in the brain mind, we can clearly separate the speed and efficiency of the background autonomic functions, and the speed and efficiency of each individual application (task) learned. If we wake up one morning and, for whatever reason, feel slow and sluggish, all the tasks (applications) we undertake that day will seem difficult, slow and hard work.

Equally, if we have only partially learned some new subject or activity, and still have a lot to learn to be proficient, the background autonomic operating system can do little to come to our aid.

However, the outside world only sees the performance of both systems working together. In everyday life, it is often almost impossible to separate the two.

If we woke up feeling ill on a day that involved sitting some exam or easily defined task and we scored only 20%, we could re-sit that exam or task, say a week later, when we had recovered. If we scored significantly differently, we could legitimately blame our background autonomic operating system. The exam, or task is unlikely to have changed in that week. The change in the performance of the background autonomic operating system could have been neural, or some problem with the endocrine, immune or cardiovascular systems; or some totally unconnected emotional problem; collapse of self-confidence; or possibly even just overindulgence the previous night!

Thus, when we look at intelligence we are always studying at least two separate systems and often three, four or more applications interacting or trying to carry out very different tasks. Hence defining intelligence is very difficult.

Variety of Definitions

We have explored how all the many definitions of intelligence from some of the best brains from the distant past to the present day are all so different. We have concluded that they are all probably correct in their own environment but are incomplete. We can see here how they also tend to define just one or more of the functions or processes — neural applications — that intelligence facilitates. They do not define the underlying facilitation but enable ability itself.

It is important to emphasise that the autonomic operating system is responsible not only for the neuron networks in the brain and the neuron networks throughout the body but also for the smooth running of the other systems like the glandular, cardiovascular, immune, digestive, endocrine, enteric and energy organisms. Thus, if an emergency occurs, messages are not only quickly on the way to the brain but also, in parallel, to the glands to secrete hormones, to the heart to raise pumping levels and the energy system to raise general activity. By the time the brain mind is activating appropriate muscles, they are already being primed and optimised to act.

Intelligence is a multi-faceted full-body activity. Human intelligence is part of all solutions.

In Control 24/7

Similarly, the autonomic functions of the central nervous system are operational whether we are awake or asleep. It continually monitors the outside world through all the sensory organs and monitors the internal world and coordinates all the other body systems.

We have explored the etymology of the word intelligence and run into all sorts of problems. However, if we set the boundaries of intelligence as the great facilitator — the whole extended autonomic functions of the central nervous system, we can solve this dilemma. We can say that we use all our inherited intelligence background capabilities to facilitate all our library of learned intelligence: to read; to write; to manipulate numbers; to acquire information; to work out and store its implications, its meaning; to extrapolate meanings to solve solutions, predict, and make decisions. We must go one step further. Intelligence is not only about executing all these activities, but also crucially about executing them *faster.*

The more efficient the background autonomic system, the more efficiently it facilitates, and makes possible, the many categories of specific individual processes and functions — the applications we execute. The better the autonomic system, the better the facilitator, the better our intelligence, the faster we execute tasks; because all the functions of the body are involved, it contributes and, in many cases, is part of the solution.

The term intelligence describes the perceived quality of the efficiency, and particularly speed, whereby the whole-body processes support and assist in executing all the individual neural activities we learn from experience. The autonomic functions are essentially hereditary being largely in place at birth. As part of its tasks to allocate resources, it continuously monitors the sensory and other organs and systems, establishing priorities, including defence and reproduction, and warning of shortages of water and nutrients by generating conscious sensations of anger, arousal, thirst and hunger.

One of the problems of understanding and defining, and particularly measuring intelligence, is that we cannot access these autonomic functions directly. We can only observe and measure the efficiency of the various learned applications indirectly as a result of the use they make of the autonomic functions. For instance, the difference between a general knowledge test and an intelligence quotient test is that the former is measuring functions like memory — the ability to acquire, store and retrieve information, thus, is maximally cultural — learned from the peerhood and minimally dependant on processing, whereas the latter is measuring, say, the ability to identify patterns, sequences or logic, and thus is minimally cultural and maximally dependent on processing. Neither directly measures the intelligence of the background autonomic functions of the central nervous system itself.

To move forward, we need to analyse and deconstruct intelligence through the medium of the individual systems that general intelligence supports and, indeed, makes possible.

History

All civilisations have appreciated that some people are observably "brighter" than others. Generally, this tended to be the richer, better fed and better educated top 10% of the community, but there have always been plenty of examples of the opposite to modify this simplistic theory.

Intelligence is one of those concepts that everyone feels they know what it is, yet any description, let alone definition is remarkably illusive. It is similar to that group of concepts like beauty and the redness of a rose that we bundle together and call *qualia*. However, intelligence does not quite fit into this category of qualia. Intelligence not only describes functions but also processes them. As we have noted above, the problem is compounded because intelligence has meant different things to different people at different times doing different tasks. Perhaps we can begin to see how these are coming together.

Theory of General Intelligence or "g"

A long debate has gone on over the last half century between the cognitive neuroscientists who argue that intelligence is fluid and depends on many influences both hereditary (nature) and experiences of life (nurture). The others see a system fixed at birth much as height and eye colour. Some see one comprehensive system, and others argue that each sensory organ and system have an individual intelligence including an emotional intelligence. Arthur Jenson, a Californian educational psychologist argued that we are all born with a general level of intelligence "g", which was fixed for life. James Flynn, a New Zealand academic argues the opposite that our experiences in life determine our level of intelligence. He makes the valid point that "IQ tests measure ability and the likelihood of success solely in the kind of society that sets IQ tests". But then that is a general rule that applies to all examinations!

Like so much in science, as one delves ever deeper into the detail, one appreciates that the entire system is far more complex and sophisticated. We can say the Jensen concept of a general intelligence or "g" is at least incomplete.

We argue that the beginnings of intelligence are observable deeply rooted in some of the earliest life forms, and evolution and our inventive brains have created ever more powerful extensions of intelligence that have built on each other to create the sophisticated complex people that we are today.

We have explored above, the evolutionary development of *survival intelligence.*

In the process of monitoring, the outside world, the autonomic functions learn to respond to incomplete information, by executing the best available solution as fast as possible, and survive. In the famous example, our eyes glimpse suspicious waving grass that might be a predator, and we activate our muscles to run and survive. Evolution has selected autonomic systems that are the fastest and most efficient, following the rule: *minimum information, maximum speed of response.*

The substantial bulk of neural processing nowadays is all about learning new information. We have noted above, but it is always useful to repeat, that one of the principle functions of the brain mind is to be the learning system of the body. We can observe four categories:

(1) As soon as we are born, we start to learn a variety of physical functions — control of input and output bodily functions, crawling standing, balance, walking, running and talking — by curiosity, imitation, experiment and endless repetition.

(2) As soon as we can talk, we can start on the long progression of learning information — reading, writing and arithmetic, throughout the whole school curriculum, and on into life-long learning. The key is much more than the acquisition of facts but includes the implications of information: what we call *meaning*. When we go further, we begin to extrapolate information to widen its value and begin to gravitate towards *thinking*.

(3) Then there are the whole range of physical and personal skills, of which good examples are writing, swimming, riding a bicycle and in due course driving a car.

(4) Finally, there are all our experiences: what happens to us, how we reacted and the repercussions.

All four have one thing in common. Watch a baby to struggle to stand up and walk; master a vocabulary of words, then the multiplication tables, recite poetry; then struggle to hold a pen and write clearly; balance a bicycle. The learning process is difficult. Every scrap of concentration is deployed. It appears the whole brain — and body — is completely engrossed. Then, suddenly — it often seems, everything falls into place — it even seems easy. We walk, and run without a thought, chatter away, use the multiplication tables, scribble away while concentrating now on the text and ideas — the writing is automatic. We can automatically ride a bicycle for the rest of our lives. We have actually grown the neural networks that drive the muscles that do the work, and those networks of physical neurons are there for life. Those new efficient neural networks now operate in what some people call background. All these learned networks are integrated into the whole system and often into each other, but, in effect, they are a series of applications, and they form a library of all our skills, attributes and abilities.

They become part of the autonomic functions. We mount a bicycle and ride away completely automatically, while our whole attention is, perhaps, concentrating on chattering to a companion.

Responsive Intelligence

Over a relatively short time, we have evolved additional skill to those inherited from our ancestors.

So far we have concentrated on the speed of reaction — responding fast. However, when we have the luxury of time, we can pause and reflect on our experiences and contemplate and evaluate alternative behaviours to solve problems. In the first place to avoid predators, or catch prey or partners more imaginatively — and survive longer. Next time we glimpse that predator or prey, we execute the new, improved response we have learned and the predator or prey is outwitted. This gradually expanded into the discovery of new information not already known to the community — prediction, invention, imagination — creativity and follows the rule: *maximum information, no time constraint, whatever time is needed to think of a better, superior, innovative, response.*

We began to use our ability to observe and monitor the world for another purpose. We began to notice recurring events and behaviour — the sequence of night and day, the progression of the seasons and their importance to farming. Long before building the pyramids, the ancient Egyptians had observed and recorded the patterns of the behaviour of the Nile to predict the annual floods and when to sow the seed corn — an early example of responsive intelligence.

Identifying patterns is the basis of information and the beginnings of science. It is an area of processing where computers can easily outperform the brain mind. Computer programs can process complex algorithms on very large databases of statistics way outside the capacity of the brain mind. It is by far the most exciting and potentially valuable aspect of artificial (or machine) intelligence (AI).

Out of these two aptitudes, we have extended our base abilities to respond — *extrapolating known information to create new solutions.* This is essentially an internal brain mind skill, with established neural networks processing neural networks to create new ideas and concepts, and *monitoring, recording, analysing and identifying patterns in streams of events and behaviours in the environment, and thereby discovering new information.*

The development of language greatly advances both skills as it enables us to reminisce, debate and compare experiences with others and so multiplies the ability of the group to decide how best to behave today, and then predict the most likely of possible future developments, so that the community can make provisions to mitigate potential difficulties — hence, we have begun to be able to start the long journey to modify and control our environment. Speech enabled *Homo sapiens to discuss and think about the significance of recurring events and invent hypotheses to explain how our environment works; to think in the abstract.* Observation suggests thinking is unique to *Homo sapiens.* It appears to have grown very slowly as a supplement to speech, accelerating with the invention of writing, and again with the arrival of printing, which in turn animated the renaissance, then the enlightenment and then the industrial revolution. Computers give us the tools, and intelligence and thinking give us the means, to turbocharge the burgeoning computing revolution on which we are embarked.

Speed of response — to react fast or recall something quickly is always a key attribute but of increasing importance in our ever more complex world is the quality of our decision making and judgements. This ability to create alternative solutions is, at least as critical, if not of greater value. Speed of physical response is less life threatening. Major longer term judgments are increasingly crucial, possibly to the survival of our race.

Other Sentient Systems

Let us broaden our view of the underlying foundation or the reactive systems of the brain mind.

Sensory Organs

The sea slug *Aplysia,* which, thanks to Eric Kandel, we know a lot about, has a tiny number of large neurons but only the sense of touch. It is increasingly clear that all the sensory organs are derivatives of touch. The very earliest life forms are thought to have been able to survive only because, in their first habitat they could develop, and their nascent neurons cooperate, in crevices that later were able to be replaced by a membrane, the ancestor of skin. The skin holds all the organs of the whole body together, and sensors in the skin are attached to dendrites that transmit patterns of signals to the brain. Smell and taste sensors evolved to recognise pheromones and chemicals like salt and sugar. The eye is a very specialist piece of skin that has evolved to be able to convert patterns of energy in the form of light or photons — the smallest measurable unit of light — into various types of patterns of neural signals. The dedicated pads of skin in the eardrum convert the patterns of sound waves as they sweep by.

Two important observations are as follows: (1) Streams of photons continuously hit the retina. The stream of photons, particularly from the shifting scene, is continuously changing, yet we perceive and experience the sensations of a stable image. (2) Sound waves flow over the eardrums and are instantly gone for good, yet we can, in microseconds, decode the patterns of signals the ears send to the brain and "hold" a record of those sounds.

Selective Concentration

In normal circumstances, the five sensory organs continuously monitor the external world and transmit patterns of signals to the brain, which may well ignore 90% of them. If we are, say, driving a car, the flow of signals from our eyes has priority on our concentration, and we focus on the traffic in front, road signs and so forth. However, the autonomic system is processing much more. It picks up images from the corner of our eyes — a car coming up fast in one of the mirrors; sounds coming from a side turning, but out of sight. "Could that be a problem?" The taste of a chocolate a passenger has just offered us: mayhem on the back seat. A part of the spectrum of our concentration is aware of the music playing. Our concentration switches as the music is interrupted by a traffic announcement, "Was that important to me?"

Evolving Abilities

The extended autonomic functions of the central nervous system are by far the oldest function of the brain mind, but it has evolved ever faster to cope with events. Speech and writing, not only gave us a means of communicating but also gave the brain mind the problem of coping with decoding sound waves; decoding symbols and shapes of letters and numbers; storing and recalling hundreds of thousands of words, singly and in phrases, in potentially many languages — the whole of mathematics — representations of where we are, and how to reach our destination; moving the muscles of our lungs, vocal chords, mouths, lips and tongues in an exact and precise sequence to enunciate words, even giving each special emphasis; moving the muscles of our arms and fingers to draw meticulously exact symbols — writing — to a degree of accuracy not attempted by any other life form.

There has been much debate about whether elements of grammar have evolved in the brain which would explain how very young children learn the complexities of speech apparently with such remarkable ease. It is quite possible that we have evolved much more sensitive and sophisticated networks to control the speaking and writing muscles. Given the explosion of words, it is a very good thing that language is as fluid as it is, or we could not have advanced so fast.

Physical Dexterity

One of the great paradigm shifts, or game changers in the history of *Homo sapiens* were discovering and then inventing tools — in effect, supplementing our arms, legs and muscles. Perhaps it was picking up sticks to knock down fruit. Later, the ability to throw some sort of projectile, gave those who were good at this a great advantage — the first glimmerings of technology. The largest part of physical dexterity is coordination between the eyes and the hands and feet. On every sports field, every day one can witness talented young people who run towards a ball, kick it exactly where they intended and direct onto their target, whereas an awkward neighbour may run awkwardly towards a ball, strike it crookedly and see it dribble off in an unintended direction.

Very successful athletes, cabinet makers, sculptors, artists, musicians and so many others have to work extremely hard to scale the heights of their professions, but no one would disagree it is almost impossible to make a star out of someone who has no underlying talent.

Everyday Operation

In everyday background mode, the autonomic functions monitor every organ, screens our environment and flags up any inconsistency or abnormality. In a perceived emergency, it responds as fast as possible. It has an ever increasing library of responses and applications — our accumulated knowledge and experience, to call on to react to events. It monitors our own behaviour to check our body has done what our brain mind ordered and feeds-back the reactions of the outside world to our own activities. This all happens in what we can call background mode, or in autopilot, or, what has been called for some decades the subconscious, meaning that we are not necessarily aware of all this activity. It happens "below the radar" is another descriptor.

In addition, we can consciously pause and reflect, and evaluate alternative courses of action, predict future possibilities and initiate activities to mitigate risks. In *foreground mode*, we can observe curious facts, discover new information, ponder and discuss with others how these observations and discoveries might relate — conjecture what these concepts might imply and imagine innovative new theories, ideas and novel solutions. We can conjure up complete plots of novels, practical or fantastical, terrible or utopian and invent whole new branches of science. Apart from the notes we exchange, string theory only exists in human imaginations — an entirely abstract concept.

The brain mind is by any definition a very intelligent system.

Language, Linguistics and Semantics

One of the problems of defining intelligence is that the generally accepted meaning of the word has evolved over time and, more recently, has become a portmanteau word that means different things to different people in different circumstances. There is another dimension to etymology from the one in Chapter 9.

Over the millennia, our ancestors could easily recognise that there is both a rainbow of abilities in the human race and a wide spectrum of levels of efficiency in each attribute. They knew nothing about neurons and patterns of electrochemical signals with networks working together sometimes in one group, sometimes another, so they amassed a whole lexicon of words to describe this most prized skill: brainy, ability, acumen, wisdom, academic, bright, smart, keen, talented, skilled, exceptional, remarkable, gifted intellectual, knowledgeable, rational, logical, cerebral, scholarly, quick, able, capable, clever ingenious, resourceful original inventive inspired imaginative shrewd, perceptive discerning insightful, wise, astute, judicious, nimble, quick witted, adroit, adept, crafty, cunning and eloquent. There is a more comprehensive list at Appendix 47 (all appendices are hosted on www.BrainMindForum.org/appendices). To cover all these attributes, they came up with the portmanteau word intelligence to identify people who appeared to have greater acumen were brighter, smarter, more gifted and so forth. In other words, *intelligence is all about the quality of our neural systems.* Reactive systems, built upon our survival intelligence, initially relied on speed — quantity — now the emphasis begins to shift towards quality. Speed and quality remain equal partners in the acquisition of knowledge.

One of the Fundamental Attributes of All Intelligence: Systems

One of the advantages of the arrival of computing is that it has introduced the concept of systems to the cognitive neuroscience debate. Neurons are wonderful, but they appear to be very similar across the community, so it was difficult to see how a neuron could be intelligent. However, neurons operating in systems are a very different matter. We might have indistinguishable neurons, but those very same neurons can work together in widely different systems in many different ways, and their efficiency depends on many things such as nature, nurture, hormone balance and diet for starters.

The efficiency of systems can vary widely, and it has positive variations from the average that we call intelligence; it is this capability that we strive to understand, define and if possible learn to augment. The ability to measure intelligence has been the holy grail of cognitive and educational scientists for a long time. We have devoted Chapter 13 to exploring this subject when we have explored all the different manifestations of intelligence.

Deconstructing Definitions

We have noted above how the definition of intelligence in dictionaries helped us expand our understanding of intelligence. Defining the meaning of the words intelligence and intelligent as "mentally apprehending something *quickly*" raises the all important aspect of speed — how quickly exactly? Against what criteria? However, we have identified intelligence as the differences between different people's diverse levels of ability. We come back to the same point that it is not so much how quickly, or well something is apprehended, understood or comprehended, but how much faster or slower than everyone else. All the intelligence words always refer to these abilities being at the top of the spectrum. An Intelligence quotient of 100 is average for the age group. Someone who is given a score of 150+ is said to be intelligent. Someone on 50– is thought not to have much intelligence.

We have defined the boundaries of two brain mind systems that exhibit wide variations in their level of capability.

(1) There are the background autonomic functions of the central nervous system common to all our relatives in the animal kingdom.
(2) In this chapter, we are exploring the first evolutionary extension of that survival intelligence — the ability to cope with the unexpected. Then the *reactive* applications we learn to help us cope with life generally. This ancient system has evolved over the millennia to monitor the world and react to events as fast and as efficiently as possible — minimum information and maximum speed.

There is a broad consensus that the brilliantly clever computer programs to beat chess masters, win the jeopardy quiz and learn how to play the game Go are very intelligent applications programs indeed. Everyone also appreciates that a computer loaded with one of these programs can do exactly nothing else. These programs replicate the genius of the people who designed and wrote the programs. The focus has shifted. Christof Koch refers to general artificial intelligence. Pedro Domingos argues in favour of designing a "master algorithm". Nick Bostrom calls for a "superintelligence" and suggests how gene editing could produce people with this sort of enhanced capability. All three suggest that strong AI, as these concepts suggest, is a computer program that is so fabulously clever that it could design and *write programs that could beat the human generated chess programs,* play jeopardy better than the existing human program and learn to play any game, not just Go, and, of course, *do everything else.*

There is a very powerful argument that something so stupendously comprehensive already exists in the human brain mind.

The "master algorithm" is effectively machine learning or broadly acquisitive intelligence. The chess-playing program is a vast store of the experiences of playing, or responsive intelligence. Learning Go is observing and identifying the patterns in the behaviour of many "Go" players or creative intelligence. This in no way limits or criticises these dazzlingly clever programs. They highlight the huge strength of computers and their potential to revolutionise the prospects of humanity. However, what they have done is replicate the functions of the brain mind, but they have done it hundreds of times better — one could almost say, more intelligently.

The brain mind can do all these tasks: play chess, participate in quizzes and learn to play Go quite competently. "Strong AI", "the master algorithm" and "superintelligence" are already well established within the brain mind. It is surely no less than the humble background autonomic functions of the central nervous system.

Perhaps the objective of strong AI, the master algorithms and superintelligence should be to emulate the background autonomic operating system, but perhaps multiplying its abilities a hundred or even a thousand-fold.

It follows that the first step on this path is to return to the definition, delineation and specification of the reactive intelligent system, as it is the foundation of all the subsequent acquisitive, creative and other brain mind systems explored in the next chapters.

For the sake of clarity, we have used the word intelligence to refer to the level of quality and efficiency of the background autonomic operating system of the brain mind, where the performance of each individual can be variable. Thus, people can be said to be more or less intelligent than others.

Speed

Speed of reaction of the background autonomic operating system is always the key attribute. We might do everything else right, but unless we respond as fast as possible we will still be breakfast. Thus, the key attribute for which natural selection has always been optimised is speed of response. If we are caught with no preferred response, we respond as best we can — we do something; dithering will always lose. Speed is the winning feature, from the deepest past to today's IQ test.

Experience and Support

Memory is essential. Without memory, we cannot learn from what has happened in the past. The background autonomic functions activate stored patterns of neural network activity that manipulate the muscles of the limbs to run, climb, or whatever. We also need to be able to activate the glands to flood the system maximising reactions and putting everything on high alert. Equally, we need to activate the generating system to release energy and prime the nutrient path in case this emergency might be prolonged, and put the lungs into action mode to increase oxygen uptake and the heart to pump both to where they are needed. Some of these basic skills are inherited, some we have to learn. They are the attributes and behaviour of our species. But we had to learn to walk and then run; best if we pay attention and practice.

Recognition

Recognition is the next key. To be able to realise that something is behaving in an unusual way, we must have a means of comparison with the norm.

Thus, a foundation of intelligence is that we can store, modify, retrieve and process patterns of behaviour (information) by the five sensory and other organs. In addition, the glands generate sensations like hunger, thirst, anger, fear and arousal, all of which stimulate physical activity. These feelings and emotions in our deep and distant past are the first glimmerings of our vast panoply of sentient experience and behaviour.

Five Senses

Our best guess is that the five senses evolved in sequence. The *Aplysia* has only touch. Then came taste and probably smell, all to service food acquisition. For a long time, the eyes were dominant as the crucial sense to monitor the outside world. However, in recent times sound has moved up to near equality, with the advent of language. The conclusion is that, although all five receive very different input signals from the external world, like photons and sound waves they behave remarkably similarly once converted into brain mind patterns.

Language

The great paradigm shift, or game changer, or epoch transformation was the development of language, which we have explored in Chapter 5. We began to unravel how information is represented and presented and began to explore the probability that the beginnings of speech — the first words — were spoken to try to express our emotions, sensations and the dawn of our conscious awareness. We have over the millennia successfully mapped words onto our experiences generated by the many multi-mixtures of hormones. This coverage is not complete as we have still not found the words to define and describe things we call *qualia*.

In other areas, we have been much more successful. For instance, we are quite good at picking out the words someone is speaking from a noisy background of, say, many people talking — *the cocktail party effect*.

As we noted above, the recognition of sounds, and later symbols, is not dissimilar to being alert to the potential of being stalked by a predator. Incomplete information is often a problem listening to see if someone is trying to attract our attention, or speak without wishing us to hear, or just listening to someone speaking especially in noisy surroundings.

However, the processing behind the initial recognition machinery is much more complex. We have discovered that there is no simple neural pattern representing a word and discussed this in Chapter 6. As we learn a new word, we start to build up a cluster of related networks. Then there are multiple languages and the processes of translation. Language engineering is a major industry in its own right.

It is interesting that considerable effort was poured into speech recognition programs to analyse and build up the components of sounds; however, better results are being obtained by scanning vast databases of spoken texts to identify recognisable patterns.

Music

The sound of music is difficult to distinguish on an oscilloscope from the sound of a speech. A well-known tune appears to activate the glands directly to generate hormones that can almost instantly change the hearer's mood, often quite dramatically. Alliteration, onomatopoeia, rhyme and rhythm play significant roles in coding and decoding sound to transmit and express subtle meanings. There is a plausible argument that words are a hybrid development of music. The general emotional impact of tunes (analogue) was surrendered in favour of precision and accuracy of words (digital).

We have explored the extraordinary world of silent speech in Chapter 6 and Appendix 25 (all appendices are hosted on www.BrainMindForum.org/appendices).

Text

Last but not least, is the facility to assemble a string of words to make a presentation, or speech, or even participate in a discussion, or prepare to write (or keyboard) a series of sentences to reflect one's thinking. There is no objective of committing these words to memory as we might learn a poem, but it seems likely we use a simpler version of the same mechanism to link a string of words together, but only temporarily before we hold forth, and abandon them immediately thereafter. Thus, the neural mechanisms that helped us safely survive the millennia have evolved to service far more complex tasks.

There is a major difference between the ancient skills of monitoring the outside world for predators, prey and partners, and the prodigiously more modern skills of language processing and machine manipulation. The library of skills available for us to learn has grown considerably in recent centuries as we have invented more gadgets and machines. However, this pales into almost insignificance beside the vast encyclopaedia of language facilities we have learned to build. The system of an average adult has anything up to 100,000 words or more, just in one language.

Evaluation

Recognition comes in at least three modalities, which again are part of the basis of knowledge:

(1) Firstly, we need to identify some form of evaluation, how significant, important or irrelevant may this new pattern of information be?
(2) Secondly, what are the *implications* of this information? Am I seeing a predator or potential food? Rather important in the scheme of things.
(3) Thirdly, and of progressively more importance over evolution, is the potential *extrapolation* of information. The ability to use past experience to predict the future is a skill unique to the human race. However, it is important to appreciate how deep its roots are.

Thus, a definition could be that:

General and reactive intelligence is the relative quality and efficiency of the autonomic functions of the central nervous system that coordinates, manages and operates the physical systems of the body: the endocrine, cardiovascular, immune and enteric systems and the dexterity of all the muscles. In particular, the brain, mind monitors and analyses all the sensory inputs from the surrounding environment, comprehends the significance and meaning of incomplete information, and respond with the most

efficient reaction available, as fast as possible, to outwit predators and the peerhood, to relate to other people and control behaviour.

It provides the framework for all the learned skills to operate, grow, develop and be executed. It allocates resources and organises all the organs and systems of the body to behave and function as one cooperative, coordinated, synchronised whole and provides the means to cope with the world, and survive.

CHAPTER ELEVEN

AQUISITIVE AND CREATIVE INTELLIGENCE

Acquisitive Intelligence

Throughout our lives, the brain mind is a massive learning machine. From the moment of birth, we start to build on the basic autonomic functions of the central nervous system — the background operating system, to feed ourselves, recognise people and things around us, control our movements and begin to speak and understand words. We associate and link all the sensory information together: the word 'mother' to her visual image, warmth, smell, taste and voice. We struggle to imitate and say her name, and feel pleasure if we get it right and get cuddled. We get to know everyone around us and go to work on our vocabulary. By six we have as many as a 1000 words, by 20 we have 100,000 words and possibly a second language. That is a phenomenal rate of growth, because we do not just identify, store and retrieve individual words, but we develop networks of connections to some or all of the five senses and other words to give us a sense of the meaning of that word, first alone, and then as part of phrases and ever more complex structures.

It is easier to identifying *meaning*, where words map directly to multimedia images, but very soon we encounter abstract words that do not map to any specific information such as adjectives, adverbs and then all the words to describe ideas and concepts. We acquire information about things and algorithms about how to do things. It is extremely difficult to list how much information an average teenager might have stored after an average education. The words average in each case being almost impossible to define, to start with. Far from coming up with a value, even working out a formula to calculate a value has stumped many a brilliant brain. Likening the brain mind to a knowledge pump does not stop when leaving full-time education. Many people would argue that their education started when they left the present school system.

By volume, the acquisitive intelligence functions are by far the largest of the three intelligent systems. Reactive intelligence may be operational for more time, and creative intelligence may be the most exciting, but acquisitive intelligence wins hands down on sheer volume of capacity and processing.

How do we process all this information, store it, retrieve it and make use of it?

There are broadly five theories about how we acquire, learn and understand information. Some people use the term *machine learning*.

(1) **Symbolism:** This suggests that all intelligence can be seen as manipulating symbols in much the same way as mathematicians solve equations. Terrance Deacon has written extensively on this hypothesis. In *The Symbolic Species*, he explores the co-evolution of language and the human brain.

We are very familiar with both the concept of manipulating numbers into expressions and developing equations into mathematical models to seek out and extrapolate meaning, and so predict the possible future course of events. We are equally familiar with grouping words into phrases and concatenating phrases into ever more complex structures to generate subtle meanings and variations on meaning.

As we learn more about the representation of words and numbers in our brain mind, this seems eminently likely. It is very probably how number manipulation grew out of language anyway. Hence, as language developed, words have developed as symbols — literary equations. This also neatly solves the problem of words for abstract concepts — the concepts are bounded by the definition of the symbol.

One strength of this argument is that it provides a solution to the problem that it is very difficult to learn new concepts from scratch, and some pre-existing knowledge is needed to build upon. Intelligence is the process of combining new and old knowledge — existing symbols, to solve new problems — new symbols. In a form of inverse deduction, symbolic thinking makes it possible to work out what information is missing and find a symbol to fill the gap and deduce a new solution.

(2) The **Connectionists** build on the well-established view that creating and growing memory as the basic algorithm of learning can be usefully extended. In addition to growing new neural links to assist with generating meaning, networks can be extrapolated to grow new solutions. The very clever twist is to identify the goal then set up a network to reach that goal and iterate the process to get closer to a good answer. Another name for this is *back propagation*. The network is manipulated going backwards and forwards continually trying to reach an ever-closer answer, until the goal is achieved. Having secured the source and goal, it is then possible to continuously manipulate the network to be increasingly efficient. Programs can replicate this iterative process relatively easily. We have explored this concept in describing how a gymnast, for instance, can move a synapse along a dendrite to fine tune the timing of exercises that require immaculate balance. This is a modern variation on Aristotle's bottom-up induction approach.

(3) **Uncertainty:** Broadly opposite is the Bayesian top-down Platonic deductive approach. Start with a possible hypothetical solution and refine it using the Bayesian concept of updating the probability of that hypothesis as more evidence and information becomes available. Hence some people argue that Bayes' theorem converts information into knowledge. More recently Andrei Markov goes further arguing that hidden Markov models disclose the relationship between strings of data with the first influencing the second and the second influencing the third and so on. Because this is essentially a learning process of identifying and reducing multiple uncertainties, it is often referred to as the uncertainty processing system. This can also be described as the Socratic approach — in effect, learning by asking questions.

(4) The **Evolutionists** believe in the pure Darwinian theory of natural selection. The basic problem they aim to solve is to follow the back-propagation route but try to manipulate the whole algorithm not just the parameters. They argue that whole programs can migrate and compete with other whole programs in the same way that nature competes and mates and evolves whole organisms.

(5) **Learning by analogy** is a very different approach all together. Storytelling, drama, parables and analogies have been the principal method of teaching and learning back into prehistory and antiquity.

Thus a definition of acquisitive intelligence is:

The efficiency of the brain to develop, grow and execute neural systems to identify, obtain and retrieve the meaning of information and the processes to convert and extend this into knowledge.

Creative Intelligence

Every single idea, every single concept, every single piece of information we have about our world and how it operates has been conceived originally in a human brain.

Leonardo da Vinci

Of all the skills and attributes of the human body and brain mind, surely the most exciting is the ability to think of something for the very first time. This major frontier of science is arguably our most important attribute: creative intelligence — our ability to think. To be able to push out the frontiers of human knowledge is qualitatively and quantitatively different to all our other sentient capabilities. There are two fundamental ways in which we can identify and create new information and add to the total wealth of human knowledge.

Firstly, we can work with the information that exists and try and reorganise and re-combine concepts and ideas in novel ways, and extrapolate new solutions to solve existing problems: induction, deduction, logic and thinking.

Secondly, quite separately, we can search through the vast volumes of information that exists all around us, produced either in the natural world, or by our own agency, and look for regular repeatable patterns. This is arguably the way *Homo sapiens* began to learn how to convert information into knowledge. It is the basis of the birth of science. It is the means by which we create new information. We can note a very significant difference in scale. There is a limit to how much information the human brain can accommodate at any one moment to analyse, especially as these patterns are likely to get larger and larger. As computers get more powerful, let alone the potential of new technologies like quantum processors and, in particular, quantum databases, patterns of ever greater size and complexity can be discovered. This is the most exciting and successful development of artificial intelligence (AI).

Thinking of New Ideas, Concepts and Solutions: Neural Processing

Let us first explore creative intelligence by the processes of thinking of new solutions by intelligently reformulating existing information. It goes without saying that to process information we need to have it available. Passing information through the system directly from input to output does not help. We need that information accessible in our memory systems.

Memory — the ability to learn, to store and retrieve information is the basic building block of all our intellectual capabilities. Concentration is about application and persistence to complete tasks. Intelligence includes the crucial skill to co-ordinate all the functions of the body to execute responses to every situation as quickly and efficiently as possible. However, "thinking" is the ability to push out the frontiers of our knowledge — how we solve problems and create innovative ideas and concepts.

However complex the procedures and however difficult it might be to understand intricate concepts, it is one thing to learn to replicate information that is already known. In most cases, we have someone else to consult to help us clarify whatever appears beyond our grasp. The very fact that somebody somewhere has thought they understood the solution to a problem indicates that a solution already exists, whatever form of storage media it might be in — stele, papyri, manuscripts, encyclopaedia, paper, silicon or biological memory system. But a completely new idea? Where does that come from? How does it arise? How can we train ourselves to maximise our chances of identifying such advances?

All forms of history are fascinating subjects to study, but surely the history of invention, of discovery, of detection, of origination, of initiation or of innovation is the most exciting and rewarding? It makes us human.

The history of all life forms is about innovation. Competition and the survival of the fittest, based upon the continuous process of variation and difference, we call evolution. Darwin's great conjecture is the basis of most modern science. It had been debated for some time before he developed his theories into a palatable form that could withstand the counter attacks of those who are fearful of new ideas in general, and inventions in particular, especially if these new ideas are demonstrably right. Yet, as with all the great stepping stones of knowledge, the present theory of evolution may be incomplete. Is the whole of life, is the miracle of the human race, purely the result of an accumulation of mistakes, transcription errors and accidents? Is the entire body of human knowledge, art, culture and commerce the sum total of chance? If we can shed light on the latter, it might illuminate our understanding of the former.

How Do We Set About Thinking About How We Create New Ideas Ab Initio?

In the earlier chapters of this book, we have tried to expand and formulate our ideas and understanding of information; what it is and how we process it. What is its meaning? We have explored how we draw information into our neural systems and learn to store it, cross-reference it and retrieve it in a myriad different ways — to learn, to remember, to retrieve, to understand the implication and explore the extrapolations of the meaning of the information we acquire, and to use one set of knowledge to illuminate another set of problems. We have explored how the mass of neural networks processes all this information. But why do we do all this? Have we explored our desire for knowledge, thirst for knowledge, curiosity, imagination, adventure, exploration, resourcefulness, study, investigation, search, quest, examination, survey, probe, analysis, and scrutiny and, perhaps the most important, initiative? What is our target? What is our goal? Why? What? When and How?

This appears to be a skill unique to *Homo sapiens*.

Self-Organising Systems

All physical and biological systems in the universe we know about are self-organising systems — *selfortems*. They have no way or process to forecast the future and can only respond to events and circumstances. The ability to predict the possible course of events is the most powerful skill in the intellectual armoury of our race. It enables us to prepare for possible eventualities, which in turn enables us to modify our environment and begin to take control of our existence on our planet and in due course, perhaps, beyond.

The facility that makes this possible is language. For the first time in the history of our planet, we could communicate with other members of our own race in intricate detail. It gave us access to the fourth dimension. We could reminisce — we could discuss how we might use the experiences of past events to help us cope with current events and problems. We could think, discuss and debate abstract concepts and contemplate how current events might develop in the future.

As we have discussed above, the key to successful reactive intelligence is speed of response — minimum information and maximum speed. Stopping to think does not enter the equation. Quite simply the physics would not support interfering with the transmission of an electrical signal. However, thinking starts with the ability to appreciate alternatives. Faced with a novel situation and the luxury of time to contemplate our response, we can interrupt the inherited or learned reaction, reflect on recent events, evaluate alternative solutions and select the best course of action — so learn from experience and be better prepared and respond more effectively in the future. We have evolved the skill to extrapolate what we know of the 'here and now' to predict possible eventualities. We continuously ask ourselves and debate with others the question "if this happens what will follow?"

The brain, specifically the neural networks of the brain, like all other systems in the universe, is also a self-organising system. The neurons have no way of knowing whether some new piece of information will be extremely useful in the future, or never be used again. Therefore, every time a neural network or structure is activated, it is strengthened so that, if it is used again, it will operate more efficiently. Axons and dendrites are insulated, and synapses-strengthened. New links will be established relating each repetition to the circumstances of that repetition, widening our facility for future recall, even enabling us sometimes to recall when we previously remembered a memory.

When we explored language, we observed that, initially, we learned words that are labels for things linked to sensory experiences — we relate the word "mummy" to her image, smell, taste and touch. Then we learn words for actions linked to muscular activity. Then we begin to learn and use words that do not map to things and actions — words for *abstract concepts and ideas*. These neural structures are not anchored to neural structures associated with the impressions and sensations input by the sensory and other organs but *are independent of physical things*. The neural structures for abstract words are just linked to other neurons and only have meaning in terms of other words. We have a foundation for thinking — a cerebral activity independent of the current immediate hurly burly of survival and the pressures of everyday life.

What Tools Do We Have to Achieve This Feat?

The stimulus of a visual image creates a new neural structure in the form of a new neural pathway. If an image is repeated, it follows the same pathway. A new "neural record" or "memory" has been formed, and if this neural structure is stimulated in the future, it is able to generate a similar impression and sensation to the impression and sensation that originally created it. Antonio Damasio argues that memory is all about feelings, sensations and emotions, and what operates for vision applies to all the other senses.

The Evolutionary Foundation of Thinking

It is a long stretch from this basic facility to the highly sophisticated structures we all take for granted today. Over millennia, we have evolved the ability to create ever more sophisticated links, relationships and cross references so that we can not only recognise previously seen images (and other sensory experiences) but also we can recall and retrieve information from different sources. For instance, from a system's point of view, it is one thing to recognise a picture of London we have seen before. It is an order of magnitude more complex to retrieve the answer to the question "What is the capital of Britain?" Furthermore, it is substantially more complex to work out the implications of experiences and extrapolate one set of experiences to solve other problems. There is one intriguing possibility. As soon as animals could move around, survival began to depend on being able to tell if a predator, potential meal or mate was travelling towards, or away, and at what speed, accelerating or decelerating, or changing direction. Having two eyes and two ears helps, but a far more accurate and precise skill depends on comparing a succession of images, and that infers that the brain evolved the ability to hold one image long enough to compare it with the next. This basic ability to "interrupt" and pause the automatic response may provide a window of opportunity to be able to pause in decision making and evaluate alternatives — the evolutionary foundation of thinking.

This gives us all the properties of a processing system. New sensations grow neural structures that can reproduce those sensations. Experiences are cross-referenced together so that memories can be recalled and retrieved from an ever-widening range of related information. We can pause and evaluate alternatives. We can create and experiment with "virtual" experiences in the abstract. We can create memories of events that have *not* happened like the design of a plot for a novel, and predict alternative possible developments and build innovative neural responses to, and make provision for, future eventualities.

However, this does not solve the conundrum of how simple neurons — even if there are trillions of them — apparently capable only of generating electrochemical signals can create the staggeringly sophisticated capabilities of our twenty-first century brains. Here our experience of computing provides an answer.

Turing Universal Machine

Alan Turing demonstrated that a universal machine, capable only of adding, subtracting and jumping to a new instruction, is capable of being programmed to forecast the weather, beat chess masters, navigate satellites and win quizzes. In doing so he created the age of computing.

The brain could be said to be a biological universal machine. Its simple basic functions can be programmed to execute almost anything. Programming in human terms is initially about learning and experience — acquiring as much of the accumulated knowledge of the community as practical. Subsequently, it is using that knowledge to conceive, tease out and test innovative new ideas and concepts: what we call thinking, or creativity.

Neurons and synapses operate rather like a biological analogue version of a semiconductor — like a transistor. Transistors in our ubiquitous digital binary computers can do only one thing. They can be in one of two states. Two transistors, therefore, can be programmed to emulate four states — 00, 01, 10 and 11, or the more familiar 0, 1, 2 and 3. Neuron nuclei can transmit a quanta of electrochemical energy along their axons and across a synapse to the dendrites of an adjacent neuron (muscle, gland or other organ). The strength and efficiency of each pattern of signals in every message is modulated by the ambient state of the surroundings. Transistors can respond precisely and only to their program. Any other result is an error. Mitochondria in each neuron nucleus generate electrical energy from nutrients pumped into them by astrocyte cells from the blood stream. Neurons exhibit some of the attributes of living organisms in their own right. There is, therefore, an element of uncertainty on how each neuron reacts. An unexpected reaction might be an *innovative new idea.*

When synapses receive a signal along the axon from their nucleus, they may, or may not, transmit a signal to an adjacent dendrite, dependent upon the ambient chemical mix of neurotransmitters, messenger molecules and hormones — our current emotional state. Having once transmitted a signal, synapses tend to go into closed mode for a variable length of time. It is possible that the capacity to transmit a signal, the strength of that signal, is also modified by the width of the synaptic gap. This gap may be variable according to the tension across the synapse. The tension across individual synapses, local groups of networks or conceivably the synapses of the whole brain may have implications for whether we are partly, fully or deeply asleep; anaesthetised; partly awake, alert or concentrating hard; or executing tasks semi-automatically in "autopilot".

The genius of the electronic binary digital computer is the facility to use completely standard groups of transistors (connected together to form registers or bytes) for many different purposes. What the number in a register stands for depends on what the programmer designates it for, including which instruction it is, whether a character or the dots of a digital image, which colour that dot is, which subroutine, which operating system or even which program. An operating program is nothing more than a stream of 0 s and 1s but usually involves trillions of them.

Over the Past Few Thousand Years We Have Developed a Rather Similar Facility

We have learned to grow neural networks which can generate strings of electrochemical signals and assign them sounds — words! Every time one of these networks is stimulated, the pattern of electrochemical instructions activates the vocal chords, lungs, mouth and tongue to say that word out loud. Every time our ears hear that pattern of sound, the mirror image of that neural pattern activates all the cross-referenced and related neural links, giving us a rich impression and sensation of the "meaning" of that word. More significantly, when a person speaks that word it stimulates a similar pattern of neural activity in the brains of everyone who is in earshot.

Most research on language has concentrated on the immense advantages of language as a medium of communication. Important as this is, there are two other fundamental benefits:

(1) The brain has had to accommodate 100,000 words and more — and that is only in one language — recognise them instantly with their meaning and link them together in myriad combinations. No other species has evolved any facility even in this ballpark.

(2) Secondly, as we noted in Chapter 5, words allow us to reminisce, relate the past to the present and extrapolate our experiences into predicting possible future eventualities. We can ask questions and exchange ideas. Possibly alone in the universe, we have found a way of overcoming the inherent weakness of all self-organising systems.

We can speculate what might happen in the future and make provision for contingencies. This has enabled us to modify our environment and so dominate our world.

Computers can only execute the programs, uploaded by the designers. We design programs to help us write program, we design programs that learn from experience and we design programs that, in turn, write program. We secure all this with software locks. But every software lock has a software key. However sophisticated the programs we develop, a more refined program will always be able to exceed it, or "hack" into it. On the other hand, the hardware is always fixed.

The brain mind has neither restriction. There is no outside programmer — except in the sense of the parent, teacher, coach, professor or tutor, but in the end, they can only advise. Ultimately, we can only program ourselves. However, the brain has two attributes that put its way ahead of any computer existing or conceived. Repetition and usage strengthens and makes more efficient the neural networks involved. The hardware is enhanced. Furthermore, electrochemical activity creates new links: the software actually grows new hardware — some trillion structures of new hardware. Observing this phenomenon carefully, we can see that the *brain* — the neurons, glia, etc. only transmit signals, reinforce themselves and grow links entirely automatically in response to their usage. The brain is still only a self-organising system. It is the electrochemical activity over those networks that do the work. That electrochemical activity is what we recognise as our *mind*. The best example is our invention of words — it is our mind that can link words to memories, link words to present events and link words to describe possible futures, think and create.

Writing

Only some 3,000 years ago, we learned to write — to draw images and shapes to represent sounds, so that when we see the image of a written word we hear it in our heads. When we want to write a letter or word, we have learned to extend the neural representation of that word to include a set of neural instructions that are able to activate the muscles of our hands and fingers to draw that image, or hit the appropriate key on our computer.

It is important to observe two things. Different communities assign different shapes and sounds for letters and words — writing in Arabic or speaking in Chinese — same neurons but different designations.

Silent Speech: The Language of Creative Intelligence

Secondly, within the last 1,000 years we have learned to short-circuit speech. Chapter 6 and Appendix 25 (all appendices are hosted on www. BrainMindForum.org/appendices) have introduced the concept that, instead of speaking and hearing words we can talk silently in our heads. We hear the words with absolute clarity, yet we have not moved the muscles of the vocal chords at all. We have the sensation of having heard the words yet no sound has activated our ears. This has transformed our capacity to think. (Thinking previously was out loud — many people report that the act of writing helps and contributes to generate innovative ideas.)

Thinking

Thinking, therefore, is the stringing together of groups of words in an ever more complex hierarchy of ever more sophisticated meanings — working out how the natural world works, how others may react to our actions, what may happen tomorrow and writing a better program to beat a chess playing computer. Then we assign novel words to represent phrases, sentences, even complex new hypotheses. The two words 'string theory' embrace more than 100 years of thinking about physics.

As we debate one with another, both our brains are only activating neural structures and synapses and activating glandular activity to generate meaning. We can communicate because we have both assigned similar neural structures and patterns of structures to have similar mutually agreed meanings.

Computing systems from Babbage's difference engine, via punched cards and programmable electronic digital computers to iPads, can use the same hardware to carry out an infinite variety of tasks. Babbage did this by adjusting a series of disks. Tabulators could change packs of punched cards; computers upload a new program. The human brain goes one step further.

Every idea and thought we have, generates neural activity, and, as we have shown, neural activity creates new neural links and structures. Every idea and thought we have ever had are recorded in our brain. Just as we store every sense — image, sound, smell, taste and touch, so we store every thought, idea, concept and ambition. If that thought appears irrelevant, inconsequential or transitory, it may not be developed and fade; although if we have that same thought again or if someone else articulates that same thought, we will remember and recognise it.

Just as we develop, widen, strengthen and elaborate simple memories into complex structures, which we can recall in different circumstances, and retrieve for different purposes by adding and widening their relationships and cross references, their meanings and their implications, and extrapolating them into different situations, we can develop and augment abstract thoughts into ever more complex structures, We can then try and explain them to our friends and colleagues, hoping that they will be able to build similar structures and so begin to see how these innovations will help better understand problems both are interested in solving.

Thinking in Modalities

We do not only think in words. If words were the sole medium of thought, then that would indicate no other species have any such capability, however modest. We can think in many modalities. Architects think in shapes and spaces, musicians in chords and harmonies, programmers in patterns, designers in symmetries, chefs in tastes and textures and so forth. This helps us understand the neural processes of both thinking and memory that this builds upon. The neural representations of both our memories and our thoughts are not binary digital structures. They are analogue representations of impressions, sensations and emotions. Words have enabled us to overlay these structures with fixed and definable meanings we can all agree upon. However, we find it very difficult, if not impossible to articulate shapes, harmonies, patterns, symmetries or tastes. Similarly, we have not yet found words to adequately define beauty, leadership, and famously, the redness of a rose, and the things we group together and call *qualia*, which we discuss further in Chapters 13, 14 and 17.

The most exciting implication of this hypothesis is that there is no limit to the capacity of the human brain to think. Some people understand new information and ideas more slowly than others, some people create new ideas and concepts more slowly than others, some people may react and recognise patterns and solve riddles more slowly than others, but everyone has an unlimited capacity to learn to think. There is no limit to the ingenuity of those thoughts — in art, science, medicine, economics, engineering, literature, jurisprudence, invention and business.

There are many different techniques to help us improve our ability to remember. We can learn to concentrate. There is much debate as to whether we can learn to be more intelligent. However, there is no doubt we can learn to think. Now that we are beginning to understand the fundamental neural processes, we can begin to develop techniques to structure our natural capacity to think. Like the programmer, we can begin to design how we will solve a problem — amass the information, the evidence, past experiences — and begin to group ideas together: much as the coder writes subroutines to execute basic functions, categorise, rank, define and name these constituent parts, then build ever more complex hierarchies of these *neur*al mod*ules* (neurules) to execute ever more sophisticated functions.

And this is a skill we can help everyone to learn. Like the programmers, we can devise ways to think about thinking — ways to communicate thinking so that groups can think together, so that individuals can specialise and the whole group can think more powerfully than the sum of its individuals.

Thus, we can begin to see a pathway from the simplest memory structure to the most complex human capabilities. And all just neurons linked together by synapses: quadrillion electrochemical signals over trillions of neurons modulated by waves from myriad electromagnetic fields.

Unlimited Capacity

Just as a computer is useless without a program, so a brain is useless without electrochemical activity — in fact it is no longer alive. Equally a program is useless without a computer to run on. Similarly, patterns of electrochemical activity, however sophisticated, are useless without a brain, and for that matter, a body. No body, no impressions, no sensations, no emotions.

We can now say with some certainty that the *brain* — that mass of neurons and glia awash with chemicals — cannot think, any more than it can feel pain. It is able to transmit electrochemical signals, strengthen existing networks and grow new links and structures. That is all.

It is the *mind* that exclusively does the thinking. It is the electrochemical activity over those neurons that do what we recognise as thinking. And it does it in impressions, sensations and emotions generated by, and in turn generating words, supported by other modalities — spaces, harmonies, patterns, symmetries but predominately in words.

And there is no limit to its capabilities.

There is an alternative way of describing the process of creative thinking and problem solving.

Logic versus Innovation

Logic is about finding a new answer to an existing question given all our current knowledge.

In these chapters, we have explored a number of possibilities. We know that we can silently initiate assembling a string of words. The poetry effect describes how we do this. We can rearrange these words till they generate the particular meaning we are seeking. We can do this with sounds. It is how composers come up with a tune, or how architects design buildings. This is where the concept of symbols can be so powerful. A string of words can be given a label, a new symbol. A string of sounds make up a symbol of a tune and a string of spaces the symbol of a new structure.

We can rearrange all these symbols into new patterns from which a new solution may emerge, where the whole is greater than the sum of the parts, and we have an answer to our question. Thinking introduces a new element to this process. We can rearrange a number of words, then give this group a label — invent a new word and symbol. We do the same with all the other modalities. Now we can do more than just rearrange all this at one level. We can build hierarchies of multimedia symbols. Thus, we can build a mass of apparently unrelated information into an elegant new proposition — the pinnacle of a pyramid of information sculpted by Occam's razor.

We have noted in Chapter 14 and Appendix 25 (all appendices are hosted on www.BrainMindForum.org/appendices) the power of emergence and will do so again. Now we can add another very powerful tool to our neural abilities, which often gets a bad press — the ability and process of creating jargon and sound bites. Like so much in life, so easy to criticise and so difficult to create.

The ancient background skills of general intelligence have facilitated the ability to learn an ever widening panoply of specific individual intelligent skills. They are the relative ability to acquire information and understand its meaning — to recognise the sound patterns of words, phrases, music and their meaning; then, more recently, the optical patterns of written words, phrases and the visual arts; assemble words and phrases to speak, write and contemplate concepts and ideas cogently and logically to think, make decisions, solve problems, innovate, imagine and predict the possible future course of events.

A definition of creative intelligence is thinking of new ideas, concepts and solutions. The neural processing is the efficiency and capacity to pause, extrapolate existing information, explore, evaluate and compare alternative solutions to identify new, better more effective and efficient results; recognise this as an improvement and organise this new information in a coherent manner that is understandable and useful to others.

Observation, feedback and repetition enable this library of specific learned intelligent abilities to be continuously improved, expanded and executed more efficiently.

CHAPTER TWELVE

PHYSICAL, EMOTIONAL, HOLISTIC AND MEDICAL INTELLIGENCE

Intelligence is finding good resolutions to three sets of factors: your concerns, your capabilities, and your circumstances.

Guy Claxton, *Intelligence in the Flesh*

Physical Intelligence

While the subject of intelligence has been debated since the seventeenth century, it has only been the centre of attention since Darwin's *On the Origin of the Species*. Therefore, it has tended to be thought about and discussed exclusively as a function of the intellect. This coincided with the growing wealth of the industrial revolution and the beginning of universal education. Less than 5% of the population went to the universities, which were beginning to broaden their studies away from purely religious instruction. The land owners, farmers, squires, parsons, doctors and knights of the shires dominated the countryside and sent their sons to the public boarding schools to be educated. The lawyers, tradesmen and merchants dominated the towns. Every self-respecting town had a grammar school for local boys, often well-endowed by generations of alumni, which took care to teach the brighter boys in their community whatever their birth status.

The heroes of the nineteenth century were the factory owners, engineers and the Royal Navy, the men who governed the empire and the entrepreneurs. Britain was very proud of the men who generated its vastly expanding wealth. The farm labourers, by far the largest numbers, and the mill and shop workers and domestic servants were largely ignored. It did not occur to Britain's elite that this clear majority of the population had any intelligence at all, even if anyone thought about it. In 1909, a parliamentary commission thought that only 10% of the population would ever be able to learn to drive a motor car. (In 1980, it was a big surprise to everyone in Whitehall that the whole population could operate computers and even have them in their homes!)

The twentieth century began to see changes. The Trades Unions and Labour Party initially had as one of their principle objectives universal education as the way out of poverty — in fact to implement the demands of Cromwell's Army Council in 1648. In the first half of the century, the idea of an "intelligence test" was seen as a way children from poor backgrounds could obtain a good education. An academic, Cyril Burt, produced evidence that the IQ test was the ideal method of selection. Sadly, it turned out he had falsified his statistics and the IQ test fell into disrepute. In the 1960s The Robins Commission led to the building of new universities with upwards of 25% of the population attending them. In 1990, the polytechnics were rebranded as universities, so by the twenty-first century nearly 50% of the population enjoyed an academic education and the curriculum of the schools replaced the controversial 11+ tests with 16+ and 18+ tests to select the academically inclined for further education.

It is a curious fact that *equality* is now considered more important than *excellence*.

It is ironic that it is this cohort that is being groomed for the careers that the computing revolution is on the cusp of making redundant.

Throughout this whole saga, it has occurred to very few that intelligence is very far from being only the province of the intellectually inclined.

Sport as a Full-Time Career

From the 1960s, sports of many kinds have been growing as full-time careers. If anyone has been prepared to look, it is very clear that nearly all the rules of intellectual mental ability apply equally to physical ability.

Observe two young children kicking a ball. One easily kicks it straight to the target seemingly effortlessly, the other is all over the place, nearly misses and the ball which goes nowhere near the target.

Eye muscle coordination is a natural phenomenon very like the ability to manipulate words or numbers. Watch a tennis player adjust their handling of their racket to return an opponent's volley, hoping to adjust for very sophisticated details like the spin they hope to notice in time, and so on. Watched in slow motion skilful players seem to anticipate their opponents move before that opponent has struck the ball. In other words, responding to incomplete information as fast as possible. Trying to build identical skills, in another dimension, to predict the future and identify patterns in streams of information.

Ball games generally emphasise the ability to quickly predict the opponent's moves and respond exactly correctly with clinical skill. Little different from chess? Just muscle control in place of imagination.

The whole subject of intelligence and intelligence testing have been so dominated by the academic community, particularly over the last century that people even express surprise that there is any other sort of intelligence.

Torbjörn Vestberg at the Karolinska Institute in Stockholm has been assessing footballers over a 3-year period "When you are more successful in soccer, you have cognitive flexibility, you can shift focus, you can supress behaviour, you can be creative and find solutions very fast" (*PLoS One*, doi.org/bz 95). Jocelyn Faubert at the University of Montreal comments "It is on the fly decision making. Reading all the inputs, taking all that in and acting on it does require fundamental cognitive capacities."

That is only the tip of the iceberg of physical dexterity — physical skill and physical intelligence. There are a wide variety of input skills associated with the sensory organs. Wine tasting — training the taste buds to identify a great vintage: the ability to blend scents to achieve a standard product; ability to identify and match colours. Then the incredible dexterity of the output skills — the skills of the cabinet maker, the designer, the maker and decorator of exquisite china, and the ability to cut and sew clothes. And we have not mentioned the musicians, artists, actors and the entire range of designers, inventors, researchers, entrepreneurs, programmers, engineers and architects, and all the creative professions that the computing revolution is releasing into the community.

Watch a pianist play a whole piano concerto entirely from memory, with exquisite timing and passion. That is physical intelligence of a high order.

Computers can do 90% of the work of the accounting community, 90% of all legal work, 80%, at least, of administrative work, and the latest news suggests 100% of driving vehicles.

Computers may do many things, but they are unlikely to excel at research, innovation, design and entrepreneurship.

A significant value of intelligence is the ability to plan strategy and implement tactics both on the grand scale, down to the minutia of everyday living. Clearly intellectual skills are valuable to consider the possibilities and decide on the best solution, but so are physical skills to carry out the agreed actions. If we look more closely are these abilities and aptitudes so very different?

There is another psychological observation we can make. There is a strong body of opinion that young people, in particular should not suffer the indignity of failing examinations, yet all sport is predicated on competition. Surely there is a disconnection here?

Emotional Intelligence

Emotion, passion, sensation, impression, perception, feeling, enthusiasm, eagerness, pleasure, enjoyment, reward and gratification, play a significant role in all our neural activities. Until recently, these attributes were thought to modify intelligence rather than be a type of intelligence in their own right and to a great extent this is true because they play such an important role in giving meaning to information. However, there are distinct areas that although emotion is very much integrated, it does stand alone.

Interpersonal behaviour, or empathy, is a major part of human experience. How we behave towards each other is one of the principal subjects that every religion has high on its lists of instructions. It fits into our general definition of "responding to incomplete information fast".

Across a Crowded Room Effect

One experience most people have experienced once or twice in life, when they enter a crowded room and see another person and instantaneously feel attracted to them. The first curious fact is that it is almost always reciprocal — just between two people. This is different to the person who turns all eyes or the person with such a strong character that instantly commands attention. People talk about being on the same wavelength. There is no doubt this effect exists, and powerfully so, but none of our sophisticated measuring systems are sufficiently accurate to pick up what this might be. We know quite a lot about the electromagnetic fields that active neurons generate. We are aware of the waves that sweep across the brain. This phenomenon also works with film actors so it cannot be a physical communication, more to do with visual images.

This effect can work the opposite way, and two people may meet and instantly feel repelled and cannot stay in the same room together. There are plenty of examples where one person seems to develop a very powerful influence over another or group. Surveys of young children in school environments exhibit a variety of behaviours in this general area. Some children are naturally gregarious and are in all the gangs, and are generally popular — some are natural leaders, some naturally followers, some adventurous and some cautious, risk adverse; some risk takers. Others seem not to mix and are upset by this: others are loners and are entirely happy with that status.

This phenomenon is part of behaviour, character and personality. We do not know much more than this, but these phenomena certainly exist. A part of intelligence? Much food for the psychologists.

Drive and Enthusiasm

A very central function of intelligence is the ability to learn. Large amounts of research, thought, effort and hard work have gone into devising ever better ways of helping (particularly young) people learn about this fascinating world. Yet none of these ideas, methods and regimes have much purchase, or effect unless a student *wants* to learn. There are many books on this subject with strong research about background, family, upbringing, peer pressure, sink schools and hopeless teaching. It is, however, worth repeating two observations.

All that we have learned about the structure and function of the brain mind is that everyone has the capacity to learn everything *if they really want to*, and if they can gain access to the relevant information. Wikipedia is a great facilitator. Google and **Massive Open Online Courses** (MOOCS) are carrying us along the path to provide just that.

If children, or adults for that matter, are told they are stupid, *and they believe it*, then they will be stupid. There are far too many examples of exasperated teachers destroying their students in this way.

Competition and being better than the other team is central to all learning. Thus, the argument comes back again to identifying each individual's talent as early as possible, nurturing, developing and encouraging it. Education will look staggeringly different in less than a generation.

We know very little about the variations to what we consider normal. Until recently, dyslexia was thought to be a sign of laziness and children were punished. Nowadays, some very prestigious architectural practices only recruit dyslexic staff. Autistic children who seem to have little or no emotional and interpersonal intelligence can have wonderful abilities in quite surprising ways. Trainee doctors are often asked what their advice should be if a parent with all sorts of problems presents a pregnancy where the foetus has a long list of complications. If they think that perhaps it would be best to advise termination, their lecturer explains why they might be looking at a future Beethoven. Read Kepler's biography. In twenty-first century Europe, he would undoubtedly have been taken into care from the moment of his birth! Delacroix, however, cautioned his students to "learn technique, it will not stop you being a genius".

In the small number of increasingly tolerant and generous communities, we are learning a great deal about the biology and neurology of sex. There are clearly physical and mental developments that sometimes are not fully synchronised and take place at various times both in the womb and throughout puberty. This can generate a wide spectrum of entirely natural effects, and we begin to realise how shockingly intolerant we have been in our ignorance to generations of our ancestors and many around us today.

Elation, Depression and Stress

These play a symbiotic role between the endocrine system and the brain. We explore this more in Section "Medical Intelligence". However, there is one aspect worth exploring here.

Strength of Formation and Accessing of Memory

We can all observe that certain memories seem to be very strong, others quite vague. Most people can recall, often in great detail their first sexual experience. We know that the brain creates a speculative neural link whenever two neurons fire together. This link can be transitory or, if not used melt away. However, if the situation is very emotional that first link can be very strong.

Similarly, in a crisis we can often recall information quickly and in considerable clarity simply because the system is throwing all its emotion and energy at the problem.

External Relationship Intelligence: Mirror Neurons

An important aspect of all our lives is our communications with others, including empathy, leadership, charisma, movement, pheromones, touch, behaviour and personality. The characteristics of our personalities are directly controlled from the brain mind modulated by cocktails of emotions generated by the endocrine system. These are expanded at Appendix 17 (all appendices are hosted on www.BrainMindForum.org/appendices).

A major part of our behaviour is determined by the characteristics of our personalities, which are as diverse as our finger prints. We have for a long time been aware of the phenomenon that there are leaders and followers. Interestingly, there are neural functions that are partly responsible. We minutely watch others and tend to imitate other people's behaviour — it is a major part of learning. We have a well-defined feedback function both to check our muscles have done what we intended and to register the responses to our behaviour by others.

We have identified a series of mirror neurons that are activated both when we carry out an act and when we watch someone else carry out a similar act. Mirror neurons are not unique to humans. They have been found to be present in most mammals. Perhaps we should not jump to the conclusion too soon that only we are properly intelligent on this planet!

Holistic Intelligence

Dissecting the human body started clandestinely in the sixteenth century. One can still see the famous theatre in the School of Medicine at Padua where an animal was strapped to one side of a reversible table and a cadaver to the other. When the religious police raided the school, the cadaver could be instantly replaced by the inoffensive animal.

It is easy to plot the gradual development of our knowledge after the renaissance in Northern Europe. Galileo in one direction, Descartes and Isaac Newton in others. Electricity and thermodynamics in the nineteenth century. Quantum physics and psychiatry in the early twentieth. Ramon Cajal found a way of exploring neurons about the time Darwin was turning the scientific world, and most other worlds upside down. Turing's *On Computable Numbers, With an Application to the Entscheidungsproblem* was published about the same time penicillin was discovered. The discovery of deoxyribonucleic acid (DNA) closely followed the first atomic bomb.

The Dartmouth conference in 1954 raised the flag for artificial Intelligence, but human intelligence and, in particular, any discussion about consciousness were definitely off limits. People find change very difficult. The education profession fought hard to keep even word processors out of the classroom. Even now, only some of the skills of the systems designers and programmers have been very grudgingly allowed into the national curriculum. Computing is having a dynamic effect on every aspect of government and wrong footing all the economists in the Treasury, Bank of England and the profession. Creeping wage deflation is accelerating and increasing redundancies are forecast by every journalist, but as the *New Scientist* comments on the manifestos of the leading parties at the 2017 election, there is no thought in any department in government to prepare to cope with the accelerating revolution. Numbers of people suggest that the Brexit vote was a canary in the mine.

The internet has been a wake-up call for the community. The politicians are reeling from the arrival of an automated agora where everyone can have their say, and old-fashioned incompetence, half-truths and bromides are ruthlessly exposed. The educational community blissfully ignores the fact that their profession will be obsolescent in the next decades.

In the mid-1970s, Jack Fincher published *Human Intelligence*, but it proved to be before its time. Douglas Hofstadter published *Gödel, Escher & Bach* in 1979. In 1994, Francis Crick and his student Christof Koch published *The Astonishing Hypothesis*, and Steven Pinker published *The Language Instinct*. The spotlight landed on the brain, but only the brain. It was studied and analysed as a quite separate organ. Almost the entire effort was devoted to using all the various scanning devices invented in the medical profession to study and analyse which parts of the brain were responsible for what activities.

Very little thinking is targeted at basic questions about the information that computers process, and how that information is represented? How memory is formed and accessed? The cognitive neuroscientists had concentrated on the hardware, the neurons, axons, dendrites and synapses, and had made considerable progress but as Eric Kandel said in his Nobel Prize presentation "the next step must be the biological systems that drive this whole process". System, of course, is what computing is all about.

In 2015, Guy Claxton published *Intelligence in the Flesh*; Craig Venter *Life at the Speed of Light* and Daniel Dennett *Intuition Pumps* whose Chapter 24 is probably the best manual for programming a Turing machine ever written. A copy is reprinted by kind permission of Allen Lane at Appendix 32 (all appendices are hosted on www.BrainMindForum. org/appendices). Anthony Grayling published *The Age of Genius, The Seventeenth Century & the Birth of the Modern Mind*.

The flood gates opened and this book is part of the result.

The autonomics functions have been known about for a long time but only recently has it been realised that it provides much of the background operating system of the whole body, encompassing, integrating and connecting up the six major systems of the body through the central nervous system. The brain is now seen as the coordinating and cooperating centre and the learning engine of the whole body.

It can be said that it is this whole-body intelligence in the brain mind that mediates the internal relationships with the immune, cardiovascular, enteric, immune and endocrine systems, and the operation of the whole body. We can for the first time, see how everything is inter-related, interconnected and interdependent on everything else. Perhaps the biggest change in our thinking is the realisation of the importance of the endocrine system, and its key role in generating all the sensations, emotions and feeling that give bald information its complex meanings to us.

Medical Intelligence

The realisation of the dynamic connection between the brain mind and the whole body and the convergence of thought between medicine, cognitive neuroscience, biogenetics, bioelectronics, the many new scanning systems and computing, both as a processing and research support facility, and as an analogy and model of medical systems are generating a flood of new ideas in the medical community.

Acupuncture, Ancient and Modern

The stimulation of specific neurons in the central nervous system by inserting needles into various parts of the body is first reported deep in Chinese history. It has been the subject of much debate throughout the centuries. Growing knowledge of the immune system and reported recent research into direct links between the brain and the vagus nerve paves the way to enable direct brain stimulation to treat various disorders from depression to arthritis. Currently such brain stimulation is by electrodes on or inserted in the brain. However, it opens the possibility of stimulating various neural networks by initiating positive neural activity by disciplines associated with thinking, decision making and creativity. Perhaps these could be lineal descendants of meditation. There are plenty examples of fakirs who can achieve remarkable levels of control over the body entirely controlled by the brain.

Psychosomatic Illness

Intuition tells us that the state of the brain can have a dynamic effect on actual real illnesses; however, it is remarkably difficult to prove in properly established tests. The biome is very complex and any hormonal imbalance could easily upset this system. This is an area of considerable research. Stress and trauma initiated in the brain clearly generate toxic effects to many organs of the body, especially the glands that secrete hormones that generate anxiety and fear *et al.*

A great deal has been learned from the wars of the twentieth century from shell shock to post-traumatic stress disorder. Considerable success is being reported using neural modulation of critical hubs using transcranial magnetic stimulation techniques. In a parallel field, cognitive neuroscience is learning a lot from work done on the neural control of prosthetic limbs.

It might seem a shame that these advances have had to be stimulated by so much human suffering, but it is a fact that warfare has been one of the two most potent drivers of the advance in human knowledge.

Placebo and Will Power

The fact that placebos have well-proven beneficial effects is one of the more fascinating aptitudes of the whole human system. It is what presumably underlies the claimed effects of homeopathy. The comment that patients lying apparently comatose in hospital beds are fighting for their lives is often very accurate. Equally there are many reports of people "giving up" and slipping quietly away.

It is relatively understandable that someone believes that medication will help them, when it is just a placebo. Close attention by nurses and friends may play a part. But it is also proven that people who know they are receiving a placebo seem to benefit equally. Mind over matter. Is that part of intelligence?

Hypnosis

Again, this appears to be a very real phenomenon, but extremely difficult to prove. It does not help that hypnosis has been the subject of many music hall acts that are just arranged for entertainment.

As with the crowded room effect mentioned at the beginning of this chapter, this may hint at aptitudes we have that we are simply unaware of.

The Discovery of DNA Has Opened Up a Whole New Science

There is the whole extraordinary process from the formation of the zygote from two parents, right through to the birth of the foetus, and the development of an adult.

Reading the coding system of DNA opens up the potential to edit this set of instructions — genetic engineering. New techniques like Clustered Regularly Interspersed Short Palindromic Repeats (CRISPR) are making it possible to change the DNA of a foetus to break the hereditary link to reproduce illness, disease and disabilities. Everyone is aware that as we learn more about these procedures, learn more about which combinations of genes produce which results, it is more likely than not that we will be able to select various traits in subsequent generations. Selecting hair colour is one thing, but selecting levels of specific abilities quite another. Major ethical problems lie in wait for us.

Two points are worth mentioning here.

Observably, the genome is a remarkably sophisticated information memory system. The well-known double helix is made up of four base pairs or nucleotides: adenine, cytosine, guanine and thymine. One possibility is that while some of these codes, possibly indirectly, are for the construction in due course of proteins or *hardware*, others are for spacing and on/off switches, or *software*, and yet others for the generation or conduit of energy. One possibility is that the fourth might be part of an intelligent error-checking system.

Sophistication of Drugs

The discovery of antibiotics opened the flood gates on the research and development of new medications, and this new industry has grown almost as fast as the computing industry. Huge advances have been made in the health of many communities. Perhaps the discovery of the ability to control our own reproduction is the most important development in civilisation — before we overwhelm our planet with more people than it can support.

We have learned one other very important point. We have always suspected that every single individual is unique. We are finding that medical preparations that save lives for the majority have little or no effect on a minority and can actually do harm to a few.

Tailoring Drugs to Individuals: Genetic Engineering

Most drugs operate through the immune system interacting with the cardiovascular system, which, in turn is influenced by the endocrine system and back to the functions of the central nervous system. The whole, in nearly call cases is modulated and activated by the autonomic functions.

In other words, the whole system is involved. Thus, an industry larger even than the pharmaceutical industry now will develop to match medicine to individuals. To do this must involve our individual DNA becoming public knowledge.

Another massive series of ethical problems. It has been technically possible to hold patient records centrally, so that patients can be treated safely from wherever they are, and potential epidemics quickly identified, since the 1970s. However, the National Health Service spends remarkably large sums of money annually as individual health organisations continue to operate incompatible systems.

This opens up major areas of development to the medical profession. Inevitably it is only possible to test the efficacy of new drugs in a degree of isolation; however, it is becoming increasingly apparent that cocktails of drugs administered with the best of intentions may be doing as much harm as good.

Future Perfect

DNA profiles and family histories will increasingly become a standard part of an individual's records.

Similarly, as we begin to take on board the implications of our realisation that the whole body is one single system, of which the brain is just one part, completely new ways of approaching life-long health care will become a major priority, in parallel with life-long learning. Life expectancy has nearly doubled over the last two centuries. 100% continuous permanent monitoring of every citizen, technically feasible today, could extend life expectancy by another 50 years over this century. Prosthetic brain interfaces and synthetic biological engineering could well take pressure off the memory systems and so extend the vibrant life of the brain to match the vibrant life of the body.

It is difficult to see how medical intelligence will affect robots, but it will have a major impact on the development of human intelligence. Prosthetic neural links may open the door of the human body to foreign bodies whose effects we may not be able to conceive at the moment. Similarly, synthetic biology may inevitably generate new variant symbiotic life forms.

Medical intelligence, prosthetic and synthetic interfaces in harmony with other aspects of human intelligence may vastly improve the health of future generations of *Homo sapiens* — the exact opposite of the doomsayers, Hollywood film makers and science fiction authors who predict singularities and the reduction of humans to slavery.

CHAPTER THIRTEEN

MEASUREMENT, IMPLICATIONS AND EXTRAPOLATION OF INTELLIGENCE

Measurement of Intelligence, Aptitude and Ability

Most people agree that it would be useful to have a reliable way of measuring ability. We can select people who are tall, people who are strong, people who can run fast, people who will be good leaders and many other specific attributes. For more specific complex abilities, we have devised a pantheon of tests and interview techniques, but, curiously, we do not have any agreed comprehensive schedule of human abilities. In an ever more complex, competitive world, it is increasingly important to be able to identify everyone's talent, nurture and develop that aptitude for the benefit of, not only every individual, but also the whole community. Surely it is time to begin to address this deficiency?

Some aptitudes are relatively easy to recognise. The army, the Regular Commissions Board, has experimented with various methods of selecting potential officers for training. The test that has worked the best over time, is the simplest one — to give a group a task and just watch who leads and who follows. It is known as the Bion leaderless task test.

In the early days of computing, all sorts of tests were tried to identify potential programmers. What worked the best was to describe a problem and provide several possible steps to solve it and see who assembled the steps and found the answer, i.e. to program. It is easy to test if someone is a competent cook, driver or pilot. We have a clearly defined objective.

Measuring intellectual aptitudes like "intelligence" is, observably, far more complex, especially as we have had so many different definitions of what we think intelligence is.

For most of the last century, the only method of measuring intelligence at all was the intelligence quotient (IQ) test. This test is broadly targeted on some limited aspects of the responsive systems; the system that has evolved from survival intelligence as the foundation of our sentient systems. It includes some pattern-matching aspects of acquisitive intelligence, but not the more creative aspects, largely because we have not had much success in defining and measuring creativity.

We can learn a lot about the attempts to devise tests from the people who have invented what we have, what their skill sets were and what their objectives were — and still are. We noted in Chapter 9 that frequently the attributes that are considered to be the most attractive change over time, much like fashions.

Ability has been a valued commodity, much prized down the millennia, but a serious study of the intellect has only really been the subject of serious study since Darwin published *On the Origin of Species*. From that point onwards, almost all the thinking on this subject has been centred on intellectual, academic and memory skills to the almost complete exclusion of the practical and physical skills. Similarly, any research on testing has been closely related to theories of education, which, in turn have been subject to the political, ideological and social engineering pressures noted above.

The situation is changing fast. In the last few years, our understanding of intelligence has begun to offer some new solutions, and the pressure to find better answers is beginning to increase as we realise the educational model that suited the industrial revolution needs radical changes to be fit for purpose to enable the community to prosper and flourish in the computing age.

Our growing understanding of information has helped us realise that to be intelligent one must have information to be intelligent about. As we have seen above, information and intelligence are inextricably linked.

The key to understanding information is to be able to identify patterns. In the definition of "survival intelligence" we refer to responding to *incomplete information* fast. One aspect of intelligence is how quickly we can identify a pattern in that incomplete information.

We have also learned that the skills we learn — our individual library of applications, operate partly in background mode as part of the autonomic functions of the central nervous system, of which we are only partially aware, and partly in foreground mode of which we are fully aware.

Existing IQ tests and their derivatives can only measure the efficiency of the foreground applications as they operate on the autonomic platform. Thus, we are measuring general "G" intelligence indirectly, which introduces all sorts of problems. Which applications do we chose? Number sequences? Pattern Extensions? Odd man out? Magic squares? Noting variants, identifying series, following logical arguments and so on. Whether we can answer them depends on whether we can identify these applications and then how quickly we can execute them. Who does the selection? What prejudice might that introduce? Can these be learned and/or gamed. Clearly a student can be coached in recognising which type each question is. The student still has to answer the individual question as fast as possible but recognising which application to use provides a significant advantage.

A lot of work has gone into trying to exclude cultural bias, but inevitably the wider a student's general knowledge the greater the advantage.

Longitudinal Studies

The University of Edinburgh unearthed some IQ test results from the 1930s. They were able to follow up many of those that took these tests and analyse their subsequent life experiences. There was a clear bias that those with higher QI scores had enjoyed higher paid careers, more stable family relationships, and, intriguingly, better health. Do these findings suggest that IQ tests are measuring a lot more than simple intelligence — whole body capabilities in some way? Or do these results suggest that IQ success led to better teenage education? Did higher IQ suggest more healthy lifestyles or more healthy inheritance? Alternatively, did more healthy lifestyles or more healthy inheritance lead to higher IQ scores? Cause or effect?

Games or Reality?

One problem that it is difficult to overcome is that the actual test experience is rather like a quiz game. It does not emulate real world experience. In everyday life, the vast majority of practical problems are not packaged up in neat little questions. In life, making decisions and cracking problems often depends on identifying what the difficulty is that one is trying to solve. Often framing such problems almost as though they are IQ type questions, indicates the answer.

There is a strong argument that identifying the category of each question is the real measure of intelligence. Once having established this, executing the answer is relatively straight forward.

Comparative, Not Absolute

In all IQ tests and their derivatives, a number of questions have to be answered in a given time. Therefore, this is a test of quantity not quality. Equally, the number of questions answered correctly in the time allowed is not that person's IQ. This number is compared to all the others taking this test of the same age. Thus, the IQ quoted is based on the average of the peerhood. 100 is average. 130 suggests that person is in the top 10% of their cohort. Below 80 suggests that person is in need of assistance.

Young people, in particular, tend to advance in fits and starts, definitely not at a smooth rate throughout puberty, and so at any one time a cohort of the same age will have members at different stages of development.

Birth Skills

If we observe the first few months of life, every baby's first priority is to identify, recognise and remember the pattern of mother's face from the stream of signals from the eyes; her smell and her taste. An important next skill is to learn to balance — stand up and walk. For *Homo sapiens*, a high priority is to identify, recognise and remember the pattern of mother's words, and to learn to imitate, copy and reproduce sound patterns to speak their first words. If baby is looked after by a variety of carers, all sorts of problems arise.

These are all semi-automatic learning processes and are firmly embedded in the background autonomic functions of the central nervous system, strengthening the argument that intelligence is very much connected with the efficiency of the extended autonomic system.

A few years later, many children extend these skills of balance to learn to ride a bicycle and add a new application to their library of abilities. Once they have learned what to do, the balancing part migrates into the background mode, and steering, and where to go into foreground-awareness mode.

This suggests two ways of measuring intelligence more efficiently. First, we can add a far wider spectrum of applications to even out the bias of the present very limited skill set. Alternatively, we can try and remove the bias of the applications to reveal the underlying general intelligence. For instance, as balance is part of autonomic intelligence and part of the cycling application, could its value be computed separately and deducted from both sides of the balance sheet isolating the "pure" intelligence?

General Intelligence, a Stable Quotient

Many people are surprised that their quotient remains constant from 11+ to 50+ and further, which suggests that intelligence is not a learnable skill. If general intelligence is the efficiency of the autonomic functions, this implies that what we are actually measuring is the physical signal speed of the axons, dendrites, synapses and nuclei. It is the library of myriad applications that we learn, which accumulates over time and which we can be intelligent *about*.

Application Intelligence

There is every reason why each of these applications should individually be competitively more efficient, faster and more accurate, but these applications are about acquiring information, recalling information, carrying out tasks and making decisions. The key is that we are marrying two attributes: (1) the efficient, faster and more accurate autonomic function of the central nervous and (2) the efficient, faster and more accurate functions of each application.

Thus, from every point of view, it is a very rough and ready tool. It seems extraordinary that intelligent people could, and still can, believe that a one hour test taken just once on a random day, could possibly measure accurately the skills and abilities of a human being. However, it is effectively all we have. Well, not quite.

Speed

We have identified speed of reaction as a key component of intelligence. It is particularly important in comparing relative performance. The IQ test depends on answering questions designed by others, and therefore, inevitably, will be biased according to their perspectives. We can explore alternative ways of measuring the speed of processing that are not dependent on human questions and measure the function directly.

Alternative Measurements of Speed of Intelligence Reactions

Being able to pick up new information quickly is an undoubtedly valuable skill.

A number of research projects show unequivocally that every image we see for at least 20 seconds creates a minimal neural trace. (See Appendix 28, all appendices are hosted on www.BrainMindForum. org/appendices.) This research could be extended to vary the time exposure of the original images and so establish a value for the minimum time it takes for each participant to form a basic trace. One would expect this to vary between individuals, and over age. It would be very interesting to see if this value correlated with standard IQ. If it proved to be sufficiently sensitive, it could be used to measure the efficacy of treatments for various types of dementia.

It has been observed for some time that if a person looks steadily at a three-dimensional outline image of a box it will continuously reverse back and forward. It would be useful to measure the time delay of switching, and see if this value correlated with IQ and memory formation.

It is entirely possible that patterns of electrochemical signals are transmitted along axons and dendrites at varying speeds. It would be expected that these speeds would be varied by the state of the hormonal ambience — the person's emotional state.

Patterns of electrochemical signals travel along the axons and dendrites at approximately 4 feet per second. It would be very valuable to carry out some serious studies to use the latest scanning technologies to measure far more accurately the speed of these signals, particularly in various emotional and stimulatory states.

Synapses

Similarly, the speed of transmission by neurotransmitters across the synaptic clefts impacts the overall transmission speeds of signals across the brain and neural system generally.

The time it takes for neurotransmitters to cross a synaptic cleft, or gap, must be influenced by the width of that gap. It has been very difficult to measure the width of synaptic gaps because the distance is very small and individual synapses are difficult to isolate, particularly in real time. However, we can conjecture that some form of magnetism must hold them in suspension. Some form of energy must determine the strength of that *magnetic attractive effect*. We can call this magnetic attractive effect *synaptic tension*.

Thus, we can determine that synaptic tension determines the width of the synaptic cleft, which in turn determines the time it takes for a signal to be passed across this cleft or gap.

The next question is what energy source controls synaptic tension? At the moment, there appear to be two possibilities.

(1) The first possible energy source is the mitochondria in the nucleus of the transmitting neuron. It is possible that the electrochemical signal patterns transmitted along the axons and dendrites contains both information and energy, perhaps at different wavelengths. We explore this hypothesis later.

(2) Glia cells close to, or attached to the dendrites and axons are thought to be able to contain mitochondria which can generate energy.

It is a significant observation that, if the energy source varies then the synaptic tension will vary, the clefts or gaps will vary and the speed of transmission of signal patterns will vary, which determine the efficiency of the whole neural network.

This conjecture has implications as it might be the actuator of whether we are asleep or awake, which we explore in Chapter 18. Of more concern to us in designing effective and accurate methods of measuring intelligence, it can also be speculated that the resting state of synaptic tension may be the variant that determines the speed of neural processing and therefore everyone's IQ result.

Other Tests and Selection Systems

Over the last half century, successive governments have sought to centralise control and standardise the education delivered. Examinations have proliferated as the means of comparing the performance of schools and to measure the performance of teachers. Thus, the whole education experience is concentrated on two sets of public examinations roughly at 16+ and 18+.

To have a series of standard national public examinations, education system requires a standard national curriculum. These examinations attempt to fulfil two objectives. One is a test of competence of information learned. The other is a selection system for entry to higher education, and so is a form of aptitude test. Over the years, the emphasis has swung between these two, effectively incompatible objectives.

One effect has been that the whole state system sets the same kind of academic, as opposed to practical, examinations for the whole population, irrespective of their talents, skills and potential.

In addition, two powerful external pressures have been in play. The negative pressure has been the collapse of mining, manufacturing and heavy engineering and all the associate careers broadly dependent on muscle power, strength and fitness. The more powerful, positive pressure has been the rock star remuneration of the traditional careers in management, law, accountancy, administration, lecturing and teaching, regulation, and particularly financial services.

Thus, from every direction the pressure has been to concentrate on an academic, desk-based, theoretical curriculum and public examination system. Curiously, although the scientific world has been advancing at breakneck speed, this has not been reflected in the interests of the clear majority of teenagers. Computing is a subject that individuals have progressed in their spare time and even now is not thought to be a priority. Some of the skills of computing have been included in the curriculum in 2015!

As the national education system adjusts to the fact that the traditional careers in law, accountancy, administration, lecturing and teaching, regulation, and particularly financial services will largely be made obsolescent within the coming decades, there is a persuasive argument to deploy our growing understanding of intelligence to devise a better method of preparing succeeding generations for multiple careers and lifelong learning.

Homo sapiens is moving from the imperative of speed of reaction towards the quality of our thinking and creativity. To match the growing skills of our robots and cyborgs, we will need to use all our ingenuity to develop tests that will be more useful.

For centuries, the primary objective of education was to pass on the accumulated wisdom of the community, and so the ability to acquire, memorise and recall information was an essential skill. The profusion of knowledge means that modern youth can only possibly acquire a tiny minority of the information available, while the entire body of human knowledge, art, culture and commerce is already instantly available. Within a few years, excellent lessons in every subject will be given online by the world's leading experts. The principal objective of adolescent education is moving towards the identification, nurturing and development of each individual's talent.

Way Forward

One way forward is to start designing an ever wider set of tests, perhaps in the form of competitions, which might typically be at least of a week long duration, exploring all the types of intelligence we are beginning to understand, including both the physical, emotional, musical, artistic, aptitudes and abilities like dexterity, craftsmanship, leadership, languages and the many other creative skills that contribute to the rainbow of human ability, and will be the necessary base of the high value careers of the future.

These "funfests" might start at a simple level around nine and ten and be repeated annually with an ever-broader remit, opening the eyes of young people to the ever-widening range of opportunities stretching out before them, guiding them to the careers they will each personally find most rewarding. Taken together, the national results will provide factual feedback to enable the whole national educational offering to be steadily improved and widened.

Influences on Neural Performance

Diet and Nutrient Path

Very little research has been undertaken into the effect of diet on the efficiency of the brain mind functions. In addition to the variety and regularity of food intake to the digestive system, there is the efficiency of the nutrient path to the brain mind and glands. It is generally believed that the brain mind uses between a quarter and a third of the total nutrient supply of a healthy body. Neurons and glands all need trace elements and a wide array of vitamins for optimum operation. Considerable research has been done on nutrition and diet for the whole body, far less on the optimum requirements to maximise the energy for a healthy brain, especially a mature brain that contains a lifetime's memory structures. Given the obesity epidemic, nutrition and diet research can claim very little success. Given the profusion of chemicals we use in agriculture, horticulture, animal husbandry and marketing presentation, it would seem wise to study what effect these chemicals might have both individually and in combinations. Is one of the reasons why so many of today's grandchildren are so much taller a result of the volume of growth hormones fed to the animals whose meat they eat?

Energy

We have noted that the nucleus of every neuron generates its own supply of energy. Astrocyte glia cells are thought to pass nutrients from the blood stream to *mitochondria* bacteria parasites in the nucleus, which "pay rent" for their presence by converting the nutrients to energy. In addition, they use adenosine triphosphate (ATP) as a form of battery to store energy and release it in an emergency. Mitochondria add a phosphate ion to adenosine diphosphate to store energy by fusion as ATP and extract an ion to generate energy by fission. All these functions may materially affect the final speed of transmission of signals across the nervous system generally and the brain mind in particular. There is nothing to stop us finding out (see Appendix 18).

Efficiency

Finally, it is possible that neural networks are better organised in different people. In the years before puberty, trillions of links and structures are grown, but large numbers of redundant neurons are edited or even completely excised. It seems logical that the efficiency of these processes could have a significant impact on the speed of reactions of the system as a whole. It is entirely feasible that the way in which information is learned could also affect the structure and layout of the neuron networks which could impact on their efficiency. Organised methodical learning or random peripatetic learning? Most likely, is that different people learn in different ways. Trying to make students who are naturally random learners to be methodical, may do considerable damage and vice versa, of course. These traits will not be absolute but on a gradient and most likely will conform to a bell curve.

Other Factors

One of the most difficult aspects of the operation of the brain mind to understand, is the very observable impact of self-confidence, self-reliance, and other psychological personality traits and attributes like introversion and extraversion. Logic suggests that we have tended to underestimate the complexity of the effect of the ambient hormone mix at all the various stages of neural processing. If the immune system, cardiovascular systems or the digestive systems are under stress, for whatever reason, it seems probable that this will directly affect various glands in different ways. Just as the neurons transmit complex patterns of electrochemical signals, we may not have given sufficient attention to similarly complex patterns of hormones both in the brain mind and other organs of the body.

Learning from Experience

In our definition of intelligence, we draw attention to "responding to incomplete information as fast as possible", that is "with the most efficient reaction available". Similarly, we have noted that "at birth we can do almost nothing". Between the two is the process of the acquisition of knowledge. Babies learn to control their digestion systems, crawl, walk, run, say words by imitation, curiosity, exploration, observation, concentration and endless repetition. Thus, every child builds up what we have called a library of applications.

Learning a skill is very different from executing that skill. Few people have a detailed memory of learning to walk or talk, but later skills are easily recalled. Most people remember learning to swim, ride a bicycle, or drive a car. We have noted above that initially we are all over the place. Our whole brain and total concentration seems to be trying to do a variety of things at once. Gradually we become proficient, then we wonder how we could ever have found the task difficult. We dive into a pool, jump on a bike, sit in a car and away we go, without much conscious thought. If we are thinking about anything, it is who we are swimming with, who we are cycling to meet and what we are going to do at our destination. People refer to this swimming, cycling and driving function as being carried out in *autopilot*.

So, we can make a very significant distinction.

Learning a skill is very different from executing that skill.

Learning will certainly benefit if we have an efficient brain as explored above, and speed of operation is useful, but nothing like as significant. Many other considerations come into play. Feedback from past experience begins to play an important role. Thus, for instance, we build up sub-libraries of cycling experiences and how to respond.

So, intelligence is different from learning. True, the more experiences we have at our disposal the more reactions we can select from, and therefore the better our response, but this observation tends to strengthen the argument.

Equally, learning and executing skills are different again from acquiring information. Intelligence is very different from being able to recite facts, whether that is a set of instructions or a poem.

Autonomic Monitoring System

Reverting to our definition, we can see that the capability to respond is a function of the background autonomic operating system. It is the background autonomic functions — the autopilot — that is permanently monitoring the signals from the sensory organs, and when these throw up an event it is the autonomic functions that selects and executes the best reaction available. We can observe that all these activities have often been put in train before we are consciously aware of what is happening.

This is no time to stop and think. This is no time to learn a new skill. Speed and the best reaction available is how we survive to tell the tale and reproduce descendants as intelligent as us.

Programming Our Robots

One conclusion is that it should not be too difficult to design comprehensive operating programs to mimic the autonomic system to driving our robots, *monitoring* events and selecting the appropriate programs to respond to circumstances as they arise. Arrays of programs can then be included into libraries of application (*reaction*) programs available to suit the needs of individual robots.

These individual programs can either be written as free standing applications like traditional systems or like the more recent apps. However, there is no reason why system designers should not seek to build systems that learn to build these types of application program. This would be better described and for the avoidance of doubt, called artificial or *machine learning*.

Reinforcement (Learning) versus Innovation (Thinking)

There is an interesting contradiction at the interface between the execution of applications and the design, developments and learning of new, innovative application. Nothing in the brain mind (nor in the body) happens in isolation. We can observe how the brain grows and strengthens memory structures, by usage and repetition — strengthening and multiplying neural links and networks, then, in due course, insulating them (myelination). On every matter the *exact same answer* is increasingly confidently given.

Yet at the same time we need to keep our minds open to new innovative ideas. On every matter, we want to open our minds to consider, possibly diametrically opposite, *different answers*.

Intelligence as we are defining it can do this. And it is one of our most valuable skills. The leaders of the ancient Greeks certainly had this facility. It was largely lost as Rome and Europe collapsed into barbarism, but was coming back in the seventeenth century and an increasing number of the population has made good use of it since the enlightenment.

Earlier in this chapter, we used swimming, bicycle riding and driving cars to illustrate how we learn skills, then "file" these patterns or algorithms in a library of applications, which are the background to be used on autopilot on demand. We also noted that we grow multiple variations on the basic skill as a result of experience.

Birth of Thinking

Among that array of skill variations, we have learned both to grow *and accept* contrasting, even conflicting algorithms.

We have to make a positive effort to accept that there may be more than one response to any question. John Stuart Mill in his *Essay on Liberty* talks about "everything being open to question". Edward de Bono coined the phrase "lateral thinking". Socrates established one of the fundamental principles of civilisation with "the only thing I know for certain is that I know nothing for certain" or as the quantum physicists could say *constructive uncertainty*. The antithesis of *infallibility*.

Thus, we have two opposing mental systems. The gradient of stasis where ideas become opinions, opinions become prejudices, prejudices become certainties, certainties become belief systems, belief systems become dogma and non-believers are persecuted. This has been the life experience of the overwhelming majority of humans over the millennia and still far too many to this day.

Alternatively, we can open our minds to new innovative ideas.

Concentration

Being able to concentrate, contributes to all the tasks we undertake, and intelligence is no exception. If a specific group of neural networks are active — coping with some problem or crisis, perhaps, it is observable that we cannot lose interest and start doing something else. If we are running to save our lives, it is essential we are well and truly safe before we start thinking about the fact we are feeling very hungry, for instance. There is evidence to suggest that concentration has similar characteristics to our understanding of consciousness, which we will explore in detail later.

Personality Traits

Long-term Over Short-term Gain

Some behaviour traits are so different, even in very young children that it seems probable they are hereditary. One example is self-control, and the quality of intelligence is related to the ability of individuals to apply themselves to the activity in hand. This can often depend on the ability to put off some pleasure or advantage now, in order to gain a bigger benefit later. Some entertaining research offers young children the choice of eating a marshmallow in front of them now, or not eating it and receiving two or more later. Those with the self-confidence to resist immediate temptation in favour of future benefits consistently register higher IQ scores later in life.

Follow a Logical Argument

The ability to hold a number of concepts in the forefront of our minds is another aspect of both intelligence and the ability to think and be creative. There is a famous old chestnut that regularly appears in IQ and derivative tests. A man stands looking at a picture and says, "Brothers and sisters have I none, but that man's father is my father's son". Who is he looking at? It is very easy for the various statements to interfere with each other, oddly and especially because of the rhymes and repetitions. The solution is to carefully keep separate the statements and answer one question at a time. Solve the last question first. "My father's son" is me. So, if "that man's father" is me, I am looking at my son. The side issues are interesting. The "brothers and sisters have I none" phrase obviously excludes "my father's son being a brother", but it also muddies the waters. It can help in understanding the role of rhyme, rhythm and repetition in memory formation and meaning. Multimedia is always helpful in learning, recall and processing. It can help to imagine looking at the picture of a man. This example suggests that thinking is a parallel not a serial activity.

Boundaries

It is much easier to process tasks with clearly defined boundaries and rules. Thus, the first artificial intelligence (AI) tasks that have been programmed successfully, are games and their sisters, quizzes. It does not really matter how complex are the rules because computer programming thrives on complexity. The reason is that programs don't forget, while humans, even specialists do forget, not only small details but often major items.

Also, computer programs are cumulative. Once a program was able to beat a chess master, better and more sophisticated programs could be designed. It is now not possible to beat a chess program.

In real life, there are boundaries and rules, but they are much more general and often very flexible, contradictory and opaque. At the macro scale, the US *written* Constitution has been hailed as the apogee of democratic politics, yet, now in the twenty-first century, a quarter of a millennium later it is showing signs of stress. Perhaps Britain's *unwritten* constitution and reliance on *case law* has its advantages. It is more flexible. Somebody has joked that the regulations of the European Union are over a million times greater than the *Ten Commandments*.

Intelligence is often about identifying the boundaries and rules, long before one can begin to process them meaningfully.

Orientation

We have learned a great deal in recent decades about how migrating species find their way. This has drawn our attention to a very useful skill that *Homo sapiens* enjoys in varying degrees. Almost the first skill a new born baby needs to master, is how to find the way back to the nest. One of the advantages of language is that it enabled people to describe how to follow a trail. Bees and other insects have extraordinarily sophisticated means of telling the hive where to find food or a new hive site.

The history of maps and map making is both fascinating and illuminating. The Greeks began to produce the forerunners of maps to navigate the Aegean, then the Mediterranean. The Romans engineered roads and aqueducts all over their empire, yet made little progress with map making. Solving the problems of cartography and navigation arguably was one of the drivers of the renaissance. There is evidence to suggest the Chinese got there first as maps circulating in Europe a century before Columbus show both the Americas and Australia. England had a full set of county maps with insets of town plans over 50 years before the civil war. They showed few roads but they did show the bridges over the rivers. Maps, map making and the information that maps imparted played an important role in the enlightenment — both to enable travel, and to help a growing public try and understand these curious ideas about the world being a sphere!

For 200 years, we have enjoyed the Ordnance Survey maps. We can read maps in a similar way to reading books or follow equations. We can look at a two-dimensional image and "see" a three-dimensional landscape and vice versa. More significantly, we can "orientate" a map by rotating it so that we can more easily see where to go. We can "hold" that map in our memory and rotate it as we travel along a trail. There is much hilarity over the fact that the ability to orientate and read maps is not a universal skill. Perhaps we have not learned how to teach it to everyone. Birds can allegedly follow the equivalent of a magnet in their heads. It is likely we have a similar facility, if everyone knew how to use it. There is an apocryphal story that Churchill favoured invading Germany from the Mediterranean, because the army would be advancing from the south, and so would be able to read their maps and find the enemy more easily!

There are many examples of where we orientate information in our brain mind to help us understand its meaning.

Is Intelligence a Fixed or Learnable Skill?

Few subjects generate as much debate and heat as whether intelligence is effectively fixed at birth as the colour of our eyes or our likely eventual height or our chance of contracting a hereditary disease. Alfred Binet argues that it is almost heretical to suggest that intelligence might be fixed at birth, and then goes no to argue that the foundation of all education should be to teach everyone how to learn. This seems to misunderstand the present meaning of intelligence, because, surely, everyone would agree that learning to learn should have pride of place in every curriculum. However, it is observable that some people learn faster, or comprehend the meaning of things quicker, or retain that knowledge better. Thus, it can be said that they "learn more intelligently" or they are "more intelligent learners".

It is for this reason that we have quite deliberately bounded reactive intelligence from acquisitive and creative intelligence. Both the latter depend on the former, but the speed and efficiency of the former can be the difference between survival and demise, whereas neither learning nor creativity is so speed dependent. Also, and perhaps this is the most important lesson to learn from this whole subject. Learning to learn and even more so, learning to think are learnable skills. Neural memory systems are unlimited. The ability to think is unlimited. In neither case it is significant if it takes longer.

From the analysis above, it seems almost certain that the physical transmission speed of signals along the neuron networks is fixed for each person at birth. Whether we can influence synaptic tension and therefore the speed of signal transmission across synapses, is open to question and research. However, while we may not be able to learn to speed up our neurons, poor food and maintenance may reduce their potency. Equally, it is observable that between individuals, speed of processing is variable for a number of reasons at different times. Therefore, some people will react more quickly than others. Clearly the ability to process *quantities* of information quickly is useful, but the *quality* of our thinking is far more important in the long run.

That is the fundamental weakness of the IQ test for the twenty-first century. If one student scores 80 out of 100 answers in 1 hour, and another scores 90 out of a 100 standard answers in 2 hours, and a third comes up with one *better* answer in 3 hours, who is the most intelligent? Our ancestors on the prairie needed to be in group one; the others did not survive. In the twenty-first century, it might be better to put our money on the third student.

Thus, the meaning and significance of intelligence has migrated again. The future lies with those who can think the most intelligently. Let us put our effort into how to learn to do this and how to teach these skills. And our biggest ally is our computers.

Implications of Aging on Intelligence

There is much speculation now about the effects of aging, as increasing longevity starts to take effect. This longevity is drawing attention to problems like the various forms of dementia, like Alzheimer's syndrome.

Pluses

As we work our way into old age, we have the increasing benefits of our wealth of experience. The pure volume of information is phenomenal. Often with ease, we can recall events that happened 60 or more years ago. Equally, some recent events do not seem to be accessible. It is an entertaining party trick to ask a sceptic if they can remember the name of their first teacher — often when they were four or less. Most people respond immediately and comment that they had not thought of that person for 40 years. So that piece of information had been present in their heads for all that time, unused, but available in seconds. If people cannot remember a name ask collateral questions. "What do you recall of the school room? Where was your desk?" These usually spark an answer. Some people report the teacher's name surfacing unbidden hours or even days later.

This is useful evidence when we look at memory failures below.

How much information can any one person store? No one has every reported any sort of "system full" message appearing before their eyes. Even trying to design a formula to calculate capacity is incredibly difficult. We could start with how many words we know, in how many language? How many phrases? How many hobbies? Very challenging. The answer seems to be that our ability to store information is truly unlimited.

One can observe that it is often progressively easier to learn a completely new subject as time goes. This may be because the actual process of learning has been honed over time, whereas the process of learning is all very new and difficult in one's youth. Also, mature people have found the optimum process for themselves. Many people in the computing world and, entrepreneurs in particular, realise that, while they have little difficulty learning, *if they want to*, they find it very difficult to be taught. School for them was a battleground of mutual incomprehension. The arrival of computing was a godsend to this cohort. If school had not destroyed their self-confidence, they quickly found they could teach themselves this new technology with ease.

Minuses

Some people are born absent minded, some people achieve absent mindedness and some people have absent mindedness thrust upon them. Some people report a progressive deterioration in the ability to concentrate. An operation accelerates this, but we don't know why. A minor problem is what we are calling senior moment syndrome; the major problem is dementia and alzheimer's. Is the former a precursor to the latter?

These latter are causing increasing concern. Are they all part of the same problem or are they different? Considerable recent research has been hampered by the difficulty of measuring manifestations of the problem. Doctors can measure our temperature and blood pressure in minutes. What is each person's starting point? Historic IQ scores appear to be of no help. How do we measure if any palliative is effective?

Autopsies have shown that the brain accumulates amyloid plaque among the neurons much as water systems get clogged up with chalk. This would seem to be an obvious candidate. So far, we have not found anyway of stopping these growths; however, professor George Perry from the University of Texas at San Antonio, and professor Rudy Castellani at Western Michigan University School of Medicine report that, to add to the problem, they have found that many people with similar levels of plaque infestation report no adverse effects.

Logic would suggest there are alternatives.

We can all observe that both the formation of memories and the recall of memories are hugely variable, but that if the information is highly emotionally significant, this has a dynamic effect on the strength of the memory formed and how efficiently we are able to retrieve it. The strength of the memory formed is largely determined by the strength of the ambient hormone mix. Separately and in combination, the strength of the neural signals — the energy levels — have a major impact.

Let us look at the senior moment syndrome first, because it is the easiest to observe and it happens from time to time to most people throughout their lives. How many times have we known the answer to a question at school but that illusive word just will not pop out? A subject touched on in Chapter 7.

The Mechanism of Memory Recall

We know that when we are seeking some item from memory, we stimulate the most likely associated neurons. If that memory trace is present, then it will be stimulated directly or indirectly by one, or many connections. When the answer is identified, the neural network will initiate the transmission of a signal along its axons then across the synapses. We also know that when synapses fire they promptly close down and unused neurotransmitters are disposed of to avoid confusion. This mechanism is described in Chapter 18.

If that signal is not strong enough, it will not penetrate consciousness. We think we do not have the answer, but often we have the impression that we do know the answer, but it is just out of reach — "on the tip of our tongues". Concentrating on looking for this answer tends to exacerbate the problem, because the circuit is temporarily closed. Later that circuit reopens and the answer may now pop up. Teenagers barely notice the event, but pensioners can panic and the stress generated maximises the problem. If you look for trouble, you can usually find it.

This suggests that memory loss is at least partly caused by a failure of the energy system. Plaque or other refuse may exacerbate the problem, but the sheer volume of accumulated information certainly does. The volume of information in the brain of a twenty-first century 70-year-old is significantly larger than at any time in history. Similarly, there are more cross reference and other neural links that all must share the available energy supply. Recent research on mitochondria and myelin destruction support these conjectures.

Palliative Exercises

It is a curious side effect, but if we fail to recall a fairly often used word of some significance, then the brain registers that recall failure, and this can precondition us to fail to recall it in the future. The solution is to make a note of that word in a lexicon on one's i-pad. Knowing that the miscreant word is within reach, a couple of clicks away often solves the problem without having to access the lexicon. All to do with confidence. It almost becomes a game to see if we can outwit ourselves!

Similarly, when we establish a new memory of some current event in later life, it may be stored with very little energy, thus the trace is very weak, hence we forget why we have just walked upstairs.

Observably advanced dementia and alzheimer's are very different from mild absent mindedness or irritating senior moments, but the question is "are they a similar problem in different stages of development?" It would seem to be worth studying.

There are a number of tests to measure and perhaps vary the nutrient path. The problem could be associated with diet or the astrocyte glia interface between the blood stream and the neuron nucleus. It could be the efficiency of the mitochondria. How could we introduce new energetic mitochondria into the neuron nucleus? It might be the plasticity of the synapses and a growing inability to vary the width of the synaptic gap, due, again, to a lack of energy.

If we think the problem could be associated with less usage — the use it or lose it theory, then perhaps we could develop some therapies.

Measuring Memory Formation

We know that minimal memories are formed automatically, if we see an image for a few of seconds (see Chapter 7 and Appendix 28). We could vary the exposure time, which would enable us to identify the cut-off point. We could carry out a similar test at definable time later and see if the cut-off readings changed.

Variant Brain Types and Intelligence

Everyone has unique fingerprints, eye patterns and so on. On the balance of probabilities, it seems certain that everyone has a unique brain. Furthermore, the neural patterns of every single piece of information we have ever learned are also likely to be unique. It seems to be equally likely that within this diversity there are many groupings spread over a wide spectrum. It follows that there are likely to be various qualitative and quantitative levels of intelligence.

Left and Right Brain Debate

There has been, and still is a debate over the idea of different left and brain types. There are two hemispheres connected by the corpus collosom, which adds credibility to this conjecture. Most people claim they are either numerate or literate. Whether this is hereditary or the influence of adolescence is far from clear. Some claim one side is creative and the other is rational and logical.

What does seem to be true is that, if one side is damaged the other progressively takes over. Some brain damage has little effect on character, some causes major changes immediately and some significant changes progressively over time.

There is little doubt that building a formula to solve a numerical, or dexterity-type problem is a very different task to assembling a sequence of words to produce sensations and emotions.

Major Variations in Personality

The majority of people in any one group tend towards the average with outliers at each extremity — the bell curve. Over the centuries, small groups that have populated the extremes have often suffered ridicule, discrimination or worse. A physical example is the occasional albino. This "fear of the different" seems to be true across all animals.

Gradually we are beginning to better understand the autism spectrum, dyslexia and the plurality of sexuality. For a long while, these examples were thought to be disabilities, but increasingly we have appreciated that this is far from the truth. Two of the most successful architectural partnerships only recruit dyslexics. Whatever deficit dyslectics might suffer, many more than make up for in creativity and design talents. Some people on the autism spectrum are brilliant programmers. Their capacity to concentrate can be phenomenal.

Gradually we are beginning to celebrate their talents rather than feel we have to compensate for their differences.

Up until relatively recently, physical illness was something to be ashamed about, and a family might care for an ill relative but would try and keep the matter quiet. Mental problems, or instability is still a pariah state for many, even in the more developed communities. One possible culprit was the fear that whatever the problem, it might be hereditary. One of the original drivers of the earliest religions was to stop close relatives marrying, because very soon it was obvious that the offspring tended to be increasingly weaklings.

Another interpretation of survival of the fittest is that, homosexuality, for instance, must have some evolutionary advantage or surely that community would have disappeared long ago.

More recently we are learning that the selection of sex takes place in the womb and throughout adolescence in fits and starts and that physical developments of the shape and parts of the body follow a separate path to mental attributes. Thus, it is possible for a baby to look like a boy or girl, but to feel the opposite, or neither. Now that intelligent communities feel able to discuss these subjects rationally, we are beginning to learn that a major development phase usually around 11 years can, in the majority of cases, reinforce the original specification, or reverse that specification, and every combination in between. We also learn that there are some 100,000 transgender people in the UK, which may be a relatively small percentage of the population, but a very large number of individuals.

It is encouraging to note that open, generous, tolerant communities, who are able to debate contentious matters in good will and without prejudice, are the most fertile of new innovative ideas, which carry our civilisation forward. That has been true from age of Socrates to the age of Turing. One feels Socrates would have said that he could know nothing for certain, and that on the balance of evidence, it might just be possible that, in this case the scribes who wrote down those ancient scripts might, just possibly, in this special case, have misinterpreted their instructions. On the other hand, Alan Turing was also effectively murdered by the state.

A Word About Qualia

The word we use for things like the redness of a rose, beauty, leadership and charisma. We usually know exactly what we mean, but we have no words to describe let alone define it. The general view is the words we have are inadequate. Words came first and we try to use them to describe emotions and feelings.

The situation may be the opposite. It is quite plausible that ancient mankind had plenty of emotions; fear, hunger, elation, arousal etc. Living in a community, it became increasingly frustrating not to be able to communicate basic orders to the peerhood thus certain simple words developed to identify things and actions. We have made a great job of creating languages to do all this very well, but we have been less successful in developing words for abstract concepts. Perhaps evolution has not given us enough time. We have only been able to think comprehensively in the abstract since we could write.

We have not created a language for qualia. Perhaps we should work on developing one. We might learn a lot.

One possibility to explore is to enlist the power of emergence. If we could conceive of a verbal definition that is close in an emotional sense, then, perhaps, the rest of the definition of some qualia, at least could be completed by an emergent element. If we could break qualia up into groups, we might find solutions more quickly. There are references to qualia in Chapters 11, 14 and 17.

Repository of All Human Knowledge

We have argued the case that Intelligence is dependent on the flow of information, and the meaning of information forms the basis of all human knowledge.

Since the beginning of recorded time, mankind has realised the fragility of human knowledge, thus the original purpose of education and the early schools had as a priority the preservation and passing on of knowledge to the next generation.

Archaeological evidence suggests the first schools, libraries, or public record offices were built about the same time as the early development of cuneiform in Sumer on the Euphrates some 3,000 BC.

The adoption of the alphabet, more or less as we know it today, quickly led to the accumulation of knowledge in libraries in the Mediterranean, of which perhaps the most famous was the Great Library of Alexandria.

It is interesting to note that even the great Socrates worried about the arrival of writing which he feared would weaken human memory.

When the ancient Roman religion merged with Christianity, the new leaders soon closed down the academies of Greece and all the wisdom of that great civilisation was nearly lost. Fortunately, the Muslims preserved as much as we know about, adding to it and in due course building great libraries. Perhaps the best known was at Istanbul, although it was burnt a number of times by marauding Crusaders.

In Muslim Spain, Toledo held copies of all the major Greek texts plus those they were able to extend. Algebra is one famous example, and the invention or importation of zero from India is another. When Ferdinand and Isabella reconquered Spain for Rome the Great Library was saved from being burned by the Medici family who bought the whole library and had it transferred to Florence. Together with many works from Istanbul, these famous bankers had copies made as they had been for centuries. Many people argue this had a major impact on stimulating the renaissance. Within a few decades, Gutenberg and the fast expanding printing industry were printing them and exporting them around Europe providing ammunition for the reformation. However, some of the exquisite Medici volumes of works of art like Aristotle's *Physica* can be seen today in Libraries like The Malatestiana at Cesena.

All the universities of Europe were built around their libraries. Books were treated with reverence and only available to be read by a limited few, hence the title that survives to this day of "reader".

Printing and the various technologies of reproducing pictures led to an explosion of encyclopaedias, dictionaries and other works of reference. In the late twentieth century, children probably learn as much from their entertaining television sets and iPads as they do in the boring old classrooms in their schools — so very last century.

So far, the computing tsunami has not reached the world of education. However, we are on the cusp of having the entire body of human knowledge, art, culture and commerce instantly available, fully up to date on our wearable, possibly even prosthetic personal terminals. Not just pages of print, but interactive online lessons teaching the meanings, implications and extrapolations of facts and video clips of how to do or execute tasks and skills, as well as films of human experience, difficult decisions and how to cope, emotional situations and how to resolve conflict. We are coming full circle to Greek theatre and drama.

There are already major problems of authenticity, accuracy and safety. Online distance learning is about as efficient as a Boulton and Watt steam engine compared to a supersonic jet. Then there are moral and ethical difficulties. One that is not so insignificant, is what do we do, if all human knowledge is exclusively online or in "clouds" and our technology fails or is invaded?

New technologies always throw up new problems.

There is one important consequence. We noted above that the principle objective of the education of each younger generation for the last 5,000 years has been to pass on intact the accumulated knowledge of the human race to succeeding generations.

We Now Have a New Opportunity

Our vast store of knowledge is safely stored and instantly available to everyone. Thus, the objective of education can now change. For economic reasons for generations, if children were taught at all, a one-size-fits-all approach was the only practical way forward. Particularly in the last 50 years, students have had to memorise an ever-greater volume of detailed information, which, however, is an ever-vanishing percentage of the information available. This seems increasingly irrelevant to young people.

We have the tantalisingly wonderful opportunity for the first time to prepare succeeding generations for life-long learning by helping each young person to explore the world of knowledge and identify their own personal individual talents and develop them. To help them build on these abilities and encourage them to think and be creative.

CHAPTER FOURTEEN

THE MANY LANGUAGES AND POWERFUL TOOLS OF THE BODY

Languages of the Hormones (Chemical Neuroscience)

Verbal Language

Chapter 5 explores the crucial importance of language: its central role in communication; as a means of passing on knowledge, working together in groups, the medium of thinking; and also, its impact on the development of the brain to recognise, store, access hundreds of thousands of words, phrases and their meanings.

We touched on the possible history of the development of language, and the construction of words and phrases: syllables, alphabets, spelling, phonemes and grammar. We noted other domains. The written language of music, medicine, mathematical and scientific formulae — all very familiar.

However, as we widen our studies of the whole-body operation of the extended autonomic functions of the central nervous systems, we begin to realise that there are other languages upon which the smooth running of our bodies depends.

253

The Language of the Hormones

The first is the language of the hormones. We have explored in Chapter 8 the significant role of the endocrine system and the key role of the hormones that its network of glands secretes, in determining the meaning of information to us. We have known about the significant role of the major glands for 100 years or so, but only recently have we discovered perhaps as many as 200 hormones, neurotransmitters and messenger molecules, and the leading specialists are suggesting we have barely scratched the surface of their complexity. Only in the last few years have we begun to appreciate the significance of the effects of the delivery of complex combinations of hormones. It is far more than just the impact of individual hormones which has been generally accepted.

Immediately we can see the resemblance of hormone mix to the language of putting together words to make phrases and sentences, and also the very powerful force again of emergence: the whole being far greater than the sum of the constituents. Words and mathematical terms have value through their meaning, but the language of the hormones is much more powerful because it resembles the notation of music, introducing the length and strength of the participant notes.

Current thinking favours the likelihood that there are some 200 glands, thus we have the potential for a hormone alphabet language of some 200 letters, where each constituent "letter" is variable in volume, strength and duration — more than adequate to represent nuanced meanings to every word in our dictionaries and every phrase in every thesaurus.

The Language of Chemical Cognitive Neuroscience: A New Field of Research

This opens up an entirely new field of chemical cognitive neuroscience and hormone research of which we have been previously unaware. The paragraphs above target the endocrine system, but the other body systems also play a major role. In particular, the enteric gastrointestinal system contributes a range of neural signals related to our food and liquid input. The sensations associated with hunger, thirst and being satiated are some of the first and most powerful feelings all animals experience.

Similarly, it seems likely that we have underestimated the hormone and other inputs from the immune systems. Taken together, the enteric and immune systems are likely to be the source of our general sensations of feeling unwell, of feeling well, and could well play a major role in our more nuanced sensations of being cheerful and of being depressed.

There is a compelling argument to start to study the combined effects of the endocrine, enteric, immune and energy systems and the inter-related roles they might play in those many areas that we find most difficult to understand and address, like autism, dyslexia, dementia, obesity, anorexia and those areas of medicine where imbalances cause faults to occur.

Musical Languages

We have touched on the notation of music, but having opened our minds to the concepts of an extended hormone language, it seems possible that we could explore a musicological language. Could we explore the same with a language of the visual arts?

Could this be the beginnings of building a language and notation to help describe and define qualia?

Mathematic and Scientific Languages

Mathematicians in particular, but scientists generally have developed their own branches of our universal verbal language, and sheer practicality has reduced the number of national languages. Science, like the airline industry speaks in English for purely practical reasons. As complexity and the volume of our knowledge expands ever faster, it may be that the language of science will migrate away from English, but the result would be more like a lingua franca, or more particularly Latin, where the scientific language of English drifts away from the vernacular English of the streets.

Body Language

Equally we can identify body language, where the movements we make and the poses we strike convey information very efficiently. This language has been well explored. It certainly adds a footnote to conveying meaning, reaction and opinion.

Programming

In Chapter 1, we explored the development of programming languages. We noted they evolved to help programmers write programs. Much more interesting is the potential to design programs than enable programs to write programs. This opens the potential for computers to learn from experience — a potentially very powerful tool.

Robots

As robots, AI and prosthetic brain interfaces begin to mature, we will need a form of language to communicate: brain to robot, robot to brain, robot to robot and brain to brain. Traditional languages may not be anywhere near precise enough, at least to start with. We explore this in Chapter 19.

Tools of Intelligence in the Body

Emergence

One of the most powerful tools and concepts in cognitive neuroscience is the notion of emergence, i.e. the concept that the whole is greater than the sum of the constituent parts. Initially this concept can seem to be a form of convenient catch all. When we are unable to identify some cause and effect, we suggest that this effect is emergent. However, in Appendix 25 (all appendices are hosted on www.BrainMindForum.org/appendices) and in examples all over this book, emergence is for real, and is a very potent force.

Sound Bites: Jargon, Icons

The same is true of sound bites: jargon. When we come up with a complex, difficult to describe concept, we can give the whole concept a label. In debates, we can discuss with the peerhood in this shorthand and so discuss more in less time. The political sound bite along the lines of "tough on crime, tough on the causes of crime" summed up, in just nine words, a whole complex policy in a form that was instantly understandable.

Similarly, we can make use of icons, symbols and indexes, everything that can help structure information so that is easier to store, access and process.

Positioning and Sequences

We have noted the importance of the position of information in a sequence as being an essential part of mathematics; however, the same is equally important in the positioning and sequencing of words. It is of equal importance in team games.

Simplicity and Clarity

It is an important discipline to try and explain things as simply as possible. There is one group in the community that see intelligence as second guessing every possible eventuality and trying to provide for that, however, this becomes a game, as the more complex any description, the more it becomes a target to circumvent the rules. We used the example of regulations for major bureaucratic institutions, particularly treasuries and tax collectors.

Many people claim the credit for the quotation that, in accompanying a letter they say "they were sorry they did not have time to write a short letter". Not just philosophers, but many programmers have realised the importance of simplicity. The more succinct a program, at the same time as being comprehensive the easier it is to follow if, at some time in the future a program needs to be amended and updated. Hence, William of Oakham is the favourite to be the patron saint of computing.

Hierarchies in Processing Neural Signals

In this context, it is worth looking again at the architecture of hierarchies, because upon this principle the construction of most computer systems are built, and most neural information processing is grown.

As far as we know, neurons can only transmit one signal at one time. There are a number of different types of neuron, but they mostly follow the same pattern. Numbers of dendrites input information to the nucleus, which can output a signal, usually down just one axon. However, many axons divide up near their target like the delta of distributaries as a river nears the sea. Most neuron axon and dendrite filaments are connected to organs, muscles, bone, glands, other organs and other neurons by synapses or narrow gaps, which we explore in Chapter 18.

Cognitive neuroscientist tends to think and talk about neurons transmitting *patterns of signals*. We have used this phrase often. However, this may be incomplete, possibly misleading. We have observed that neurons have their own independent energy-generating system. Mitochondria convert nutrients into a steady flow of energy. If more energy is generated than is immediately needed, then energy is stored in adenosine triphosphate (ATP) molecules. In a crisis or if the arrival of nutrients is unreliable, this stored energy can be called upon. There is no evidence whether any of these transmitted signals are strong or weak, or whether the messages are of variable length transmission. There is also no evidence of any Morse like dot, dash type code.

There is, however, ample evidence that the hormone mix in the fluid surrounding the neurons and their dendrite and axon filaments is constantly variable and directly affects the behaviour of the nucleus and its input–output activities. Similarly, the ambient mix around each synapse affects the efficiency of the signal transmission. There is also no evidence of the nucleus being able to select which axon, if there is more than one or which distributary if they are present, down which to transmit signals. It appears to be all or nothing.

Current thinking is that a nucleus can transmit an output signal down the available axon, if it receives an input signal from one of its dendrites. In a normal resting state, the nucleus may not react to one input signal and only transmit an output signal, if and when it has received several input stimuli. This is thought to depend on the ambient hormone mix. Thus, in a state of high emotion, the nucleus might be very sensitive to a dendrite signal and transmit a signal down its axon(s) immediately. Alternatively, in a state of low emotion, the nucleus might only respond and transmit a signal after receiving numbers of dendrite input signals. Thus, we can observe the mechanism by which emotion affects behaviour.

This raises questions about exactly what neurons are capable of transmitting. The actual transmission process of the action potentials, or electrochemical signals, along the filaments is well known. Sodium and calcium ions pass backwards and forwards across the membranes of the filaments is a continuous "pass the parcel" stream along each axon and dendrite. These signals can only be transmitted in one direction. So, precisely, what are neurons transmitting? Is this action potential information or energy?

What Do Neurons Transmit?

We do know that this electrochemical activity generates electromagnetic fields around the filaments and that these magnetic fields are capable of attracting glia cells.

We are left with the tantalising question of how the brain transmits the patterns of signals that we have presumed enables it to transmit complex information.

It is a disruptive thought to suggest that it does not. To say a word, the mind transmits a stream of signals to the muscles of the lungs, throat and mouth: the lungs to expel air; the muscles in the throat to adjust the vocal chords; the muscles of the mouth to adjust the tongue, lips and cheeks to expel the desired pattern of sound over the airwaves. So, the pattern of each individual word emerges from the multitude of single signals, from a multitude of single neurons, all firing in exactly the right sequence with exquisitely correct timing.

A syllable is a hierarchy of phonemes. A word is a hierarchy of syllables. A phrase is a hierarchy of words. A speech, instruction, concept or idea is a hierarchy of phrases. A neuron can do one job and one job only. It can transmit a single, fixed, standard electrochemical signal down an axon, and nothing else.

Neural Behaviour

Whether it does so is a matter of probability. In a stream of identical circumstances (if that were possible), it might respond identically n times the same way, but in every next time it might behave differently.

Of such is evolution, of such is intelligence, of such is thinking, of such is creativity.

On this analysis, we build the argument that the presence of a neuron at that position in that neural network, capable of receiving signals and transmitting signals at that strategic position to contribute to the speaking of a word, is what we understand as memory — *potential* information. When that neuron is activated and contributes its signal to the articulation of that word, we understand it to be intelligence — *kinetic* information. We can conclude that neurons transmit energy. The hormone mix that this activity generates is the meaning that makes that information live and valuable to us. By this natural process, we create words with meanings. Once we have created words, we can link them together into phrases, concepts, ideas, aspirations and ambitions.

Donald Hebb called these *engrams*. A computer programmer calls them *subroutines*. A software designer calls them *neu*ral mod*ules* or *neu-rules*; Richard Dawkins has suggested *memes*. Other observers have suggested a range of terms listed at Appendix 12.

How Neurons Invent Jet Engines

We argue that this simple process enables us invent jet engines and computers. The brain mind is a neural version of a Turing engine, which, we have reiterated many times can only add, subtract and jump, yet we can program a computer to beat us at chess and Go. The neurons of the brain mind can only transmit an electrochemical signal, but that is enough for us to write those programs! Both employ pure logic. We have invented them in our computers and developed and learned to create them in our brains.

CHAPTER FIFTEEN

DEFINITIONS OF INTELLIGENCE

At the beginning of Chapter 9, we posed the question:

Is Intelligence an abstract evaluation concept or a measurable neural process or can it be both?

We argue it is both, simultaneously. We have observed that the autonomic functions of the central nervous system are in continuous operation at every moment of our lives coordinating the whole body, whether we are awake or asleep. We have explored how these functions continuously monitor all the sensory and other organs, and generally manage the various operations of the brain mind. We have put forward a compelling case that acting as a background operating system they can be defined as general "g" intelligence. Throughout life, we learn a library of information and skills — part specific to that individual foreground application — part adding to the autonomic background functions.

The more individual information and skills we learn, the more they add to the vibrancy and sophistication of our general intelligence. All these additional information and skills increase the volume of our knowledge system, *but do not affect the speed of processing of the whole.*

The intelligence quotient (IQ) and similar tests measure the speed and efficiency of the system — the background operating system — literally the speed of the patterns of electrochemical signals transmitted along the axons and dendrites and across the synapses. The volume of knowledge we accumulate and the skills we learn — the mass of additional neural links and structures we grow — vary greatly according to each individual's circumstances and opportunities.

Thus, the IQ and other evaluation test scores vary little over a lifetime, but general knowledge, the panoply of skills, wisdom, problem solving, decision making and creativity vary greatly. The former provides the evaluation the latter the measurable neural processes. They both occur together.

It is generally thought that electrochemical signal patterns tend to travel along axons and dendrites at very much the same speed of some 4 feet per second, although this may be modulated by the current ambient hormone mix. The synapses play a much more significant role. The overall relative quality, efficiency and speed of the neural processes flowing over the networks depend on the width of the synaptic clefts that depends on the level of tension across the synapses, which, in turn, is regulated by the level of energy available in the neurons individually or in networks.

Everyone can observe from their own personal individual experience that whether we are learning a new piece of knowledge or a new skill, there are two phases. We struggle to master the intricacies of Pythagoras's theorem and the latest twists in string theory, and we wobble around learning to balance a bicycle, until they become almost automatic, operating in the background, or as some people say, on *autopilot*. They are "filed" in our library of neural applications — stored as individual discrete abilities.

In addition, they contribute to our store of general skills, and so are available to make future learning easier. Pythagoras's proofs are useful across the rest of geometry. We began to learn to balance when we learned walk. Therefore, cycling was not difficult. Sophisticated balancing is a crucial skill for gymnasts.

We can *evaluate the abstract concept* of the efficiency of the background general intelligence. In Chapter 13, we suggest there is a rainbow of ways of measuring the rainbow of intelligences. We are by no means limited to the traditional IQ test. And we can measure the individual neural *processes* of each application. We *can* define intelligence.

The Architecture and Relationship of Information and Intelligence

Information is the identification of patterns of observations — patterns that mean things. Intelligence is the identification and processing of patterns of activities — patterns that do things. Knowledge is the identification and accumulation of patterns of meanings. Memory is the means by which we record the past so that we can improve the present and predict the future. The meaning of a unit of information is the cocktail of sensations, impressions, feelings, perceptions and emotions generated by the hormones produced by the glands in the endocrine and other body systems.

The earliest glimmering of intelligence is about a mechanism to respond to events. Thus, the first expression of intelligence is a means of coping with the unexpected.

The Source, Foundation and Evolution

of Survival Intelligence is the Ability to

Respond to Incomplete Information Fast.

General and Reactive Intelligence

The description, the processes, the mechanism and definition of general and reactive intelligence are as follows. General and reactive intelligence is the relative quality and efficiency of the extended autonomic functions of the central nervous system that coordinates, manages and operates the physical systems of the body: the endocrine, cardiovascular, immune and enteric systems and the dexterity of all the muscles. In particular, the brain mind monitors and analyses all the sensory inputs from the surrounding environment, comprehends the significance and meaning of incomplete information and responds with the most efficient reaction available, as fast as possible, to outwit predators etc., to relate to other people and control behaviour. It provides the framework for all the learned skills to operate, grow, develop and be executed. It allocates resources and organises all the organs and systems of the body to cope with the world and survive.

Acquisitive Intelligence

These ancient background skills have facilitated the ability to learn an ever-widening panoply of specific individual intelligent skills. They include the efficiency and speed of the brain mind to develop, grow and execute neural systems to identify, obtain, retrieve and process the meaning of information to extend knowledge. To recognise the sound patterns of words, phrases, music and their meaning, then, more recently, the optical patterns of written words, phrases and the visual arts; assemble words and phrases to speak, write and contemplate concepts, ideas and formulae cogently and logically. To think, make decisions, solve problems, innovate, imagine, speculate and predict the possible future course of events.

General extended autonomic intelligence was, and is the driving mechanism of evolution.

The personal libraries of ever more efficient, learned, specific and individual applications of intelligent skills and abilities are the driving force of civilisation.

Creative Intelligence

A definition of creative intelligence: thinking of new ideas, concepts and solutions. It is the ability to pause neural processing; extrapolate existing information; explore, evaluate and compare alternative solutions to identify new, better more effective and efficient results — recognise this as an improvement and organise this latest information in a coherent manner that is understandable and useful to others. Observation, feedback and repetition enable this library of specific learned intelligent abilities to be continuously improved, expanded and executed more efficiently.

Physical Intelligence

Physical intelligence is defined as the efficient and precision control of muscular movements — dexterity. It is the ability to learn and execute sequences of physical activities that includes efficient eye muscle coordination and the efficient comprehensive processing of the information from each of sensory organs.

Emotional Intelligence

It is the ability to recognise the behaviour and reactions of others to events in general and to one's own actions in particular, and respond appropriately and constructively; to cooperate in a group, to be able to lead and give and accept orders; to motivate oneself and others.

Holistic Intelligence

It is the efficient organisation by the extended autonomic functions of the central nervous system to manage and mediate the relationships between the endocrine, cardiovascular, enteric and immune systems to organise the whole body as one coordinated, cooperative and synchronised organism.

Medical Intelligence

It is the efficiency of the dynamic psychological relationships between the immune system and the functions of the brain mind to maintain the equilibrium of the emotional systems and the effect of will power on health.

Neural Modules (Neurules)

A syllable is a hierarchy of phonemes. A word is a hierarchy of syllables. A phrase is a hierarchy of words. A speech, instruction, concept or idea is a hierarchy of phrases. Knowledge is a hierarchy or pattern of phrases.

Neurons Generate Meaning

A neuron can do one job and one job only. It can transmit a single standard electrochemical signal down its axon(s), and nothing else. Networks of neurons transmit patterns of energy. These patterns stimulate the glands of the endocrine system to secrete the mix of hormones that generates the sensations that makes information meaningful.

Potential Information

The presence of a neuron in a particular position in a neural network, capable of receiving signals and transmitting signals at that strategic position to contribute to the execution of a particular function, is what we understand as *memory — potential information.*

Kinetic Information

When a neuron in a particular position in a neural network is activated and contributes its signal to the execution of a function, we understand it to be *intelligence — kinetic information.*

We can conclude this section by saying that intelligence is the relative efficiency of the application of energy to enable patterns of neural instructions, or algorithms, to store and process information to make decisions, solve problems and create knowledge that defines our culture (defined by Mathew Arnold as "the study of perfection" and by Oscar Wilde as "sacrosanct and sublime").

PART IV

CONSCIOUSNESS

CHAPTER SIXTEEN

UNDERSTANDING CONSCIOUSNESS

Conscious awareness and the sleep/wake cycle are separate functions.

Brain Mind Forum 2017

All Knowledge is Provisional

Perceptions of Consciousness

We spend about a third of our lives asleep, hence it has always been a subject of much speculation. When we are awake, we are conscious of the world around us, of participating in that world and of being alive. Both being awake and being aware of the world, interact and conflate together. However, let us study these attributes of the sleep wake cycle and being consciously aware separately to start with.

Consciousness

Down the ages, there has been near universal agreement that there is some "force" in addition to the visible brain. Great minds deep in our ancestral past have suggested *Ka*, vital essence, atman, mind, soul and consciousness. All these observers had one thing else in common but none had the privilege of programming a computer! For the last 50 years, we have thought of computers only as useful information processors. However, as we are now just beginning to realise, they can do so much more. Computers give us a means of seeing things for the first time. This different perspective has enabled us to isolate the brain from the mind and opened a plethora of new possibilities. Let us pull together the old ideas of the past and the new ideas of today and see where that leads us.

Some of the earliest records are from Egypt where around 5,000 years ago there are references to *Ka* which they described as the "vital essence" — the difference between a living and dead person. In the sixth century BC, one of the central religious concepts of Hinduism, Buddhism and Jainism was the concept of the *atman,* the immortal perfect spirit of any living creature. Around 1,600 René Descartes' dualism thoughts of the body are working like a machine, while the mind (or soul) was non-material and did not follow the laws of nature. Around the same time, Spinoza disagreed. In *Ethics: An Outline*, he argued that "neither can the body determine the mind to think, nor the mind determine the body to motion or rest or anything else".

A 100 years or so ago, Ramon Cajal worked out how to stain neurons, so that we could begin to study them, identifying a nucleus, axons and dendrites. More recently, Nobel laureate, Sir Charles Sherrington (1857–1952) in *Man and His Nature* argued that the mind is invisible, intangible; it is not a thing. "Physical science…faces us with the impasse that the Mind *per se* cannot play the piano — Mind *per se* cannot move a finger of a hand". However, Erwin Schrödinger (1887–1961) in *What Is Life?*, argued that "The brain operates to the rules of physics". In recent decades, consciousness has been dubbed the "hard problem".

In the 1920s, Sherrington identified the very sophisticated way in which neurons are linked to all the muscles, glands and other neurons, namely by small *clefts* or gaps, which he named *synapses* from the Greek "to clasp". Only in the last few years have we begun to appreciate the significance of this complex connection system. Professor Lulu Xie of the University of Rochester reported in 2015 that the width of the synaptic gaps increases during sleep. Researchers at the University of Pittsburg are attempting to measure the width of synapses in their resting state. The variability of the synaptic gaps may be determined by the tension generated across the synapse. The current best guess is that this tension is a combination of energy transmitted down the axons and dendrites and the ambient state of the hormones — our emotional state.

The Current "Standard Model" of Sleep and Consciousness

The present consensus of our understanding of consciousness is built on Daniel Dennett's ground-breaking 1991 book *Consciousness Explained*, which was the first major work to move away from Descartes concept of consciousness being a theatre. In the last three decades, we have learned a great deal about the power of emergence and its mechanism. We have explored the remarkable scale and complexity of the endocrine system — still only partially discovered; and most recently the structure and hitherto unsuspected capabilities of the synapses.

Let us look again at what we observe as sleep and consciousness. What, perhaps, we can call the standard model of consciousness? This conflates being awake with being consciously aware and is thought to be all one neural process. Similarly, we conflate being asleep with being unconscious. In addition, we have the concept of the subconscious, which appears to be permanently in operation controlling all the organs of the body and is thought to be associated with the sympathetic nervous system, or the extended autonomic functions of the central nervous system. The problem is that this theory no longer fits with observable fact. We can be apparently fast asleep, yet dreaming so vividly we seem to be almost completely consciously aware; similarly, once we have learned some new task, we can carry it out without any sense of being aware of doing so while being fully awake, for instance writing, swimming, balancing a bicycle, driving a car. If we are not conscious of these background activities, where do they fit in to the scheme of things?

Brain Functions

Perceptions of Sleep

We are all very familiar with falling asleep. We feel tired, running out of energy. Our arms and legs begin to relax, our eyelids close and recent events begin to drift away. Only when we wake up are we conscious of having gone to sleep. We are never conscious of *being asleep*. As we drift off to sleep, we have a sense of losing tension: tension in our muscles — tension in our minds. Let us explore that observation?

We talk of being asleep or awake, but sleep is a gradient, from anaesthesia, via deep sleep to rapid eye movement (REM) sleep, to the grey area where we are nearly awake or just awake and day dreaming, drowsy, through being attentive, then alert, right up to full concentration.

We can see a possible evolutionary path for these attributes. Neural activity uses up a great deal of energy. Life is often made up of long periods of little action, then phrenetic periods of extreme activity: escaping a predator, chasing food, or mates. The mitochondria in the neurons convert nutrients to energy in order to power the electrochemical signalling system and to control the tension across the synapses. Adenosine triphosphate (ATP) acts as a form of battery that can store energy in quiet periods and release it in active periods, crisis or famine. Reptiles can only generate enough energy to be awake in sunshine. Maybe one reason mammals evolved warm blood systems was to generate enough energy to enable them to operate independently of daylight.

After periods of extreme activity or just part of the daily circadian rhythms (or annual cycle of life), the energy levels drop. The tension across the synapses falls and the synaptic gaps widen. Messages can still cross these clefts but less efficiently. We lose attention — fall asleep (or some mammals hibernate). As the mitochondria in the neurons re-build the energy levels, the synaptic tension rises narrowing the synaptic gaps, facilitating the passage of signal traffic. As this reaches a critical mass, more signals from the sensory and other organs fully penetrate to the brain attracting attention: we wake up and become aware of the world around us and experience the sensations of consciousness and of being alive.

A sharp blow to the head quite literally knocks the synapses apart, rendering us instantly unconscious.

It is generally thought that we have a limited ability to force ourselves to stay awake, usually at the cost of being extremely tired afterwards.

Priority in a Crisis

Different sections of the brain may be active at different times. In crisis conditions, one section of the brain, dealing with immediate essential actions may have preference — their synapses are at maximum tension, operating at maximum efficiency. Alternatively, even if the majority of the brain is relaxing and ostensibly asleep, one or more sections may still be active, generating the sensations of consciousness. We recognise this partial state as *dreaming*. Where we have learned some task, the neural networks enabling us to drive a car, for instance, can operate with little or no supervision. We describe this as background mode. We steer, brake and accelerate almost on *autopilot,* while other groups of neural networks, perhaps, have temporary precedence as we decide which route to take or concentrate on conversing with a passenger (foreground mode). We are awake, but observably driving unconsciously. Being awake or asleep is very clearly a function of the efficiency of the neural networks of the Brain. It is a hardware task.

Mind Functions

Consciousness

On the other hand, consciousness is a series of perceptions, sensations, impressions and emotions. When very young, our first conscious sensations are of feeling warm or cold, of hunger and thirst. We suddenly feel frustrated and lose our temper, shout and cry to attract attention. We feel the warmth and security of a loving embrace. We become conscious of parents, siblings, and other people and things around us. We begin to associate certain sound patterns — words — with things and activities and grow the neural circuitry that associates the five senses to relate to each other and we begin to imitate the sounds of words so that we can begin to learn to ask for things.

We begin to search for the *meanings* of everything. Some of these words make us feel good, cheerful and happy; others might make us feel frightened, nervous and apprehensive. Music excites us. If someone smiles at us, we imitate them, and so gradually learn to appreciate the boundary of ourselves and others. We can think of a plethora of other examples of these sensations. The enteric systems generates sensations of hunger and thirst, the cardiovascular system lets us know our heart is in overdrive, the immune system signals fever and maybe much more than we realise. Some are whole body sensations, others are more cerebral. Puberty brings a flood of new sensations and emotions. Teenage brings more complex, nuanced and sophisticated perceptions, elements of comparison and criticism, hope, faith, charity, envy, arousal and desire, jealousy and respect, even the poignancy of a parting.

Consciousness is multiple streams of the meanings of all our experiences. They are a function of the continuous mass of patterns of electrochemical activity and electromagnetic fields, synchronised waves stimulating both the muscles to carry out actions and the endocrine glands to flood the system with a cocktail of hormones — a veritable language of sensations. All these are functions of the mind, the software. This mélange of chemicals generates an intricate pattern of sensations, impressions, feelings and emotions, while the incoming signals from the sensory organs generate a similar set of perceptions.

They perform one other function. We automatically deploy that most powerful attribute emergence. *This whole electrical and chemical activity is greater than the sum of all its component parts in one special way.* What we experience is an integrated coordinated experience of our whole world and our place in it. The experiences of conscious awareness are functions generated by the mind.

Coordination

Without the mind, the brain is dead. Without the brain, the mind has nothing to operate on. We can agree with Sir Charles Sherrington that we need both brain and mind working in unison to play the piano. Similarly, all computers are useless without their software. They cannot even make the tea!

We can say with Erwin Schrödinger that everything we are learning confirms that both the brain and mind are equally tangible, measurable and operate to the laws of physics. Aristotle's proposal that "the Mind shapes the inner forces responsible for the regulation of all the body's processes and goals" seems pretty close for 350 BC. So, there is an almost unanimous consensus that both the conscious awareness functions of the mind and the brain functions of being awake are essentially one complex function, and both are necessary for us to be awake, conscious of the world about us and of being alive. However, *all knowledge is provisional.* It does not follow that both systems have to work in such close tandem when we are in all the other various states of sleep.

Let us open our minds to consider an alternative and recap on our knowledge of our neural machinery.

In the previous chapters, we have studied four major aspects of our neural "machinery". We have a reasonably clear idea of what our *brain* (the hardware) and *mind* (the software) are, how they evolved, what they do for us and the differences between them. We have studied and analysed *information* which is the raw material of everything we are discussing. We have come up with some descriptions and definitions of *intelligence*, which, at least at one level, is how efficiently we process that information; finally, we have studied how we experience the meaning of everything that happens to us, and, in particular, the meaning of every word and phrase.

Conscious awareness appears to be tied up with being awake or asleep. We have observed this gradient of being awake from deep anaesthesia, to deep sleep, REM sleep, dozing, just awake, and alert, all the way up to full concentration. If we are in any of the awake phases, we hear and react, yet, even if we are fast asleep, and someone says our name or calls a warning we react, thus we could not have been completely asleep, or there is some danger warning override?

Yet, although there are many examples of conscious awareness being closely tied up with being awake, it is like so much else: *not quite*. We can note this as a clue.

The brain and mind uses a lot of energy. Is sleep the way we recharge the batteries? Both physical and emotional crises make us tired. Some animals hibernate for a whole season. If this recharge function is correct, what is the relationship to being consciously aware?

Dreaming

Subsidiarily, we have noted the curious experience of dreaming that never quite fits in to any hypothesis. People of a religious persuasion have suggested this is part of our communication system to the gods; perhaps how they try, and warn and guide us? More prosaically, it is thought it might be the brain tidying up previous experiences and sorting out the filing. We often seem aware of events happening around us, and yet we are definitely asleep: a contradiction difficult to explain. Then there is the opposite of dreaming: sleep walking. Moving around and behaving nearly normally, but quite clearly fast asleep. A sharp hit to the head may cause some synapses to drop apart: a brain function, but why does that cause us to lose consciousness: a mind function? Is this a clue?

Can our experience of the design of computers and their software help us in any way? In a negative way they can. We will soon have vastly cleverer computers: an ever-expanding library of intelligent applications, building up to versions of ever more comprehensive general intelligence, but very obviously none are conscious, awake or aware: not a scintilla, not a hint. What is it computers do *not* have?

And here is another small hint. Computers are programmed to switch off, if they are not used for a period of time, to save energy and to make sure that some pixels on the screen are not damaged. Touch the screen or mouse and they are instantly back in full action. Might this spark an idea?

Short-form Definitions

Let us summarise what we have learned about the four attributes of brain, mind, information, intelligence and meaning. We have learned a lot about the *brain* recently. It is part of the central nervous system. At birth, we have some billion neurons in the central nervous system and another billion concentrated in the brain, between them providing the communications infrastructure that coordinates the whole body — the autonomic functions of the central nervous system. There are a number of types of neuron, but they mostly have a nucleus and a number of *dendrites* receiving signals from the sensory and other organs, and one or more *axons* transmitting signals to the muscles, glands and other organs, and other neurons. The connections of these neural filaments are by gaps known as *synapses*. The brain is the physical hardware.

The *mind* is the mass of patterns of electrochemical signals that are continuously flowing over the neural networks of the brain and central nervous system. Our best guess is that these signals patterns evolved from the signals of cells and organs communicating with each other enabling the body to operate ever more efficiently as one coordinated synchronised whole.

Information is both what means things and what does things, and *intelligence* is the efficiency with which the latter processes the former.

Meaning is the sensations, impressions, emotions, passions, perceptions, cravings, lusts, urges and feelings generated by the cocktails of hormones and other chemicals secreted by the endocrine system, and the activities of the enteric, cardiovascular and immune systems. Starting in the far distant past with anger, fear, hunger, thirst, raised heart rate, fever and arousal, these have evolved to generate nuanced meanings associated with individual words and phrases, images, sounds, smells, taste and touch.

Power Supply

It is useful just to recap on the power supply of the system. The nucleus of every individual neuron contains mitochondria that continuously generate energy for immediate use with any excess being stored in ATP "batteries" and available to cope with emergences that may need strong sustained responses. This enables the neurons to transmit electrochemical signal patterns along the length of axons and neurons, and control the tension across the synaptic connections.

The Cycles of Consciousness and Sleep

The current traditional conventional view of the meaning of the word consciousness is that it tends to be used to mean two things in two contexts. It is nearly synonymous with being awake, and it is used to include all the sensations of being aware of our surroundings and of being an individual and being alive.

We are at the risk of being ambushed by our own shortage of words to describe this more accurately.

Consciousness tends to be taken to mean being awake and being aware all as one monolithic function.

Unconscious is almost synonymous with being asleep and unaware of anything (as in being "knocked unconscious").

On the other hand, *subconscious* suggests various activities being carried out in the background while being completely asleep.

Let us deconstruct these various functions in the light of what we have just been exploring.

One of the major constituents of conscious awareness is being able to communicate with others and also to be able to talk silently, even debate with ourselves: to think.

We are familiar with the concept that a part of intelligent neural activity is to assemble words into phrases etc., and generate the *verbal language* to speak those words, to write those words, to think those words, to recognise the sound of those words and seeing those words, all in exquisite detail.

Similarly, the background neural processing system is continuously monitoring the sensory and other organs, responding accordingly, and stimulating the glands to secrete the hormones of the *language of the endocrine system* to generate the sensations, perceptions, impressions and emotions of being aware of everything that is happening around and to us. We have explored how these two languages have come together enabling both neural activities to use the language of the hormones of the endocrine system to give the sensations and emotions of meaning to words, phrases, art and music of neural activity, substantially widening our conscious experience.

What we have traditionally bundled together as the conscious awareness of being awake has four major components.

(1) The continuous background autonomic functions of the central nervous system monitoring the whole body.
(2) Our learned individual library of foreground physical and mental applications many of which generate verbal language and communication with others.
(3) Thinking.
(4) The electrochemical signalling activity of the neural networks driving all these activities which are modulated by the synapses whose behaviour is controlled by the level of available energy.

Relatively minor players are the cardiovascular system that contributes sensations, usually warning, like heart beats, the enteric system contributing sensations of hunger, thirst and the need to defecate. The immune system contribution is the least known but is likely to contribute sensations associated with illness like fevers and possibly contribute experiences we associate with depression and wellbeing.

Notwithstanding our shortage of words, we can be more specific about the gradient of conscious awareness.

Conscious Wakeful Awareness

There are three variants of conscious wakeful awareness.

(1) Concentration — all systems are fully active. The neurons may be using all their available energy supplies; the tension across the synapses is at its maximum, so the synaptic gaps are at their narrowest, facilitating the maximum efficient transmission of neural signals activating the endocrine hormone language generating a full conscious awareness experience and a sense of being wide awake.

(2) Alert and attentive — probably the normal resting state of the brain. The background monitoring system is normally active. Usually, only one foreground application is active. The neuron energy use is in equilibrium and so the synapses are facilitating normal transmission, and the endocrine hormone language operating normally.

(3) Drowsiness. The background monitoring system remains in its normal state of activity, but is reporting nothing interesting. Any foreground activity is minimal, giving way to the introspection of reminiscing and thinking; the memory systems are mildly active. Neuron energy output is beginning to fall, tension across the synapses weakens, the synaptic gaps widen lowering transmission speeds, which begin to reduce the endocrine hormone output. We are still consciously aware and only just awake.

If some event occurs or the monitoring system picks up a risk, energy in the neurons can be restored rapidly to push the system back up to being in a state of alert, or concentration quickly.

Unconsciousness and Asleep

If nothing occurs to interfere with this state of drowsiness, then the energy flowing from the neurons will continue to drop, tension across the synapses will weaken, the gaps will widen, further reducing transmission traffic and lowering the endocrine hormone output. The background autonomic functions monitoring the sensory organs remain active. We are asleep, but in some parts of the brain the neural networks may have sufficient energy to remain partially active, generating some endocrine hormone output: we dream.

Subconscious

The background monitoring system remains active 24/7, as do all the other autonomic functions of the central nervous system. The neurons are recharging their depleted stores of energy; a minimal amount of energy maintains the lowest level of synaptic tension. Some neural traffic generates so little reaction that we have only vestigial conscious awareness and we experience being fully asleep or anaesthetised.

Definition of Consciousness, Awake, Aware and Asleep

Consciousness, unconsciousness and subconscious are all one continuous set of neural processes, operating 24/7 throughout our lives. Streams of electrochemical signals transmitted over the neural networks cause the glands of the endocrine and other systems to secrete patterns of hormones, which generate all the sensations and emotions that give meaning to information.

Functions of the Mind

Being awake or asleep (or anywhere along that gradient of the sleep wake cycle) is governed by the level of energy in the neurons. This determines the tension across the synapses and the width of the synaptic gaps, which varies the speed and efficiency of the signals transmitted over them.

Functions of the Brain

Detail and Amplification

Consciousness is all about processing the *meaning* of everything that is going on around us. Aware of the outside world, ourselves, what our bodies are feeling. It is in operation continuously and is independent of whether we are awake or asleep. While we are asleep this processing continues. The sensory organs continue to monitor the external and internal world. The autonomic functions of the central nervous system continue in full operation 24/7. The evidence is that if someone says our name, even if we are fast asleep we hear and wake up.

Whether we are awake or asleep is quite separate and is dependent solely on the availability of energy accessible to maintain tension across the synapses, and therefore, the width of the synaptic gaps, which, in turn, control and modulate the volume and efficiency of information transmitted. The highest tension — the narrowest gaps, accounts for concentration, then alert, awake, below which we begin to drift into edges of sleep. First, REM sleep, then deep sleep and finally anaesthesia — the lowest tension — the widest gaps.

With the possible exception of deep anaesthesia, the synapses continue to transmit signals at all times. When we are concentrating, the synaptic tension is highest, and all the electrochemical signal traffic is transmitted at top available speed and efficiency. In REM sleep, variable amounts of traffic are transmitted, sometimes randomly by various groups of neural networks — we dream. Even in deep sleep, enough traffic is transmitted to enable high emotional signals like our name, or a warning to scale the widest synaptic gaps and stimulate the system.

While we are asleep, the background autonomic functions of the central nervous system continue to operate as normal, monitoring the sensory and other organs, managing and synchronising the body. Hence, we often wake up to find we have a solution to a problem or we have memorised some poetry.

All the synapses in the brain do not necessarily lose tension simultaneously or at the same rate. Signals to the muscles and the muscles themselves use the most energy. They tend to be the first to lose power, so the memory systems can often continue to transmit patterns of signals which get through to other neurons but not to the muscles. So, part of our brain is active and experiencing the sensations of dreaming of some event, but we have the sensation that we cannot move, and indeed we cannot. A very common occurrence in dreams.

Chiara Cirelli and Giulio Tononi at the University of Wisconsin–Madison report a much more intriguing phenomenon. Their research, so far only on mice, suggests that individual and groups of neurons experience "on" periods of neural activity and "off" periods when they are silent, during sleep, and in a staccato manner while awake. This opens the possibility that the tension across the synapses of individual and networks of neurons may operate randomly across swathes of the brain, driven by a variety of changing circumstances, out of synchronisation with the main brain operation. Not only do these findings add to the argument that being awake and asleep are quite separate functions to the neural processes of consciousness, but they also open a Pandora's box of ideas. This stimulates the hypothesis that this random operation of the synapses could account for lapses of memory. Could the dreaded "senior citizen syndrome" and energy failure even be one of the main causes of the various forms of dementia?

So to conclude, the brain determines whether at any one moment we are asleep or awake. The mind continuously generates the sensations of consciousness. These are two quite separate neural functions, and they operate quite separately. Only when the brain is awake, does the mind experience sensations of consciousness. When the brain is just asleep, the mind may experience some limited sensations of consciousness: dreaming. When the brain is asleep or anaesthetised, the mind continues to generate conscious sensations, but the mind is not able to experience them.

Exploring Sensations, Perceptions, Impressions and Emotions

How do we experience sensations, impressions, perceptions, feelings and emotion? Feeling warm or cold is registered by the sensory organs in our skin, as the difference across the membrane from outside to inside generating a stream of neural signals, according to their intensity: a few if warm, and a massive stream if burning. Do the streams of electrical signals generated by calcium and sodium ions along the length of an axon stimulate this sensation of warmth, comfort and well-being, or pain? No, they do not. They do activate glands that secrete a cocktail of hormones that do generate these sensations. This is a function of the biochemistry of the body.

Adrenalin, testosterone, serotonin, endorphins and probably a couple of 100 more neurotransmitters and messenger molecules, behave like words but words of different strength, volume and persistence. They blend to generate various levels of fear, anger, excitement and relaxation etc.: clenched stomach muscles, higher heart rate, increased blood sugar levels, desire, swelling of the sex organs, pleasure etc. These are all major, not very subtle sensations that are likely to be similar in most mammals and have been present in our ancestors for many millennia. However, over the span of our species' evolution and over the lifetime of each individual's growth to maturity and our ever expanding experiences; these perceptions, sensations, impressions and emotions have grown more complex, more nuanced: crying, laughing, lonely, jealous, unloved, rejected, greedy, self-confident, introvert, extrovert, self-confident, shy and, as we noted above, more complex with puberty — plus intricate details of the inputs from the sensory and other organs, so that even individual words acquire individual discreet reactions, thus out of simplicity at every level grows complexity at every level.

Exact patterns of activity over the neurons are a form of "language of sensations" with subsets that resemble words. Thus, sequences of these subsets of feelings generate sophisticated complex sensations, particularly and explicitly in a similar fashion to the way a string of words generate complex meanings. Feelings map onto meanings in the same way. One set stimulates the other. Hence, a word we hear translates into a feeling that generates a sensation, while the feeling of a sensation translates into a word we can speak. Thus, we can conclude that the sensation, perception, impressions and emotions of conscious experience are generated from the precise neural patterns of a "language" of sensations generated by the hormones secreted by the glands of the endocrine system, in much the same way as the meanings of speech is constructed from the language of words.

This opens another intriguing possibility. Feedback between these two systems enables words to generate perception and deduce meaning, while sensations, feelings and emotion, in turn, generate words. This could be the basis of the process whereby we build up a unified model of the world.

Synchronised Waves of Meta Neuron Networks

We have noted above that waves of neural networks fire in unison and oscillate in synchronised phases. Francis Crick and Christof Koch thought these might be the basis of consciousness and described them as the "neural correlates of consciousness". However, on reflection, they are hardware functions and are more to do with competing for, and grabbing attention, and maximising efficiency. It seems likely that, as a second-order function, they generate sensations of consciousness. For instance, if a meta network grabs attention in a crisis, it is likely to stimulate the generation of more adrenaline to maximise the speed of reaction of the whole body. So, from this point of view, brain waves impact conscious experience but only indirectly.

Functions of Consciousness

Memories and Availability of Information

Neural and amended memories are new links and structures of neurons. They include synapses that have been adjusted and strengthened (as opposed to just tension variability), new patterns and networks of neurons that are edited, extended, reinforced and insulated (myelinated). On each occasion *that they are activated*, these new and modified structures generate similar perceptions, sensations, impression, emotions and neural, muscular and glandular activity to those that caused these developments in the first place.

The physical neural brain structures of all our entire information (database) are present whether we are alive, dead or asleep. Only if the mind is able to *activate these networks* by a flow of patterns of electro-chemical signals, are we *conscious of their existence*, and include them in any deliberations to make decisions.

Abstract Thinking and Prediction

Language enables us to reminisce about the past and try and apply our experience to improve how we cope with the present. However, it gave us another skill that is unique in the living world. We can think about extrapolating what has happened in the past, and think about, imagine, speculate and predict what might happen in the future. All the systems in the universe we know about are self-organising. No self-organising systems can predict, they can only respond to events. The ability to imagine the possible future course of events enables us to prepare for eventualities. Hence, we have begun to modify and control our environment: to take over the planet.

Thinking is a function of consciousness. We can think whether we are asleep or awake, but we have greater control over what we think when we are awake. The key point for this discussion of consciousness is that all predictions, all imagined futures, all speculation of the future courses of events are abstract. They only exist in the patterns of neural activity in our heads. (Similarly all computer programs are abstract.) We can make notes of our ideas, write novels, make lists and draw flow charts, but their genesis is entirely cerebral. We largely think in words, and those words will be either directly, or indirectly, anchored to the neural structures of experiences of the sensory systems, but the structures of possible future circumstances and how we might prepare for them are entirely abstract constructions of the electrochemical software activity of the mind.

We can think in modalities other than words. Architects think in shapes, musicians in chords, chefs in tastes, programmers in patterns and so on. These thoughts are directly linked to sensations. They can be powerful but difficult to communicate. We usually need words to describe and fine tune them.

We have to map the (digital) words we have on to the (analogue) neural structures we have grown. Therefore, we sometimes do not have the vocabulary to describe our sensations and feelings adequately — the redness of a rose, attraction, beauty, leadership. We call these *qualia*. Perhaps, one day, we will learn to invent new words and phrases that describe qualia sufficiently accurately that they generate these sensations. Perhaps they will stay tantalisingly out of reach. Perhaps the power of emergence can be employed to build a knowledge base of accurate descriptions and definitions of qualia.

A significant part of the meanings of things and all our thinking and the imagined predictions we create are functions, constructions and processes of the mind. The fictitious worlds we dream up in our imaginations have no basis in reality, yet we are so confident of them we store, retain, recall and modify them in the greatest detail.

As we have observed, all these functions, constructions and processes stimulate endocrine system activity causing the glands to secrete hormones, neurotransmitters and messenger molecules, which generate perceptions, sensations, feeling, impressions and emotions, and therefore, are a major part of our experience of our advanced consciousness.

Unlimited Capacity

Perhaps the most valuable attributes of our ability to think, is that it is a skill we can learn. There is no upper limit to our capability. It is not constrained with the number, speed or efficiency of the neurons we have inherited. Thinking is something we can teach. It is the basis of creativity and essential for our future wellbeing.

Monitoring: Feedback

Neurons linking the brain to the muscles and other organs are generally in pairs: axons transmitting signals to activate the muscles etc., and dendrites transmitting signals back to the brain. The sensory organs provide a feedback mechanism of how the external world is responding, particularly to our actions. We have a series of *mirror neurons* that imitate the actions of others. Taken together, we have a sophisticated feedback system. Sometimes we have the experience of somehow monitoring our own behaviour: the id checking up on the ego. This is partly to do with timing. The brain is optimised to respond fast. The mind is more concerned with the quality, rather than the speed of our responses. However, if we get involved in an argument or confrontation, our brain can begin to take precedence to protect itself. If we get excited and our glands are stimulated to flood the system with adrenaline and testosterone, we may find ourselves reacting differently — too belligerently perhaps. If our mind starts to realise we are beginning to lose, it is either time to change tactics or take some evasive action.

Many observers have commented that there is plenty of evidence that when we take some action we appear to be conscious of this only after the event. So, who is in charge? In many everyday situations, the brain gets on with controlling the body as a cooperating coordinated whole. We spend a lot of time on autopilot and our consciousness is not stimulated. However, sometimes "I" notices that "me" has just done something and I am baffled. Why did I do that? This is, surely, just various parts of the brain operating independently, with minimum effort, and the monitoring system catching up?

Great orators often provoke their antagonists to make a particular retort, so that they can impress by reacting very fast with a carefully planned riposte. As well as a monitoring function, the mind facilitates building networks in the brain to be in position and prepared for instant action. Thus, we see the mind stimulating the growth of new networks in the brain.

Characteristics of Personality and Temperament

We gradually build up a wealth of experiences: a cornucopia of memories. We grow trillions of new neural links and structures, and when we stimulate them, they generate streams of patterns of signals, which can either manifest themselves as verbal reminiscences, or some physical action, or just a mass of perceptions, sensations, impressions and emotions mirroring those we experienced the first time they occurred. Early in life, we talk about temperament. Taken together, they represent an abstract representation of our lives: our hopes, fears and ambitions, our successes and failures and how we responded. This mass of memories are our lives; our sense of self — the characteristics of our personality.

As our brain wakes up each morning and a subset of this ever-growing array in our mind becomes active, we become aware we are alive. We have the perception and sensation of a sense of self. We are conscious.

Thinking and Reasoning

Thinking is a skill that sets us apart from every other species. It enables us to review circumstances in the light of our previous experience and debate with others. We can invent alternative solutions, search for novel patterns, test theories and build whole new structures and mental edifices.

All the different aspects of our imagination are a function of thinking. The whole creative world of fiction is based on abstract thinking.

We largely think by talking silently to ourselves in our heads, so we can think anywhere, anytime, oblivious of our surroundings. We build neural structures of thoughts, ideas, and concepts and set about testing them. We assemble groups of words to reflect as accurately as we can these thoughts. As we get older, this becomes the dominant part of our consciousness. However, we can observe we have another skill very close to thinking that we call reasoning. They are different facets of creativity, but have interesting differences.

Thinking is usually a mental construction of some sort, a solution, or a formula, or algorithm that enables us to obtain a solution to something. Thoughts are often extensions, coalescences or hierarchies of other thoughts, and on rare occasions a unique new concept. Invention, prediction and imagination are usually thought of as functions of thinking. On the other hand, reasoning is usually an answer to something, or the way something happens. Reasoning is often a comparison of alternatives rather than a new unique creation. Reasons are often explanations.

Thinking is predominantly inventing *how* things happen, reason more *why* things happen. What was the stimulation? Both are activities of the software signalling systems of the mind operating over the hardware neural structures of our brain when it is fully awake and fully conscious. We have discussed elsewhere logic and creativity. They make interesting comparisons.

Recursion: The Last Piece of the Jigsaw

There is another considerable advantage of the hypothesis that being awake is a state determined by the tension across the synapses, and that consciousness is a continuous process stimulated by the activity of the neurons, sensory and other organs, causing the endocrine glands to secrete a language of hormones, generating a stream of sensations, impressions, emotions, perceptions feelings and experiences in our whole body.

It provides us with an explanation of that most difficult aspect of conscious experience — the really hard problem — to be able think about how it feels, and about how it felt, about what we were thinking, when we were wondering if we were right, when we thought. Recursive self-representation or conscious thinking and reflection of our thoughts.

We have explored above that our memories of visual, sound and the other senses, are patterns, perhaps "profiles" is a better word, of perceptions and sensations and that, when we retrieve these memories, we experience similar emotions to the experiences of the original events. With our eyes closed, or even if they are open, we are fully aware of most of the details of Constable's *The Hay Wain*. In a silent room, we can clearly hear the first bars of Beethoven's Vth Symphony.

It follows that we can store and later retrieve the profiles of the emotions, sensations, impressions and perceptions that we experienced when the original event occurred. We can recall how we felt when we were wondering "if". Thus, we can replay/process/think about previous conscious experiences in the same way as we can contemplate past sensory experiences, we can relive them at will, the sensations we experienced of taste, smell, how we felt when we lost our temper, won an argument, was frightened, cold, aroused and so on. We can then process conscious experiences as a sixth sense. This is immensely powerful. We can, at last, see how we are able to think about..., how we previously thought about...., what we felt about..., when over the years we were wondering about....

Arguably this is the last major component of consciousness slipped into place.

Summary

We can make a compelling argument that consciousness is an attribute and function of the mind — being awake, a function of the brain. We can define consciousness as the mass of perceptions, sensations, impressions and emotions generated by the whole body, and in particular, the banks of endocrine glands and the floods of hormones they secrete, stimulated by the patterns of electrochemical signals transmitted over the neural networks of the brain, initiated by the activity of our sensory and other organs monitoring the world, and our responses. We can process these conscious experiences like a sixth sense.

When we are born, we are conscious of very little, and we have very little control over our behaviour. Immediately, we begin to grow neural structures of our experiences and exploits and begin to build our perception of ourselves. We learn to actively monitor our automatic behaviour and be aware of the reactions to and by other people, and we begin to control our responses. We begin to accumulate the meanings of an ever-growing mass of information. To start with, we accept a lot of what we are told at face value, but increasingly we learn to question, interrogate and criticise, and begin to think for ourselves. We are increasingly conscious of ourselves as individuals. If we are lucky to enjoy a good education, we are encouraged to ever widen our interests, study as many subjects as possible, try new experiences, strive to identify the talents we possess and what skills we can master in the cornucopia of the rainbow of human ability and endeavour; and learn to enjoy the exhilaration of the adventure of exploring every aspect of our universe.

Thus, we construct an ever-growing abstract bank of the mass of memories of our past experiences, our perceptions of the present and our expectations of the future. We learn to widen, deepen and extend our consciousness of our world and our place in it. We can retain and understand whatever we have sufficient desire to learn. We can learn to concentrate harder. We can learn to think more clearly. We can learn to reason more logically. Thus, our consciousness is closely tied to our body of knowledge. And the speed and quality of how we access and process that knowledge is a major part of how we describe and define intelligence. We can see how consciousness, intelligence and learning all work together to maximise our knowledge, our abilities and our potential.

There is no limit to our capacity to learn, to think, to be creative. They bid each other up, and help drive forward our civilisation.

CHAPTER SEVENTEEN

THINKING, KNOWLEDGE AND CREATIVITY

We have explored *thinking*, referred to *knowledge* and investigated *creativity*; however, as these capabilities stand at the pinnacle of our civilisation, it might be profitable to reprise them together and how they impact on each other, specifically to consider how we can use our understanding to enhance our own individual personal abilities.

We have studied intelligence in all its forms and capabilities and mentioned its central contribution to thinking, knowledge and creativity, but in one aspect intelligence and thinking are quite different. Intelligence is overwhelmingly about the present and the past. 'Thinking' and 'creativity' are about the future: pushing out the frontiers of our knowledge. It is about prediction, imagination and speculation. We cannot intelligence the solution to a dilemma; we can use our intelligence to think of a solution.

Arguably, this has been the philosophical stumbling block that the computing community has encountered in designing and programming artificial or machine intelligence. The delegates at Dartmouth in 1956 thought that producing a definition of intelligence would be easy.

The Implications of the Fourth Dimension

We can write programs that process — behave — intelligently, but essentially, they all process existing information. They identify patterns in massive quantities of existing records. They analyse experience, which, by definition, is about the past. Their role is extremely important, because they can, increasingly do tasks that the human brain has evolved to do but not on this massive scale.

The great successes of the last few years — chess, quizzes, "Go", language processing — are all either analysing existing records or using histories of experience. The results are spectacular and will get ever more impressive and valuable. However, no program yet written, or even conceived, can create a new idea, because thinking and creativity are about prediction and imagination which are both abstract and the product of sensations and emotions. Different emotional states can cause different neural responses from similar information. Protagonists argue that we can design programs that simulate sensations and emotions and so invent new solutions. Programs have been designed which compose pieces of music which are almost indistinguishable from original music from the past. Specialists can tell the difference because they are variations on a theme or recognisable style. However, we should not be complacent. We have only just begun to think about these ideas. The genius of the human brain is being employed to build genius into our computers.

There is one flaw. We can build wonderful capabilities into our machines with one exception — coping with the unexpected. By definition, we have built skills and, yes, probably elements of genius into programs, but they are, and only ever can be our constructs. Thus, every event has in one sense been expected by the program designer. Build in random number generators? Hardly.

It is the central problem of the whole research community. Governments and institutions can build superb facilities and vote large sums of money to employ the best staff, but no one can invent to order. 90% of all current research is about improving on what we have discovered and turning science into products and wealth. Very laudable, but that is behaving intelligently, not thinking, not creating new knowledge. Administrators still ask the researchers to forecast how many new ideas they will have next year so the budget can be set. Entirely reasonable question. Entirely impossible to answer. The words "blue sky" come to mind. Equally, even the best administrators have difficulty accepting Bertrand Russel's advice, and many others, to employ the most unreasonable and eccentric people they can find.

So, how is it — what is it, about the human brain and mind that can invent new ideas, new concepts and new solutions? The whole process of evolution is based upon the concept that at any one time a variety of solutions to the problems of everyday life are in competition, and the best prosper, and reproduce their genes which generated their winning behaviour. So, the whole genetic system is based on variety and competition. However, at the beginning of the twenty-first century, we do not have any control over the make-up of the genome we inherit or pass on down to our offspring (at least for the time being!)

There is a compelling argument that our deoxyribonucleic acid (DNA) holds not just the genomes of our two parents but also the genomes of many of our ancestors. We come into this world only half created and are not fully mature till our teens, so that we have time to adapt to the circumstances in which we find ourselves. As well as a massive learning machine our entire system is optimised to adapt and survive.

Constructive Tension of Conservers and Reformers

We can observe that all communities tend to divide into conservators and reformers. The former council everyone to make the best of what we have and not let go of nanny's purse in case we encounter something worse. The reformers are never satisfied and are keen to experiment with new solutions. Down the centuries, belief systems have universally been conservators usually because they fear having to justify their beliefs to reformers. Reformers do not have a universal record of success!

In political terms, democracy has been a great champion of reform, because democracy at its base is about tolerance. Once a community starts to think about new ideas in one subject, it is impossible to stop that spilling over into others. In Britain, the break with Rome, then the civil war exchanged a monarch ruling by divine right to a constitutional figurehead and an elected body of citizens. This unleashed huge intellectual energy, like the Royal Society and the Industrial Revolution, spurred on by waves of immigrants like the Huguenots. Computing was led from the eastern United States but gravitated to California, partly because of the plentiful supply of "new" money and not least because of the tolerance of the west coast community.

London is rising as a centre of innovation again, thanks to its wide mix of immigrants and its social tolerance, but it is being held back by endless regulations, unsupportive governments and mostly only "old" money that always tends to be risk adverse.

In neural terms, new ideas can often be seen as errors, and the established authorities and the peer review system are often sceptical. The ArXiv publishing facility of Cornell University is a way round this inertia. Science fiction plays a valuable role, as it often plants innovative ideas in people's minds. No one thought Captain Kirk could really be "beamed up" to his space station until Professor Anton Zeilinger demonstrated "teleportation" in his laboratory in Innsbruck in 1998. Only a molecule was teleported, but it proved the technology was possible.

We have set out how logic is about assembling known facts into patterns that lead to better solutions. Thinking is about imagination, playing with ideas however implausible, role playing, and one other important constituent. Many new concepts are the result of the cross fertilisation of concepts from different disciplines. In the last few years, the convergence of cognitive neuroscience, biogenetics and computing has unleashed a flood of innovative ideas — many in this book.

There is a compelling argument that education should be moving towards producing polymaths, but away from specialism, especially as early as teenage. No one can know every subject in depth but everyone can know the basic principles of most subjects, enough to whet their curiosity or uncover an unexpected talent.

Learning to Think

Thinking is about trying to assemble a variety of ideas together, and seeing if they can form any sort of novel and useful pattern. One way to begin to learn to think, is to express a well-known situation or circumstance in the form of a problem to solve. There are many, many situations in life we have grown up with and which are so familiar that it never occurs to anybody to try and change and even, possibly improve them. A problem has parameters. How things are. Why are they that way? What are the possible alternatives? Could this be better?

There are many techniques for thinking. Edward de Bono popularised the idea of thinking "outside the box", which is often very successful. There is a plethora of alternatives. Some work for some people, some for others. One important component is to be able to recognise a better solution when one chances on one. It is often easy to dismiss an innovative idea, even our own, but often it comes back and we realise we have a solution. If often happens when we do have a good idea, we realise we have thought of this before but had not recognised its value.

If we sometimes find it difficult to recognise a good idea even when it is our own, think how much more difficult it is for a third party to appreciate this innovation? Half the difficulty of having good new ideas is selling them to the peerhood. Einstein was over 40 before people, even in his own subject, caught up and began to realise his breakthroughs. It is always a standard reaction, of even the most tolerant and enlightened, to respond negatively to any new idea, at least initially. The whole point about a new idea is that it is unfamiliar. Selling new concepts is always a hard slog.

Thinking Can Counter Stress

One considerable advantage of learning the art of thinking, is that it can be practised anywhere, any time. Computer programming is a stylised form of thinking: how to solve this problem with just these limited facilities. It too can be done anywhere. Both are very good at countering stress. If one's plane is delayed for many hours in some dreadful airport terminal, one can make the time fly by solving some tricky problem in one's head.

Another useful technique of thinking is to try and explain the problem to someone else. Similarly, trying to write down possible solutions can often clarify a vague idea into a plausible answer. Possibly this can be accounted for because we have had to rearrange the solution from another perspective and, or state the problem in another medium.

Yet another tried and tested method begs as many questions as it solves. If faced with an intractable problem, the best plan is to do something as different as possible. Come back later to that problem and a possible solution has often surfaced. This is reported so often that it must have some basis of validity. It suggests the intriguing possibility that our background autonomic general intelligence is working on the case, while we are actively involved elsewhere. Also, it appears that the more energetically we are involved elsewhere, the more likely we are to have found a solution.

Emergence

Once again, we should not overlook the power of emergence in the process of thinking and creating new knowledge. Both the process of thinking and the ability to create something new are very close to being able to assemble facts, words, ideas etc. where the whole is greater than the sum of the parts.

This recurring theme is explored further in Appendix 25 (hosted on www.BrainMindForum.org/appendices), but Oh! What a powerful one.

CHAPTER EIGHTEEN
THE SYNAPTIC CONJECTURE

Synapses are, perhaps, the most enigmatic components of the central nervous system in general, and the brain in particular. Evolution usually seems to select the simplest solution, yet here we can observe a remarkably complex and sophisticated structure, in what might have been thought to be a relatively unimportant mechanism: how neurons are connected to all the sensory and other organs, the muscles, bones, glands and other neurons. Why? Synapses have not received all that much attention. What are we missing?

We have introduced this conjecture in Chapter 1 and Appendix 30 (all appendices are hosted on www.BrainMindForum.org/appendices) outlines some of the latest research findings. In Chapter 13, we have begun to advance a theory that suggests synapses have a far more important role, and also a possible role in brain mind failures. In Chapter 16, we suggest synapses play a decisive key role in sleep and being awake. Let us look at synapses with new eyes?

There appear to be a small number of variant types of synapses, but the vast majority share the same architecture. These connections throughout the central nervous system and brain consist of a gap, or synaptic cleft. On each side of this cleft, a slight swelling contains, on the transmitting side, a source of neurotransmitters and on the receiving side, a set of receptors. Electrochemical signals arriving at a synapse stimulate the output of neurotransmitters which flow across to the receptors and stimulate a reaction. If the receptor is on another neuron, probably a dendrite, a new electrochemical signal will be generated and transmitted along that dendrite. If the receptor is on a muscle, gland or other organ, it will stimulate an activity by that muscle, gland or organ.

Once this signal has been transmitted, no more neurotransmitters are produced and any unused will be removed, probably by scavenging glia cells, effectively closing the link temporarily, to avoid a continuing signal causing confusion further down the neural networks.

What holds the two sides of this synaptic gap in such close proximity, but without touching? How wide is this synaptic gap or cleft? And the most important question. Is this gap variable? The best answer we have is that synapses are held in permanent tension. Raise the tension, narrow the gap. Weaken the tension, widen the gap.

A variable gap has significant ramifications for the transmission of the neurotransmitters. Crossing a wider gap will take longer. Crossing a narrower gap will be quicker — more efficient.

How are synapses held in tension? We know that activity along the axons and dendrites generates a surrounding electromagnetic field. It would seem that the energy generated in the nucleus of the neuron can thus be projected to provide the magnetism to hold the synapses in tension. Thus, the volume of energy available in the nucleus is the deciding factor.

Historically, it has been suggested that this complex arrangement enables the connection between an axon and a dendrite in a circuit to be more easily moved, or slid, thus enabling the time taken by a whole neural circuit to be fine-tuned. Moving a synapse closer to a muscle will cause it to contract or relax microseconds earlier. One can observe this in action with the exquisite timing of a professional gymnast, for instance.

Another suggestion is that synapses act as circuit breakers to damp down unwanted electric surges, overheating or fatigue. It certainly provides an answer to why a sharp hit to the head, a knockout blow, literally knocks the synapses apart causing instant unconsciousness. However, there are far more ambitious purposes for synaptic tension causing variable width synaptic clefts.

Wide Fluctuations in Energy Needs

The central nervous system and the brain mind have evolved a number of mechanisms to store energy in quiet times to be able to deploy maximum energy quickly in a crisis, or ride out a famine. We have explored how individual neurons generate as much energy as possible from the nutrient, storing any excess to current requirements in adenosine triphosphate (ATP) "batteries".

On a more major scale, the brain mind uses a great deal of energy — something like a quarter to a third of all nutrient input to the whole body. After an emotional, or physical crisis, or even just the cumulative effect of the passage of time, the system begins to run low of energy. We cope with this problem by falling asleep.

Here is the perfectly graduated mechanism. As energy levels fall, the magnetism round the synapses weakens, the tension falls and the clefts widen. All the electrochemical signals and all the neurotransmitters continue to flow, but more slowly. These signals no longer penetrate our consciousness and we fall asleep. As the generation of energy catches up with requirements, the magnetism round the synapses strengthens, the tension rises and the clefts close. All the electrochemical signals and all the neurotransmitters start to flow more efficiently. At a point of critical mass, we wake up. Maximum energy = maximum tension = narrowest gaps = efficient transmission of signals = concentration.

Concentration

This analogue system modulates the efficiency of the synapses and therefore the complete neural "circuits". There is an added bonus. Concentration can be optimised onto sets of neural networks and limited sections of the brain mind to give priority to currently imperative tasks and also exclude the remainder from being diverted by less important activities.

Short of full concentration, we have a mechanism to allocate resources. In many cases, we have observed that some processing happens in the foreground, some in the background. In a crisis, the background functions can be activated en bloc. We have used the example of driving a car while chatting to a friend. A pedestrian steps in front of the car and all our attention is immediately directed at this emergency. Here is the mechanism — a massive injection of energy to the whole of the 'driving networks'.

Key Role in Allocating Neural Resources

We are deep in a task, and the telephone rings and in a second we have to deal with a completely different set of activities to respond to the caller. Again, we can swiftly divert energy from one set of neural networks to another. We can wake up instantly in a crisis, or ease ourselves into conscious awareness in other circumstances.

Temporary Amnesia

We have begun to explore the whole role of energy in the processes of both memory formation and particularly memory failure. Recent research suggests that even individual neural circuits can close for short periods. See appendix 30.

It is generally accepted that neurons that fire together wire together. Two neurons may just form a new synapse between them, but we also know that a mature brain has grown a massive number of new links and structures — glia bridges. A link may require two new synapse, one at each end. A new structure may require more than two synapses. When a new memory structure is created, these new structures may be major users of energy or just bit players in the background, depending on our emotional state.

Energy plays an equally important role in the efficient and reliable accessing of stored information. It is a subject of growing importance. If we try to recall some word or fact, the neural system may well stimulate the right network to respond, but it may not deploy sufficient energy to send a strong enough signal across the synapses, so the "answer" does not penetrate conscious awareness. We have the sensation we have forgotten the answer, although we often feel that the answer is there somewhere: "on the tip of our tongues". After a while, when sufficient energy builds up, the correct "answer" is strong enough to succeed in crossing the synapse and we become consciously aware of knowing that answer.

This conjecture also suggests the reason why some people can remember things that happened a long time ago — the memory trace was laid down with greater strength, while they cannot recall recent events — the memory was laid down with too little energy.

We have speculated how these variable amounts of energy are deployed to support a wide range of brain mind functions, and the problems that can develop if insufficient energy is available. Perhaps this explains why evolution favoured our ever more wonderfully sophisticated synapses.

An Alternative Measure of Intelligence

Much effort, time and thought have been devoted to understanding our intelligence and all its associated neural functions. There is plenty of evidence that everyone's neural structures are different and operate at different speeds in different circumstances. This speed is a major component of what **intelligence quotient** (IQ) tests seek to measure.

We have a very compelling candidate and the one that cannot be influenced by the social environment. We have explored how the speed and efficiency of the neural circuits depend on the state of the synaptic clefts. How this efficiency can be maximised to cope with problems and minimised to enable us to recuperate from energetic activities. However, we can also observe the synapses in their normal everyday resting state. We can devise ways of measuring the reaction time for all the categories of intelligence and intelligent behaviour, and the background autonomic general intelligence, which we can identify both in extreme state and resting state, thus we can build up a comprehensive profile of an individual's overall competences, abilities and potential talents.

It is generally believed that electrochemical signals — action potentials — travel along axons and dendrites at fixed speeds of about 4 feet per second, governed by the laws of science. Yet observation suggests that people process neural transmissions at very different speeds. Could both statements be true? The signals may transmit along the axons and dendrites at similar speeds, but the observed difference is the performance of the synapses, which can vary greatly, even in their resting states.

There is a compelling argument to research this particular hypothesis, because if it is anywhere near true, then diet, and the whole nutrient path, energy generation complex, may have a far greater influence over neural processing than we have ever imagined. Furthermore, it may be possible to study possible medication that improves energy generation and synaptic tension. This could lead us to new ways of studying nonstandard syndromes like dyslexia and the various spectrums of autism. Could it turn out that the much-ignored synapse is the major key to unlocking our understanding of our intelligence and many of the workings of the operation of our brain and minds?

PART V
THE FUTURE

CHAPTER NINETEEN
THE FUTURE

What do we hope to gain from a better understanding of intelligence and consciousness? One argument is that all knowledge is valuable, but some people feel that something like intelligence is so personal, so wonderful, so inscrutable and so enigmatic that they would feel quite upset if it could be explained as a scientific phenomenon. For them, it would lose its mysteriousness. We can respect their opinions, but greater knowledge can only increase our respect for its genius.

What can we gain from peering into a crystal ball? Fifty years ago, only a few people directly involved with computers began to realise the implications of electronic digital computers. Twenty-five years ago — just before the internet and World Wide Web hit the street, the science fiction authors and futurologists were suggesting some exciting ideas. No one forecast the social media revolution. Hollywood usually opts for an apocalypse.

Can We Do Better?

Our observations and research over the last decade set out in this book, suggests we can make useful suggestions and some recommendations for the possible direction of research.

(1) Better brains: Top of the list to learn how to improve our own personal individual abilities. Part of this endeavour must be to understand more about the landscape of human ability. What are we trying to improve?

(2) Better computers: We can use our growing knowledge of ourselves and our potential to design ever more intelligent systems and robots.

Lastly, we can explore three specific topics, partly because they could be very valuable in their own right, and partly because, they are good examples of the general potential. The first is to draw attention to the importance of energy generation and usage in all neural activities, and the role and efficiency of the nutrient path, which our research has disclosed. The second, in the light of the arrival of gene editing, prosthetic brain interfaces and synthetic biological cells, is to stimulate discussion into the ethical, educational, employment and economic problems these advances will cause. The third could change our longevity and quality of life in this century to match the immense successes of the medical world in the last century.

Improving Our Own Personal Individual Abilities

Making the best use of our neural inheritance we can consider:

- If we understand more about how we learn, then we can learn to learn better, and we can learn more. If we can learn how to remember better, we can remember more.
- If we can learn how to control our concentration, we can concentrate harder.
- If we can learn to think, we can think more clearly.
- If we can learn to solve problems better, we can learn to make better decisions.
- If we can extend our own personal individual abilities, we can work better with our robots and the artificial intelligence (AI) systems we invent.

It seems likely that the whole subject of education, life-long learning and research may experience some of the biggest changes in the coming decades.

Education has taken great leaps forward in the last 100 years. The industrial revolution created the need, and provided the resources, for the whole community to attend schools for the first few years of their lives. There are many arguments about the difference between training to earn a living and education to broaden the mind. The excitement of the adventure of exploring this wonderful world we find ourselves in. When the first education acts were being passed in the late nineteenth century, the vast majority of the population had never travelled far from home. Today, most young people have travelled abroad for their holidays and many have explored the distant world by themselves on "gap" years. Television has widened the knowledge base, and now wikipedia, google and social media have opened up teenage eyes, ears and more to the world as never before. Sitting in classrooms even with the most inspiring teacher will soon seem very last century.

For the last few thousand years, the principle function of education has been to pass on the accumulated knowledge of the community to succeeding generations. Universities have always been sited around libraries.

Computers are taking over that task, causing a paradigm shift. We are on the cusp of having the entire body of human knowledge, art, culture and commerce available on our cell phones. Soon we will have wearable computers — in due course prosthetic interfaces. And not just the facts, but teaching, instruction, life styles, intensely personal information. These massive open online courses (MOOCS) are in their infancy, but they will steadily change the basic objectives of education.

Progressively the principle function of teenage education will gravitate towards identifying, nurturing and developing each individual's talents and abilities, and help them prepare for a future of lifelong learning and multiple careers in occupations we can only guess at.

The Variety of Brain Types

What we do know is that people have very different brains — everyone is unique, but we can identify some obvious groupings. Broadly, some people thrive in what we recognise as an academic environment, which then divides into those that tend to be the more literate and emotional, and those that tend to be more mathematical and logical. Completely different groups are more practical and technical. Their intelligence is about physical activity and dexterity. We have always known that creators, artists, actors, musicians and entrepreneurs have different skills and have cut them some slack, but we are only recently beginning to appreciate their importance and beginning to cater positively for their needs. In another dimension of this matrix are the risk takers, and the risk adverse, the extroverts and the introverts, the cautious and courageous, the leaders and the led, the explorers and the watchers.

Vanishingly, few teenagers wake up each morning excited at the thought of spending the day in a classroom. How do we remedy that?

Trends in Education

For the last 50 years, our education system only has an A-level stream, planned, organised, examined and judged by the academic community, which has successfully prepared the brightest and best to be the teachers, lecturers and professors, the lawyers, accountants, administrators, managers and bankers who supported the industrial revolution over the last century, and more recently, the new armies of regulators.

A new initiative is to try and build a T-level stream of cater for the hands-on practical, scientific, technically inclined stream of young people. However, the approaching tsunami that is so large few people can see it, is that this welcome reform does not go anywhere near what all advanced nations will need to implement — and as soon as possible. The problem is that the computer revolution is on course to make the high-value professions of the past: the A-level stream, obsolescent within little more than a decade.

We need to plan, organise and implement a C-level stream planned, organised, examined and judged by the creative, artistic and knowledge community to prepare the brightest and best for the high-value creative professions of the age of computing, who are already beginning to be visible: the designers, inventors, researchers, entrepreneurs, software designers, marketeers, engineers, and as always, the architects and doctors as well as all the arts and crafts. After the four r's of reading, writing, arithmetic and computing, key subjects should include design, logic, languages and philosophy.

How do we stimulate children to *want* to learn, to want to explore the world around them, to want to go to school and look forward to a career of lifelong learning? Classroom learning and endless exams tend to blunt the natural curiosity of many young people, squeezing out their imagination and creativity as they find that they do not fit the narrow general state education that John Stuart Mill and so many others have warned us against. It certainly does not seem to have been very successful. After 40 years of the A-level only strategy, 45% of young people leave school barely competent in five subjects. 20% are thought to be functionally illiterate (and they are gaining political power!).

Paradox of Sport

Young people who are good at one sport and bad at another are given extra coaching in the sport they are *good* at. They become the captain of that sport and are school heroes. Young people who are, say, good at maths and bad at English are given extra English lessons, end up in detention and are teased by the peerhood, and often by the teachers. Why not learn from sports and give the mathematicians extra coaching and encourage them to compete to be the captain of maths? Having built their confidence, encourage them to believe they can do everything well.

Learning from the Arts

The Royal Society of Arts is carrying our research into the relative effectiveness of different forms of cultural education, and what makes them effective. Is it the process of drafting and redrafting that is an endemic part of all the visual arts? Or the feedback, and rehearsal at the heart of drama? Or the deliberate practice and mastery required of a musician? Or the motor skills developed in the dance studio? Or the motivation and on-going inspiration drawn from a memorable experience, be it a display or public exhibition? Or performing or debating in public and before the parents and peerhood? The key is that the participants, of every age, *want* to participate in these disciplines.

Competitions might be much better than examinations at involving teenagers.

The Widest Possible Curriculum

Logic suggests that to prepare the next generation for the widest possible range of careers, they should experience the widest possible curriculum. Whatever stream any teenager takes, it would be wise to train *mentors* to help them widen their options, try alternatives, seek out their natural skills and talents. Every scientist should have a basic knowledge of our history and how our system of government developed and works, how our law operates. Every classicist should understand the basic principles of quantum physics; every mathematician should be able to express their ideas in clear English; every student of literature should be able to understand basic mathematics. They do not need to know much more than compound interest and the way money works.

There is a well-established advantage in being able to speak fluently in at least one foreign language and preferably have lived with another family in their country for a few months. Everyone should understand the basic economic rules of the capitalist system: a basic understanding of the law and accounting. An introduction to geography, astronomy, philosophy, and last, but not least hygiene and diet.

It is now fashionable, and promoted by the regulators, to concentrate school effort on getting the maximum number of students over the average grade hurdle, even at the expense of not stretching the ablest. History tells us that the top 10% in every community tend to drive it forward. To sacrifice the ablest in the interests of the average as Sir Michael Wilshaw, until recently, Head of Ofsted, has promoted, is economic suicide.

Selection Procedures

It is curious that selection, which is the basis of evolution and the driver of our civilisation, has become a shibboleth to politicians and that dread term "experts". All scarce resources inevitably involve selection procedures. Schools that gain a reputation for excellence will be oversubscribed, so are good jobs, so are attractive houses, the best holidays. Students of similar skills level who learn together tend to encourage and compete with each other to the benefit of all. Scholars have been segregated and taught together in great schools and universities for centuries. The problem is the method of selection.

Using the 1-hour intelligence quotient (IQ) test at any age to determine anyone's future education is rather like selecting people to spend a career in any type of sport by how fast they can run 100 yards. We need to give all our children, and adults for that matter, the best possible education that fits their individual talents and skills. We should give our brightest and best in every field of endeavour the maximum help, encouragement and support. In the end, we all benefit.

Selection procedures should cover the widest range of skills. We argued above, that a week-long battery of every sort and type of test would appear to be the practical minimum for all our young people, as a step towards identifying their latent talents and skills.

Accepted Wisdom

If we interrogate a computer and it does not have any answer stored in its memories, it cannot answer. If someone asks us a question about a subject which we have never learned anything about, we are hard pressed to manufacture an answer. If there is no neural memory structure, we cannot activate it. The opposite is true. If we have learned an answer, even just heard about an answer in some cases, then we will tend to reply on what we have stored in our memory banks. Generally, we do not stop and question if we think that answer is correct. There is an apocryphal tale of Darwin seeing some fish fossil on the top of an Argentinian mountain. Had he been to university, he might have learned that the accepted wisdom was that birds must have flown up there. As he had not heard this explanation, it occurred to him that perhaps that once upon a time, that mountain range had been beneath the sea.

It is important that we always teach that everything is always, on the balance of probabilities, only our best guess.

New Dispensation

If the priority is no longer to acquire detailed knowledge about a diminishing segment of our vast and increasing knowledge base, what are our priorities to teach our children? Few would disagree that reading, writing, numeracy, computing, communication skills and responsible behaviour, cooperation and team work remain top of any list.

We have drawn attention to the spectrum of brain types, so an early task is to help every child learn how their individual brain most easily learns to remember. Next, we can help every child learn to channel their natural concentration, so they can make better use of it when they need it. Then we can help young people how to find the information they want, how to interpret it, how to be critical, the implications of information and how to extrapolate it to solve problems.

One subject that may prove very useful is the history of knowledge; how we have amassed it, and hopefully stimulate young minds to experience the excitement of the adventure of exploring what we know, how we found out about it, and then encourage them to build their confidence and ambition to push out new frontiers themselves.

The Path So Far

Throughout recorded history, we can observe that civilisation has moved forward in fits and starts. Periods of intellectual ferment have been followed by periods of almost complete silence. Everything points to the beginning of the twenty-first century being a pivot of major change, not to say revolution, in almost every field of human endeavour. There are many drivers to this situation, deoxyribonucleic acid (DNA), control of our reproduction, gene-enhanced food, the first diffident steps to world government, but undoubtedly, one is the invention of computing. We thought we had invented (1) a machine that could solve mathematical problems and that could help us write, publish and disseminate text, (2) an accounting machine that could look after aspects of economics and (3) a machine that could control other machines. But we have invented a machine that can do far, far more.

We have invented a machine that can be what the optimists think can be a partner or what the pessimists fear can be a predator. And the choice is ours.

In designing our computers, we have had to solve a variety of systems problems, and these have stimulated us to wonder how our natural brain solves those self-same problems. We have closely studied the physical mechanisms of our bodies and the components of our brains in particular using ever more sophisticated scanners, but, notwithstanding all the research effort, we have to accept that we know remarkably little about how this neural *system* operates. However, the more we study our brain and how our bodies operate, the more we learn about how we might build better computers.

Convergence

In the last few years, the convergence of cognitive neuroscience, biogenetics and computing has released many new ideas. One great leap forward is how we interface our brains and our machines together to support each other, concentrating on the activities each can do best. It is neither an exaggeration to say that the problems are colossal, nor is an overstatement to say the potential possibilities are immeasurable.

Thinking About Thinking: The Philosopher's View

So how do we set about thinking about thinking about how to gain these benefits and avoid the problems?

Homo sapiens has two ways of thinking, and they have been in tension throughout history with one or other in the ascendancy from time to time.

One way is to build on the views, ideas and theories of our forebears and try, and modify and extend them to fit new information and discoveries. Alternatively, many people believe that some form of extra-terrestrial power has handed down to us great truths which we disobey at our peril.

In the fourth century BC, the materialistic Greek Stoics argued we are only "atoms, voids and sensations: make the best of it". Described by the Roman, Lucretius Carus in his *De Rerum Natura* (*On the Meaning of Things*), this is perhaps the most influential book in the history of philosophy. Also in the former corner are the followers of Socrates who think that "the only thing we know for certain is that we know nothing for certain". The great Muslim philosopher, Abu'l'Ala al-Ma'arri argued that "humanity follows two world-wide sects. One, man intelligent without religion. The second, religious without intellect". Confucius offered us "only the wisest and stupidest men never change". Winston Churchill suggested "to improve is to change. To be perfect is to change often".

Rather closer to home, Leo Tolstoy reminds us that "Everyone thinks of changing the world, but no one thinks of changing himself". T. S. Eliot warns us "that all our knowledge brings us closer to our ignorance", and Plato reminds us that "everything may just be shadows on the wall of the cave of our ignorance".

Rather more cheerfully for those who aim to push out the frontiers of our knowledge, Aldous Huxley commented that "the vast majority of human beings dislike, and even actually dread all notions with which they are not familiar. Hence, it comes about that at first appearance innovators have generally been persecuted and always derided as fools and madmen." John Stuart Mill puts this rather more aggressively "originality is the one thing which unoriginal minds cannot feel the use of. How could they?"

Charles Darwin's advice is that "it is not the strongest of the species that survive, nor the most intelligent, but the ones most responsive to change." H. G. Wells adds a warning "Adapt or perish, now as ever, is nature's inexorable imperative."

George Bernard Shaw speaks for the optimists "the future belongs to the unreasonable man, who looks forward not back, who thinks the unthinkable, and is certain only of uncertainty", or as the quantum physicists would put it — "constructive uncertainty", which neatly takes us back to Socrates.

Both groups can probably agree about one thing. Few in either camp can believe that we are the most intelligent organisms in the universe. In 1939, at the outbreak of war, Winston Churchill wrote "I, for one, am not so immensely impressed by the success we are making of our civilization here that I am prepared to think we are the only spot in this immense universe which contains living, thinking creatures, or that we are the highest type of mental and physical development which has ever appeared in the vast compass of space and time."

It is vanishingly possible perhaps, that, indeed, it is our destiny to populate the universe with intelligent life forms, but at best this is a somewhat arrogant position, and, if true we do have rather a long journey in front of us. If we both agree that there is some higher form of intelligence, then we only disagree about the means of communication. Back into two groups, one *believes* they know the answer. The other argues that there is *no proof* — emotion versus logic.

Building the Corpus of Human Knowledge: Landscape of the Rainbow of Human Abilities

One of the more fascinating observations that flows from any research into intelligence, education, or the general competence of the community and its leaders and managers, whether in government, industry, commerce, finance, the arts or the armed forces is that we know so very little about what we can describe as ability.

All these groups are concerned to identify and then train leaders, but no one can provide a comprehensive definition of leadership. We are vaguely aware that there are people who can do tasks, and those that can teach others. But what makes a standout lawyer, accountant, inventor, entrepreneur, systems designer, researcher, architect, musician, doctor, administrator or engineer? We feel we know when we see, or witness an expert, but we cannot tie down what that is. Everyone will immediately answer that, for instance, the legal profession knows exactly what makes a good lawyer, but there is no definition or even specification. The best the professions and other similar bodies can do is to point to their codes of good practice, their disciplinary systems to maintain standards, and the training and examinations they have in place.

Our future as a community depends on the quality of our community. Not least in doing everything we can to fit round pegs into round holes of careers. There is a powerful argument to start the remarkably difficult process of listing what we believe to be the skills that our community needs to navigate the existential problems of living in peace and harmony on this very small planet, as we spin through space.

The first step might be to list every known skill and ability, yet even designing a way of setting about this preliminary task is fraught with difficulty and suggests both why this is so difficult, and also why no one has attempted to do it — a task for our finest brains. If we could survey the landscape and develop a language to describe and identify ability and aptitude, we could begin to recognise the talents and skills of the individuals in our community. If we could go further and grade the value to the community of each skill and ability, we could adjust our educational and training priorities to match. It is a massive task no one has dared to even consider.

If individuals could spend their lives doing the tasks that they are best at, and gain the most fulfilment from, we could begin to change the whole experience of many lives. Even trying to set out the parameters of how we might approach this task will yield many valuable insights into the human condition.

Better Computers

The Drive to Design Ever More Intelligent Systems and Robots: The Next Generation of Software

Over the last 40 years, we have developed "operating" software, to organise the hardware and provide a platform on which to run our programs. In parallel, we have designed programming languages to help us write applications, with specialist languages for the various different categories of systems.

Given our detailed knowledge of how our brains operate, we can begin to think about developing a new generation of software. To emulate the autonomic functions of the central nervous system, we can begin to develop much more ambitious operating, or background systems that both manage the system, but also add general purpose processing functions. Similarly, we can design programming languages that do not just sit on the operating systems as an inert platform but are far more dynamically integrated into it.

In designing this new generation of software development tools, we need to bear in mind that very soon now we will have the first prosthetic links that will provide interfaces between our neural and machine systems.

Robotics is moving steadily forward, but we need to give more attention to how we communicate — a different use of the word "language", for example. It is relatively easy to offer a user a table of functions: word processing, email, spread sheet etc. Click and the appropriate software is instantly loaded. We would like to say to our robot, "I need to write to ..." — an order of magnitude more complicated for the system to interpret. It's time to start developing a stylised verbal language to communicate with our robots in the same way that we need a verbal language to communicate with our Chinese friends.

We have set out some ideas at Appendix 50 (all appendices are hosted on www.BrainMindForum.org/appendices).

The Ethical, Employment and Economic Implications of the Age of Computing

Most people would be in favour of editing our genes, if by doing so we could eliminate hereditary illnesses, but people might be less enthusiastic at the prospects of being able to design our babies. Where to draw the line? Fifty years ago, the vast majority worked a 6-day week with minimal annual holidays. Now a 40-hour week and paid fortnights or even month-long annual holidays and a rising income are rights. The French have experimented with 35-hour weeks with dire consequences. However, this basic pattern of employment has changed only marginally. How would we cope if we could produce all the needs of the whole community within a 20-hour week? With the same or rising incomes? Or with half our present incomes?

McKinsey & Company are currently forecasting that half all existing activities could be automated by current technology, let alone what is in the pipeline, saving $16 trillion p.a. in wages. No economist has dared ask how governments will cope without the income tax revenue from this money? It is a plausible argument that the failure of the Osborne Treasury to balance the UK budget during his term in office was partly due to the unexpected shortfall of income tax — *already*. Solutions suggested are to pay everyone a Universal Basic Income, as being trialled by cities like Utrecht. Arguably Universal Credit is the first step along this path.

It is instructive that the World Economic Forum (WEF) describes what is happening as the "Fourth Industrial Revolution". The first three Industrial revolutions were based on machines replacing human muscles. They created production, employment, and *created* purchasing power. What we are beginning to witness is the first computer revolution, which is based on computers replacing human brains. It will satisfy production but increasingly eliminate jobs and *reduce* purchasing power. The opposite of the industrial revolutions.

The risk of this complacent analysis of the WEF and many others, is that it suggests that what we are experiencing is just more of the same, just another phase of industrialisation. People will continue to think that all we must do is muddle through, as we always have done. All the great bureaucracies in Brussels, London and Washington will continue to take this smug view at their peril. Appendix 49 analyses this further (all appendices are hosted on www.BrainMindForum.org/appendices).

Neural Energy

One of the most important conclusions that comes out of the arguments in this book is the all-embracing role of energy in the operation of all the systems of the body. Almost every topic covered in this book involves the expenditure of energy. The signalling system of the whole central nervous system involves the transmission of energy. Whether we are asleep or awake is dependent on the level of energy in the system, particularly at the synapses. The capacity to concentrate depends on our ability to focus the maximum energy on the problem in hand. The growth of memory by the creation of new neural links and structures is entirely dependent on the energy supply. The successful accessing of information depends on the level of energy that is available. The cardiovascular, endocrine, enteric and immune systems are all dependent of a smooth supply of energy.

There is a prime facie case that Dementia, Alzheimer's and "senior moment syndrome" are all related to the imperfect availability and deployment of energy in the neural networks.

Diet, nutrition and the enteric gastro-intestinal system is a subject where, perhaps, the medical world can make the biggest contribution. While famine is still present in many parts of the world, the developed nations are faced with an epidemic of obesity.

There is a compelling case to raise substantially our joint research effort in the whole area of *neural energy*. There is the nutrient path from the intestines through the brain barrier to the neurons. There is the conversion of nutrients to energy and the "storage" role of adenosine triphosphate (ATP) in the nucleus. Least studied is the deployment of energy by the neurons along the axons and dendrites and across the synapses. The propagation of electromagnetic fields surrounding the neuron filaments and the various wave forms, and their impact has received little attention.

Variant Brain Types

A great deal of research is going on into various individual variant brain types, which we can group together as autism, attention-deficit/ hyperactivity disorder (ADHD), dyslexia, aphasia and other syndromes where we have made less progress. A very recent, major advance in the medical, cognitive neuroscience and psychological communities is to appreciate that these states are often not weaknesses, or failures, as previously thought, but the variations that may mask other attributes. There is a strong argument to group these together as one research activity, learning from each other's work. Perhaps the biggest single contribution computing can make this century.

We are close to having whole body, continuous online scanning and monitoring. Throughout history, disease and plague have regularly decimated whole communities. Children married in their teens and were often dead by 30. Only a century ago, the flu epidemic killed more people than the First World War. In the 1950s, the National Health Service (NHS) and the National Pension were designed on the expectation of a life span of around 65. Magnificent medical success is leading the profession to forecast that babies born today can expect to live to be a 100. However, as we are all well aware this remarkable success has brought its own problems. Another 20 years of life is less appealing if much is spent in care homes with either or both physical and mental problems.

The ability to read the human genome opens the possibility of eradicating hereditary ailments, but it is also emphasising the remarkable breadth of variety of the human condition. A growing obstacle for the pharmaceutical industry is that medication that helps the many can often not help, even damages the few. Thus, increasingly drugs must be carefully aligned to each person, and the effects of preparations must be closely monitored. Multiple ailments are a growing problem. The medicine prescribed for each problem may be fine, but they do not work together and interaction can cause complex problems.

Last, but probably the most important, we are now beginning to realise just how interdependent all the systems of the body are, and how powerful psychosomatic effects can be. Therefore, perhaps the greatest contribution to the human race is to be able to monitor, measure and process the myriad signals from every part of our bodies, and in split seconds identify a problem and its solution, or forecast a problem in time to take avoiding action.

Computing Can Change the Health of the World

We are not too far from having a print of everyone's genome. We can monitor the activities of the cardiovascular and endocrine systems: measure the gastro-intestinal enteric inputs and outputs, and screen an increasing range of the immune system's activities. We are already able to track where most people are and communicate with them.

Integrating all these information streams just for one individual is a mammoth task. Processing this information for whole communities to identify useful knowledge, orders of magnitude greater, and, arguably, far more difficult than merely sending people to the moon, but the potential gains are truly unimaginable. Some people may not wish to participate on the grounds of the potential infringements of their human rights. Their views should be respected, but not be allowed to interfere with, or impede this research. Everyone has the right to refuse a life-saving operation but only for themselves.

It has been technically possible to store the medical records of the whole population online in real time since the 1970s. The Select Committee of Science and Technology of the House of Commons discussed the potential advantages of every doctor, hospital and ambulance crew having instant access to the medical records of every member of the public should they be involved in an accident and be unable to tell the medical staff about any special health conditions. It is a scandal that this information is not available in the second decade of the twenty-first century and that reports have to be typed by one doctor or consultant, sent by post and scanned into another doctor's system. The cost of this waste would solve many of the NHS's problems. This also does not take into consideration the benefit of having these records to enable research and the early recognition of epidemics.

Patients in intensive care wards today are connected up to many systems designed to provide warnings of malfunctions or impending problems. All this equipment is quite large, however, 50 years ago, computers were the size of office blocks. All this monitoring equipment will also be miniaturised.

It is possible now for a user's heartrate, pulse and blood pressure to be continuously monitored and continuously transmitted automatically by cell phone to a medical centre. If the user suffers a stroke, feints or is in an accident, the emergency services can be alerted instantly, with the exact location and diagnosis. Neighbours, or next of kin can be informed.

Better: In many cases, it will be possible to register warning signs and inform the user of what might be happening and what avoiding action to take.

Standard Interface Platform

In designing a nationwide system, it would be prudent and intelligent to design the specification to provide a monitoring and communication standard interface platform. This would allow new monitoring facilities to be added with minimum additional expenditure.

Perhaps, the next monitoring system could be a standard interface to a miniaturised blood sampling and testing device. Continuous monitoring of blood sugar levels could open the door to myriad functions and not just in monitoring a user's state. It could equally be used to administer medication, exactly in the right amounts at the right times and provide feedback on the reactions.

Once in place the potential is unlimited. The potential to help with recreational drug problems is just one.

This also opens the possibility of combining inherited DNA problems with transmitted ailments and treating the body as one holistic whole — a variation of combining nature with nurture.

The potential to build a database of immense proportions of actual experience, rather than the necessarily limited testing facilities available now, could open many windows on previously intractable problems.

Whether we want to live to be much more than 100 is perhaps a personal opinion, but to be able to live out our allotted span of life in excellent health, both in body and mind is a truly great objective.

After 42

Once a national standard communications interface platform is in place, it will be relatively easy to connect the brain to this platform with a prosthetic neural link. The possibilities would even stretch the imagination of the science fiction writers. Truly a task for the super intelligent computer systems of the twenty-first century. Truly a task for our computers as our partners.

Spem Successus Alit

BIBLIOGRAPHY

1. Ableman, Paul. *The Secret of Consciousness*. Marion Boyars Ltd. 1999: London.
2. Allman, John. *Evolving Brains*. Scientific American Library. 2002: New York.
3. Appleyard, Bryan. *The Brain is Wider than the Sky*. Weidenfeld & Nicholson. 2011: London.
4. Augur, Jean. *This Book Doesn't Make Sense*. Bath Educational Publishers. 1981: Bath.
5. Baddeley, Alan. *Your Memory; A User's Guide*. Penguin Group. 1992: London.
6. Bagemihl, Bruce. *Biological Exuberance*. Profile Books. 1999: London.
7. Baldwin, *et al. Synthetic Biology*. Imperial College Press. 2012: London.
8. Barron, Frank. *Creative Person and Creative Process*. Penguin. 1969: London.
9. Bartlett, Jamie. *The Dark Net*. William Heinemann. 2014: London.
10. Bateson, Patrick & Martin, Paul. *Design for a Life*. Jonathan Cape. 1999: London.
11. Beer, Stafford. *Beyond Dispute: Invention of Team Syntegrity*. Managerial Cybernetics of Organization. John Wiley. 1994: London.
12. Bennett, Max R. *The Idea of Consciousness*. Harwood Academic Press. 1997: Amsterdam.
13. Bernhardt, Chris. *Turing's Vision. The Birth of Computer Science*. MIT Press. 2016: New York.
14. Blakemore, Colin. *The Mind Machine*. BBC Books. 1988: London.

15. Blakemore & Greenfield (Eds). *Mindwaves*. Blackwell. 1987: Oxford.
16. Boden, Margaret. *The Creative Mind*. Cardinal, Sphere Books, Weidenfeld & Nicholson. 1990: London.
17. Bostrom, Nick. *Superintelligence*. Oxford University Press. 2014: Oxford.
18. de Bono, Edward. *Letters to Thinkers*. Harrap. 1987: London.
19. de Bono, Edward. *I am Right, You are Wrong*. Viking. 1990: London.
20. de Bono, Edward. *Teach Your Child How to Think*. Viking. 1989: London.
21. de Bono, Edward. *New Thinking for the New Millennium*. Viking. 1999: London.
22. de Bono, Edward. *The Mechanism of Mind*. Jonathan Cape. 1969: London.
23. de Bono, Edward. *Five Day Course in Thinking*. Basic Books. 1967: USA.
24. Boorstin, Daniel. *The Discoverers*. Random House. 1983: New York.
25. Bor, Daniel. *The Ravenous Brain*. Basic Books. 2012: New York.
26. Brooks, Michael. *13 Things That Don't Make Sense*. Doubleday. 2008: New York.
27. Brooks, Michael. *At the Edge of Uncertainty*. Profile Books. 2014: London.
28. Cahan, David. *Herman von Helmholtz and the Foundations of Nineteenth Century Science*. University of California Press. 1993: California.
29. Cantor, Norman F. *Antiquity*. Harper Collins. 2003: New York.
30. Calvin, William. *How Brains Think*. Weidenfeld & Nicholson. 1997: London.
31. Carter, Rita. *Consciousness*. Weidenfeld & Nicholson. 2002: London.
32. Carter, Rita. *Mapping the Mind*. Weidenfeld & Nicholson. 1998: London.
33. Chadwick, Derek & Whelan, Julie (Eds). *Exploring Brain Functional Anatomy with Positron Tomography*. Wiley. 1991: London.
34. Chalmers, David. *The Conscious Mind: In Search of a Fundamental Theory*. Oxford University Press. 1996: Oxford.
35. Claxton, Guy. *Hare Brain, Tortoise Mind*. Fourth Estate. 1997: London.
36. Claxton, Guy. *Noises from the Darkroom*. Aquarian. 1994: London.
37. Claxton, Guy. *The Wayward Mind*. Little Brown: Abacus. 2006: London.
38. Claxton, Guy. *What's the Point of School?* One World Publications. 2008: Oxford.
39. Claxton, Guy & Bill, Lucas. *New Kinds of Smart*. Open University: McGraw Hill. 2010: Maidenhead.
40. Claxton, Guy, Maryl Chambers, Graham Powell & Bill. Lucas. *The Learning Powered School*. TLO. 2011: Bristol.
41. Claxton, Guy. *Intelligence in the Flesh*. Yale University Press. 2015: USA.
42. Coopersmith, Jennifer. *Energy: The Subtle Concept*. Oxford University Press. 2010: Oxford.

43. Cornwell, John. (Ed). *Nature's Imagination.* Oxford University Press. 1995: Oxford.
44. Cosmides, Leda & Tooby, John. *Adapted Mind.* Oxford University Press. 1995: London.
45. Crick, Francis. *Astonishing Hypothesis.* Simon & Schuster. 1994: London.
46. Crystal, David. *Dictionary of Language and Languages.* Penguin. 1992: London.
47. Crump, Thomas. *Anthology of Numbers.* Cambridge University Press. 1989: Cambridge.
48. Cushing, James. *Philosophical Concepts in Physics.* Cambridge University Press. 1998: Cambridge.
49. Damasio, Antonio. *The Feeling of What Happens.* William Heinemann. 2000: London.
50. Damasio, Antonio. *Looking for Spinoza*: Heinemann. 2005: London.
51. Davies, Jamie A. *Life Unfolding.* Oxford University Press. 2014: Oxford.
52. Davies, Paul & Gregerson, Niels Henrik. (Ed). (Seth Lloyd). *Information and the Nature of Reality [Physics to Metaphysics].* Cambridge University Press. 2010: London.
53. Dawkins, Richard. *The Selfish Gene.* Oxford University Press. 1978: Oxford.
54. Dawkins, Richard. *River Out of Eden.* Weidenfeld & Nicholson. 1995: London.
55. Dawkins, Richard. *The Ancestors Tale.* Weidenfeld & Nicholson. 2004: London.
56. Deacon, Terrence. *The Symbolic Species.* Penguin. 1997: London.
57. Deacon, Terrence. *Incomplete Nature.* W. W. Norton & Co. 2012: New York.
58. Dehaene, Stanilas. *The Number S.* Penguin Press. 1997: London.
59. Dehaene, Stanilas. *Consciousness and the Brain.* Viking. 2014, New York.
60. Denes, Peter & Pinson, Elliot. *The Speech Chain.* W. H. Freeman & Co. 1993: New York.
61. Dennett, Daniel. *Consciousness Explained.* Penguin. 1991: London. [Profile Scientific American February. 1996. p. 24.]
62. Dennett, Daniel. *Kinds of Minds.* Weidenfeld & Nicholson. 1996: London.
63. Dennett, Daniel. *Intuition Pumps and Other Tools for Thinking.* Penguin. 2013: London.
64. Dennett, Daniel. *From Bacteria to Bach and Back.* Allen Lane. 2017: London.
65. Deutsch, David. *The Fabric of Reality.* Penguin. 2001: London.

66. Domingos, Pedro. *The Master Algorithm*. Allen Lane. 2015: London.
67. Duncan, John. *How Intelligence Happens*. Yale University Press. 2010: USA.
68. Dyson, Fremman, *et al*. *Nature's Imagination*. Oxford University Press. 1995.
69. Eastcott, Michael J. *'I', The Story of Self*. Rider & Company. 1979: London.
70. Edelman, Gerald. *Bright Air, Brilliant Fire*. Penguin Press. 1992: London.
71. Edelman, Gerald. *Consciousness*. Penguin Press. 2000: London.
72. Edelman, Gerald. *Neural Darwinism: Theory of Natural Group Selection*. Basic Books. 1987: New York.
73. Evans, Dylan. *Emotion, Science of Sentiment*. Oxford University Press. 2001: Oxford.
74. Evans, Vyvyan. *The Language Myth. Why Language is Not an Instinct*. Cambridge University Press. 2014: Cambridge.
75. Fagan, Brian. *Beyond the Blue Horizon*. Bloomsbury. 2012: London.
76. Fincher, Jack. *Human Intelligence*. Putnam. 1976: New York.
77. Fodor, Jerry. *The Modularity of Mind*. MIT Press. 1987: Massachusetts.
78. Ford, Martin. *The Rise of the Robots*. One World. 2015: London.
79. Galbraith, John Kenneth. *The Age of Uncertainty*. Book Club Associates. 1977.
80. Gazzaniga, Michael. *Nature's Mind*. Penguin. 1992: London.
81. Gazzaniga, Michael. *Who's in Charge?* Harper Collins. 2011: New York.
82. Gelernter, David. *The Muse in the Machine*. Fourth Estate. 1994: Great Britain.
83. Gershenfeld, Neil. *When Things Start to Think*. Hodder. 2004: New York.
84. Gleick, James. *The Information*. Fourth Estate, Harper Collins. 2011: London. (Author of Chaos Theory.)
85. Goleman, Daniel. *Emotional Intelligence*. Bloomsbury. 1996: London.
86. Gopnik, Alison, Meltzoff, Andrew & Kuhl, Particia. *How Babies Think*. Weidenfeld & Nicholson. 1999: Great Britain.
87. Gordon, Barry. *Memory*. Master Media Ltd. 1995: USA.
88. Gould, Stephen Jay. *Rock of Ages*. Jonathan Cape. 2001: London.
89. Grayling. A. C. *Meaning of Things*. Weidenfeld & Nicholson. 2001: London.
90. Grayling, A. C. *Ideas That Matter*. Phoenix. 2009: London.
91. Grayling, A. C. *Seventeenth Century and the Birth of the Modern Mind*. Bloomsbury. 2016: London.
92. Grayling, A. C. *Towards the Light*. Bloomsbury. 2010: London.

93. Grayling, A. C. *The Age of Genius*. Bloomsbury. 2016: London.
94. Greenblatt, Stephen. *The Swerve. How the Renaissance Began*. Bodley Head. 2011: London.
95. Greenfield, Susan. *The Private Life of the Brain*. Penguin Press. 2000: London.
96. Greenfield, Susan. *Brain Story*. BBC Books. 2000: London.
97. Greenfield, Susan. *The Human Brain*. Weidenfeld & Nicholson. 1997: London.
98. Greenfield, Susan. *Tomorrow's People*. Penguin Books. 2003: London.
99. Gregory, Richard. *The Mind*. Oxford University Press. 1987: Oxford.
100. Gregory, Richard. *Mind in Science*. Weidenfeld & Nicholson. 1981: London.
101. Gregory, Richard. *Mirrors in Mind*. W. H. Freeman. 1997: London.
102. Gregory, Richard. *A Day in the Life of the Brain*. Allen Lane. 2016: London.
103. Gullberg, Jan. *Mathematics, from the Birth of Numbers*. W. W. Norton & Co. 1997: New York.
104. Halliday, R. J. *John Stuart Mill*. Allen & Unwin. 1976: London.
105. Handy, Charles. *Beyond Certainty*. Hutchinson. 1955: London.
106. Harari, Yuval Noah. *Sapiens*. Harvill Secker. 2011: London.
107. Harari, Yuval Noah. *Homo Deus*. Harvill Secker. 2016: London.
108. Hawking, Stephen. *Brief History of Time*. Bantam Press. 1988: London.
109. Hebb, D. O. *The Organisation of Behaviour*. McGill University. John Wiley 1949: USA.
110. Hey, Tony. *New Quantum Universe*. Cambridge University Press. 2003: Cambridge.
111. Hobson, J. Allan. *Consciousness*. Scientific American Library. 1998: New York.
112. Hobson, J. Allan. *Dreaming*. Oxford University Press. 2002: Oxford.
113. Hodges, Andrew. *Alan Turing. The Enigma of Intelligence*. Counterpoint, Unwin. 1983: London.
114. Hodgson, David. *The Mind Matters*. Oxford University Press. 1993: Oxford.
115. Hofstadter, Douglas. *Gödel, Escher & Bach*. Penguin Books. 1979: London.
116. Holmes, Richard. *The Age of Wonder*. Harper Collins. 2008: London.
117. Holt, John. *How Children Learn*. Penguin. 1967: London.
118. Holt, John. *How Children Fail*. Penguin. 1964: London.
119. Howe, Michael. *IQ in Question*. Sage Publications. 1997: London.
120. Humphrey, Nicholas. *History of the Mind*. Chatto & Windus. 1992: London.

121. Huxley, Aldous. *The Human Situation 1959*. Grafton Books. 1980: London.

122. Irwin, Terence. *Classical Thought*. Oxford University Press. 1989: Oxford.

123. Isaacson, Walter. *The Innovators*. Simon and Schuster. 2014: London.

124. Janson, Tore. *Speak*. Oxford University Press. 2002: Oxford.

125. Johnson, Steven. *Emergence*. Penguin Press. 2001: Great Britain.

126. Kahneman, Daniel. *Thinking, Fast and Slow*. Allen Lane. 2011: London.

127. Kandel, Eric R. *In Search of Memory*. W. W. Norton & Co. 2007: New York (see also Squire & Kandel).

128. Kandel, Eric R. *Behavioural Biology of Aplysia*. W. H. Freeman. 1979: San Francisco.

129. Kennedy, Ludovic. *All in the Mind*. Hodder & Stoughton. 2010: London.

130. Koestler, Arthur. *The Sleepwalkers*. Hutchinson. 1959: London.

131. Koch, Christof. *The Quest for Consciousness: A Neurobiological Approach*. Roberts & Co. 2004: USA.

132. Koch, Christof. *A Consciousness Meter*. Scientific American. March 2013, p. 24.

133. Koob, Andrew. *The Root of Thought*. Pearson Education. 2009: New York.

134. Kuhn, Thomas S. *The Structure of Scientific Revolutions*. University of Chicago Press. 1962: Chicago.

135. Lavington, Simon. *History of the Manchester Computer*. British Computer Society. 1975.

136. Lewis-Williams, David. *The Mind in the Cave*. Thames & Hudson. London.

137. Lloyd, Seth. *Programming the Universe: A Quantum Computer Scientist Takes on the Cosmos*. Jonathan Cape. 2005: Toronto.

138. Locke, John. *Concerning Human Understanding*. 1706: Edinburgh.

139. Loewenstein, Werner R. *Physics in Mind – A Quantum View of the Brain*. Basic Books. 2013: New York.

140. Lucas, Bill. *Evolution*. Crown House. 2010: Carmarthen.

141. Lucretius, Titus Carus. *De Rerum Natura*. Sphere Books. 1969: London (*C* 50 BC. Roman commentary on the ideas of Epicurus: first concept of Humanism). [See The Swerve by Stephen Greenblatt, which describes how the *De Rerum* Survived.]

142. McCrone, John. *Going Inside*. Faber. 1999: London.

143. McConkey, James. *Anatomy of Memory*. Oxford University Press. 1996: Oxford.

144. McGinn, Colin. *The Problems of Consciousness*. Basil Blackwell. 1991: Oxford.

145. McKellar, Peter. *Imagination & Thinking*. Cohen & West. 1957: London.

146. McLeish, Kenneth. (Ed). *Guide to Human Thought*. Bloomsbury. 1993: London.

147. Makari, George. *Soul Machine. The Invention of the Modern Mind*. W. W. Norton & Co. 2015: Geneva.
148. Leff, Harvey S. & Rex, Andrew F. *Maxwell's Demon: Entropy, Information, Computing*. ISBN 0-691-08727-x. Princeton University Press. 1990.
149. Maturana, Humberto & Varela, Francisco. *The Tree of Knowledge*. Shambhala. 1992: Boston. First published in 1984.
150. Maddox, John. *What Remains to be Discovered*. MacMillan. 1998: London.
151. Maxwell's Demon: Entropy. Information, Computing. ISBN 0-691-08727-x Princeton University Press. 1990: Princeton.
152. Metzinger, T. (Ed). *Conscious Experience*. Imprint Academic. 1995: Exeter.
153. Miles, T. R. & Miles, E. (Ed). *Dyslexia & Mathematics*. Routledge. 1992: London.
154. Mill, John Stuart. *Essay on Liberty*. First Edition, John W. Parker & Son. 1859: London.
155. Miller, Arthur I. *Genius: Imagery and Creativity in Science and Art*. MIT Press. 2000: Cambridge.
156. Miller, Arthur I. *Einstein, Picasso: Space, Time and Beauty that Causes Havoc*. Basic. 2001: New York.
157. Miller, Arthur I. *Empire of the Stars: Friendship, Obsession and Betrayal in the Quest for Black Holes*. Little Brown, 2005: London.
158. Miller, George. *Science of Word*. Scientific American Library. 1991: New York.
159. Mithen, Steven. *Prehistory of the Mind*. Thames & Hudson. 1996: London.
160. Mithen, Steven. *Creativity*. Routledge. London.
161. Mithen, Steven. *Thoughtful Foragers*. Cambridge University Press. 1990: Cambridge.
162. Mithen, Steven. *After the Ice*. Weidenfeld & Nicholson. 2003: London.
163. Mithen, Steven. *Singing Neanderthals*. Weidenfeld & Nicholson. 2005: London.
164. Parker, Derek. *Voltaire*. Sutton Publishing. 2005: Gloucester.
165. Pears, David. *Wittgenstein*. Fontana. 1971: London.
166. Pennebaker, James W. *The Secret Life of Pronouns. What Our Words Say About Us*. Bloomsbury Press. 2011. New York.
167. Penrose, Sir Roger. *Shadows of the Mind*. Oxford University Press. 1994: Oxford.
168. Penrose, Sir Roger. *The Emperor's New Mind*. Oxford University Press. 1989: Oxford.
169. Penrose, Sir Roger. *Road to Reality*. BCA Jonathan Cape. 2004: London.
170. Perkins, David. *Outsmarting IQ*. Free Press. 1995: New York.
171. Pert, Candice. *Molecules of Emotion*. Simon & Schuster. 2004: London.
172. Pinker, Steven. *The Language Instinct*. Penguin. 1994: London.

173. Pinker, Steven. *How the Mind Works.* W. W. Norton & Co. 1997: USA.
174. Pinker, Steven. *Words & Rules.* Weidenfeld & Nicolson. 2000: London.
175. Pinker, Steven. *The Blank Slate.* Penguin. 2002: London.
176. Pinker, Steven. *The Stuff of Thought.* Penguin. 2008: London.
177. Ramachandran, V. S. *The Tell-Tale Brain.* Heinemann. 2011: London.
178. Ratey. John. *User's Guide to the Brain.* Pantheon Books. 2001: New York.
179. Rees, Martin. *Just Six Numbers.* Weidenfeld & Nicholson. 1999: London.
180. Richardson, Ken. *Making of Intelligence.* Weidenfeld & Nicholson. 1999: London.
181. Ridley, Matt. *The Rational Optimist.* Harper Collins. 2010: London.
182. Robertson, Ian. *The Mind's Eye.* Bantam Press. 2002: London.
183. Robinson, Andrew. *The Story of Writing.* Thames & Hudson. 1995: London.
184. Rose, Steven. *The Making of Memory.* Bantam Press. 1992: London.
185. Rose, Steven. *The 21st Century Brain.* Vintage. 2006: London.
186. Ross, Alec. *The Industries of the Future.* Simon & Schuster. 2016: London.
187. Ross, Charles & Redpath, Shirley. *Biological Systems of the Brain. Unlocking the Secrets of Consciousness.* Matador. 2008: Cambridge.
188. Russell, Peter. *The Brain Book.* Routledge. 1979: London.
189. Rutherford, Adam. *A Brief History of Everyone Who Ever Lived.* Weidenfeld & Nicolson. 2016: London.
190. Rutherford. R.B. *The Art of Plato.* Duckworth. 1995: London.
191. Searle, John. *The Rediscovery of the Mind.* MIT Press. 1994: USA.
192. Schrödinger, Erwin. *Nature and the Greeks* and *Science and Humanism.* Cambridge University Press. 1951 (Reprinted).
193. Shapiro, Robert. *The Human Blueprint.* St Martins Press. 1991: New York.
194. Sheldrake, Rupert. *Presence of the Past.* Collins. 1988: USA.
195. Sheldrake, Rupert. *A New Science of Life.* Collins. 1980: USA.
196. Singh, Simon. *Fermat's Last Theorum.* Fourth Estate. 1998: London.
197. Singh, Simon. *The Code Book.* Fourth Estate. 1999: London.
198. Shlain, Leonard. *Alphabet versus the Gods.* Penguin Press. 1998: London.
199. Sloane, Paul & MacHale, Des. *The Lateral Logician.* Quality Paperback Club. 1991: New York.
200. Springer, Sally & Deutsch, George. *Left Brain: Right Brain.* W. H. Freeman. 1993: New York.
201. Squire, Larry & Kandel, Eric R. *Memory.* Scientific American Library. 1999: New York.
202. Stewart, Ian & Cohen, Jack. *Figments of Reality.* Cambridge University Press. 1997: Cambridge.

203. Stewart, Ian & Cohen, Jack. *Nature's Numbers.* Weidenfeld & Nicholson. 1995: London.
204. Storr, Anthony. *Music & the Mind.* Harper Collins. 1992: London.
205. Sykes, Bryan. *The Seven Daughters of Eve.* Bantam Press. 2000: London.
206. Tegmark, Max. Life 3.0: *Being Human in the Age of Intelligence.* Allen Lane. 2017: London.
207. Thruelsen. Richard & Kobler, John (Eds). *Adventures of the Mind.* Alfred A. Knopf. 1959: New York.
208. Tononi, Giulio. *A Complex Theory of Consciousness.* Consciouness Redux. July 2009.
209. Tooby, Cosmides. *Adapted Minds.* Oxford University Press. 1999: Oxford.
210. Turing, Alan. *On Computable Numbers with an Application to the Entscheidungsproblem.* Royal Society. 1936: London.
211. Venter, J. Craig. *Life at the Speed of Light.* Little Brown. 2013: London.
212. Wagner, Andreas. *Arrival of the Fittest – Solving Evolution's Puzzle.* One World. 2014: New York.
213. Watson, Peter. *A Terrible Beauty.* Weidenfeld & Nicholson. 2001: London.
214. Watson, Peter. *Ideas.* Orion Press, Weidenfeld & Nicholson. 2005: London.
215. West, Thomas. *In the Mind's Eye.* Prometheus Books. 1991: London.
216. Wills, Christopher. *The Runaway Brain.* Harper Collins. 1994: London.
217. Winston, Robert. *The Human Mind.* Bantam. 2003: London.
218. Wolf, Maryanne. *Proust and the Squid.* Harper Collins. 2007: London.
219. Zimmer, Carl. *Microcosm: E. Coli and the New Science of Life.* Random House. 2008: London.

LIST OF APPENDICES

Available at www.BrainMindForum.org/appendices can also be accessed via Google. Scroll down website.

1. List of appendices
2. Definitions of intelligence. Thirty examples of definitions by: Jean Piaget, A C Grayling, William of Ockham, Maria Leitner, Richard Feynman, Susan Greenfield, Erwin Schrödinger, Alfred Binet *et al.*
3. Quotations relevant to cognitive neuroscience
4. Hormones, neurotransmitters, peptides, etc.
5. History of proprietary memory systems from Simonides 5th century BC, to Cicero, J S Mill, Edward de Bono & Tony Buzan
6. Science of software. Understanding the relationship between the brain and the mind, deoxyribo nucleic acid and RNA. Stem cell & protein folding hypothesis
7. Examples of software in biological systems
8. Computer software v brain software
9. The Halting Problem, from Hilbert's questions for mathematicians in 1900
10. The Hebbian Hypothesis. The process by which the brain grows memory structures
11. Pattern formation & mathematical biology: The work of Alan Turing in the last years of his life: Fibonacci numbers

12. Growth of neural processors and algorithms in the brain. Engrams, neurules, memes and other names given them by eminent cognitive neuroscientists
13. Lexicon of terms and words. Towards a language of cognition, and convergent sciences
14. Convergence of cognitive neuroscience, biogenetics, synthetic biology
15. Quest for artificial intelligence
16. Brain waves
17. Characteristics of personality
18. Energy generation ATP DNA
19. Free will debate. Spindle, monitor feedback timing evolution
20. Contribution of Greece
21. History of software. Clocks, Jacquard. Essence of power of software
22. Definitions of learning, memory, meaning and words
23. Bibliography
24. List of proposed definitions
25. Emergence
26. Measuring intelligence: History and examples of IQ tests
27. Information. Potential for Laws of Infodynamics? Probability of relationship between information and energy. Maxwell's devil: info=heat?
28. Research into memory formation at the Royal Institution 25th July 2013
29. References to glia bridges
30. References to synapses
31. Scanners & scanning systems
32. Dan Dennett chapter on programming. Extract from 'Intuition Pumps'. 32-H program for multiplication: How programs write program
33. Professor David Hilbert
34. Description of programming languages
35. Facts and Stats
36. Greenfield's criteria for consciousness solutions
37. Diagrart
38. Information chart
39. Notation & coding systems

INDEX

Printed in the United States
By Bookmasters